Fauna and Flora, Earth and Sky

sightline books

The Iowa Series in Literary Nonfiction

Patricia Hampl & Carl H. Klaus, series editors

Trudy Dittmar

Fauna and Flora, Earth and Sky

Brushes with Nature's Wisdom

University of Iowa Press ψ Iowa City

University of Iowa Press, Iowa City 52242

Copyright © 2003 by Trudy Dittmar

Printed in the United States of America

Text design by Richard Hendel

http://www.uiowa.edu/uiowapress

The publication of this book was generously supported
by the University of Iowa Foundation. ·

Printed on acid-free paper

Library of Congress
Cataloging-in-Publication Data
Dittmar, Trudy, 1944–
Fauna and flora, earth and sky: brushes with nature's
wisdom / Trudy Dittmar.
p.   cm.—(Sightline books)
ISBN 0-87745-872-3 (cloth)
1. Natural history—West (U.S.).   2. Mountain animals—
West (U.S.).   3. Dittmar, Trudy, 1944–   .
4. Human ecology.   I. Title.   II. Series.
QH104.5.W4D58 2003
508.78—dc21   2003048416

03   04   05   06   07   C   5   4   3   2   1

To the memory of my father,

GEORGE J. DITTMAR, JR.,

and his personal legacy of

flora and fauna, water and earth.

And to PATRICK V. MCDONNELL, JR.

O Nature, and O soul of man! how far beyond all utterance are your linked analogies! not the smallest atom stirs or lives in matter, but has its cunning duplicate in mind.

—HERMAN MELVILLE, *Moby-Dick*

Never does Nature say one thing and Wisdom another.

—JUVENAL, *Satire 14*

I am the wiser in respect to all knowledges, and the better qualified for all fortunes, for knowing that there is a minnow in the brook.

—HENRY DAVID THOREAU, *Journals,* February 14, 1840

Contents

Acknowledgments

For helping make this book possible, I thank the Rona Jaffe Foundation, the Ucross Foundation, and the former Ossabaw Foundation, all of which have supported me in my writing.

I thank three esteemed friends — Edmund White, David Hamilton, Vicki Lindner — each of whom has made a cherished difference in my writing career.

Above all, I thank Carl Klaus — friend, mentor, and editor. In helping me find my way back to writing, then inciting me with his wisdom, literary and otherwise, to make the best book I could, he has made the biggest difference of all.

I gratefully acknowledge the editors of the following magazines and anthologies in which some of the essays in this book previously appeared:

"Pronghorn" appeared in the *North Dakota Quarterly*, volume 62, number 4 (Fall 1995).

"Cows, Arrogance, the Natures of Things" appeared in the *North American Review*, volume 280, number 1 (January/February 1995). Subsequently it appeared in *The Pushcart Prize XXI*, edited by Bill Henderson. In both publications it appeared as is, except for a few small changes.

"The Porcupine's Old Clothes" appeared in *High Plains Literary Review*, volume 10, number 3 (Winter 1995). It appeared as is except for a few very minor changes.

"Moose" appeared in the *North American Review*, volume 281, number 5 (September/October 1996). It has subsequently appeared in *American Nature Writing 2000*, edited by John Murray, and *Nature Writing: The Tradition in English* (in paperback called *The Norton Book of Nature Writing*), edited by John Elder and Robert Finch (2002).

"Going to Rainbow" appeared in the *Georgia Review*, volume 51, number 4 (Winter 1997). There, the endnotes appeared as footnotes. Other than that it appeared as is, except for a few small changes.

"Paedomorph Pools and Other Blighted Bounties" appeared in condensed form in *Orion*, volume 17, number 3 (Summer 1998), under the title "Teeming Pools and Other Blighted Bounties."

Finally, I thank the following friends who, through making a difference in so many other parts of my life, have all in one way or another affected my writing life: Bridget Clarke, Frank Devlin, Beverly Donofrio, Robert Lemperly, Irma Lester, Susan O'Meara, Susan Shor, Ann Kiesling Smith, Martha Turner, Norma Williamson — and everyone to whom I've dedicated an essay in this book.

And I thank my brother, the best friend I have.

Prologue

Each essay in this collection is based on three things: my observations in the natural world, my readings and studies in the natural sciences, and the insights born of the interplay of these with the more expressly human experiences of my personal life. Most focus on animals, one is a wide-ish–ranging contemplation of the world of plants, and a couple were sparked by abiotic phenomena pertaining less to earth than to the skies. Whatever its topic, however, each essay is a braiding of diverse strands of subject matter. Some weave in scientific theory. In some, environmental considerations are part of the weft. Now and then, a thread of art criticism or other cultural matter wends its way through. But while each essay is its own fabric, in every essay one strand is personal, tracking my interactions with the creatures or creations in question, and often tracing a personal story as well. For ultimately, every one of the essays reflects the importance of nature — its bearing and consequence — in this human life. And in the lives of all others, if I've managed to tell it right.

Mirrors in the Land and Sky was a title I briefly considered for this collection. I was thinking how nature's other creatures and creations have so often reflected to me meanings in human life, but I soon saw this title was wrong. It might be taken to imply that nature's role is to echo or magnify our image — and what would that suggest? It might invoke the notion of humanity at the center, with the rest of nature secondary, and this is not what I or any student of nature I can think of believes. When I hit on that title, I'd been reaching for a metaphor to suggest what I experience when I go into the nature of the other creatures and creations, and what I'm left with when I come out; but in the end, the notion of mirroring seemed too narrow to express it adequately. This metaphor, I feared, was apt to suggest that when I go into nature I see only myself.

When I go into nature, I see the cedar groves and porcupines and rainbows and moose of these essays. I see beach plums, grizzly bear tracks, meteor showers, and the cached bodies of deer. In these creatures and creations, I see details of their appearance, and of how they fit where I find them; I see details of how they move and change. Sometimes I glimpse hints, however fragmented, of their history. Almost always — in the field or in the books of others — I glimpse correspondences among one and another of them. Along with all of this, many times I see us in them, them in us. What I tune into when I'm hard in the midst of nature's other creatures and creations is a vibrant field of resonances, often between the human condition and nature at large. What I receive at those times, however, are not simple one-way reflections, but linked analogies.

It's not that a pronghorn is defeated in battle and witnessing this I see, and cry for, my own self. It's that witnessing the pronghorn's defeat I begin to fathom why I have ever cried. It's not just that a pool of tiger salamanders basking in a lush, lucky season echoes a theme in my personal history, but that my personal history prompts my recognition of the nascent predicament of those salamanders — and further, it's that the implications of a pool jammed with their fragile species speaks to me of the implications of a pool jammed with mine. Resonances. Linked analogies. Celestial phenomena flashing in the night sky reflect the loves of my life to me in only the most oblique, metaphorical fashion, stretching to snapping point the meaning of *reflect*. But as metaphors, singly and collectively, those celestial phenomena interpret my whole romantic career for me.

I don't put humanity at the center. But being human, I trace out and back from my species' point in the web. When I go into nature, I'm bounced from inklings of nature at large to inklings of my human nature. As I get an inkling of how nature works, I get an inkling of how we work in it, even as we may feel ourselves apart. Tapping into these resonances, I get an inkling of life's reaches. Sometimes, without thinking about it, I merge with a new possibility. In touch with life's wideness, sometimes something in me widens. Nature and soul, linked analogies.

A Shrewd, Obscure Mercy was another title I considered — a phrase plucked from one of the essays here. I plucked it because it says what the workings of nature, broadly speaking, represent to me. Among the endless other ways I might put it, nature is conflagrations to dust grains to planets to life systems. Self-making, self-directing — unknowingly, it knows its way. In the simultaneity of their intricacy and simplicity, their chaos and order, I find in the workings of nature meaning and miracle. What greater mercy — in the indifferent, confounding, red world of nature we're part of — than that?

This is grandiose talk, however much I believe it. This notion of a shrewd, obscure mercy is my notion, and as such it has a place here; but the title for this collection of essays on nature, it finally struck me, should be simpler and grander than that.

As I've said, these essays are about some of what I've learned from others about what they've learned from nature. And they're about some of what I've learned from nature myself. Which means, of course, that in the end the ground and bulk of these essays come from those kingdoms and realms that humanity has always learned whatever it is we know from — fauna and flora, earth and sky.

Fauna and Flora, Earth and Sky

Pronghorn

TO KIRSTEN DEHNER

t was a good-sized band, considerably larger than any I'd ever seen before. That was all that struck me as unusual about the antelope[1] when I first spotted them. We were on our way out from a camping trip in the forest, in open country for the first time in a week and driving straight at the blaze of sunrise, when I caught a squinting glimpse of them not too far back from the Forest Service road. Since so far in our travels K had seen just a few small bands of pronghorn, and those at a distance, I pulled up for her to get a good look at them.

The size of the band seemed impossible. It looked to be fifty strong. In winter, all pronghorns — does, fawns, and bucks of every age and sexual status — join in large herds, and at that time it's not unusual to see a hundred antelope together now that they're coming back strong in this part of the state. But this was not winter, and the pronghorn had not yet formed herds. This was just the end of September, the heart of the rutting season, a time when they were still moving in small segregated bands — bachelor bands of young males or bands comprising an older buck and his harem of does. Eight does were generally considered a good-sized harem for a buck, but it seemed to me it would take about twice that many, each with her offspring of one to three fawns, to make up a band of such heroic proportions as this. In a grassy field at the foot of red badlands, they stood in tawny clusters, their white bars and patches flashing in the early sun.

· · · · ·

Back then, if you'd asked me, I'd have complained that in Wyoming pronghorn antelope went unappreciated. Their elaborate, curious beauty goes largely unheeded here, and at a knotty juncture in my life

I was peculiarly stung by this. Of course, the reason is just that there are so many of them. They're like the magpie and the fireweed. If a local cowboy were to see a bird with the magpie's plumage and stature in a tropical jungle, I'd bet he'd ooh and aah and snap fifty pictures. But in Wyoming the sight of magpies is so familiar the accustomed viewer just doesn't see the green-ember glow of their feathers anymore, or the sleek, bold cut of their tails, and so instead of an admiring gasp at the electric white flash in their wingbeats, all magpies get is disparaged as scavengers. As for fireweed, favoring soil that's been burned, or ravaged by human activities like logging, and finding such soil in abundance in this part of the state, they're snubbed for being so common, seen as weeds instead of as stately tall-plumed fuchsia flowers. The old "familiarity breeds contempt" law is all that's at work here, nothing more, but that was one of a few truths of life I was having trouble swallowing back then.

Once in a saloon, its decor an array of taxidermy common in Wyoming bars, I stood looking up at the head of a big pronghorn. "Funny looking stunkers, ain't they?" an old cowboy said. "All painted up like that and them big eyes bulging out, I always thought they looked like a clown."

I thought the white bars on the throat were beautiful. Ditto, the rectangular white side patches, the white rump, and the big luminous eyes. It was bewildering to hear pronghorns called clowns. The first day I ever entered Wyoming, the first animal I saw was a pronghorn, on a rise by the road in the afternoon sunlight, looking down on the cars going by. Their hairs are hollow, against brutal plains winters. The fastest creature in the Western Hemisphere, they run like the wind.

The first settlers must have been dazzled by the spectacle of the pronghorn, but now they get called clowns and goats, a fact which bears witness that an everyday spectacle is a contradiction in terms, and that no matter how rare a thing is in the world at large, and how marveled at there, its beauty fades in everyday eyes. Be that as it may, back then, if you'd asked me, I'd have had pretty bitter words for this state of affairs, but the heated way I deplored it was probably extreme. After all, what did the pronghorn, or the magpie or the fireweed, know or care if their beauty should fade in some human's eye? If I found this situation so poignant, it was probably just an oblique way of singing some personal blues. I was entering a new season then, and something of my own was fading, something which at that stage of the game I identified as my "looks," and so the disappearance of beauty, real or imagined, or even just in the beholder's eye, was a thorny issue for me.

. . . . .

It was a big band all right, but as it turned out, that was not the most striking thing about it. There was something going on in their midst that we hadn't picked up from the road. The band fell into two main groups, a large crowd of scattered does and fawns to the west, up to forty maybe, and about four hundred yards to the east of them a smaller bunch, this apparently of does only, perhaps eight or nine in all. Normally they would be ambling about browsing, but they weren't. Instead both groups were focused on a spot midway between them, where two bucks labored in combat.

As if fused head to head, they moved as one entity, like one drunk, multilimbed, tawny body staggering back and forth, side to side, in the middle of the field. First the westernmost part of the body was back-stepping, driven by the easternmost part, and then, the tables turned, the western half would be the one pushing forward, and the eastern half, hind legs angling sharply in an attempt to hold footing, would have a turn at stumbling backwards for a while. Sometimes when both bucks managed to hold ground at the same time, they sashayed to one side and the other together, like an eight-legged creature in an awkward angular dance, until finally one of them lost his footing and they started backward and forward again.

For a while it was exciting. I'd never seen a pronghorn fight at close range before, and at no range had I seen one like this. The few I'd watched had been brief, a matter of swift admonishment and flight, but this one was long and tangled and vivid. The morning sun broke the horizon. The frost melted along the fence rails. Against the eroded red spires of the badlands the bucks toiled and toiled, as the rest of the band looked on. It was a nice piece of luck that we'd happened upon it, I thought while it lasted. A fine spectacle of nature for K to see.

. . . . .

An old friend from back East, K had come out to kick me up a little after a situation of mine had flopped. An intense situation of three years, with a man nearly half my age. My old friends had never grasped the attraction. "What are you doing with a guy half your age?" they said. But my new friends, the ones I met only after I was with him, didn't seem to have a problem with it. After all, I looked young when I met him, and felt it, and I still looked and felt young three years later when we went down in flames. Some months afterward, though, one particularly bad day I glanced in the mirror and I didn't look the same anymore. I looked again, and again, trying to see what I was used to seeing, trying to get it right, but it wouldn't come.

"We turn corners," K said on the phone, from New York. Coiled up, tail a-rattle, I said baloney to that. I was temporarily derailed by this break-up, was all; in a few months I'd get my old stuff back. In fact, once out of sight of him (the hard, smooth-skinned rounds of his shoulders; the cords standing up in his arms) I saw pretty clearly that my lost beau and I had been on mightily different wavelengths. Day by day I worked back into my old life, slowly working him out of my blood, and as far as he went, I can say that in a few months I was making good progress at getting back on track. And I was out in the hills almost daily, getting my color back. Certain days, in the mirror, I would note this color, and I would note other things, too: I had the same cheekbones as ever; I was as straight-nosed as before. So, what had changed then? What was the tragedy? Could just some lines around my eyes be the source of this dire leaden pool spreading in my chest?

Whatever it was, I still couldn't shake the mirror business. I was either nagging at it for the image it threw me or avoiding it, but never at home with it anymore. Sometimes there was an annoying frustrated feeling, like beating your fists on a wall. Sometimes there was something chilling, unbearable, that I wanted to run from fast. "How about I come out for a while," said K. I said no, she should come next summer, as we'd planned. "It's just some weird vanity trip I'm on, for some reason. No big deal," I said. But K came anyway.

. . . . .

As the sun mounted from orange to yellow, the bucks kept at it, scrambling backward and forward, legs bent at distressing angles, hooves jabbing into the clay. Heads tossing in unison, they grappled from side to side. Because they moved as a unit, while it went on the object of our watching was only the fight. But then they broke, turned their backs to each other and moved apart, one east, one west, and at that point the object of our watching became the fighters instead of the fight. It was a shocking moment. They seemed so unevenly matched. By the looks of them, it seemed a threat from one should have sufficed to send the other packing, no need for a fight, much less one as long and tough as this.

The one for whom it seemed a threat should have sufficed was lean, almost spindly, and small enough that if it weren't for the cut of his horns, I'd have taken him for a doe. His opponent was by far the more robust and regal. A tawny bulk, heading into the morning sun, his white bars were gleaming, and his black horns were polished with light. Broad of chest and barrel, and wide of skull, he had such big horns it looked like just one of them might fill both my hands at its base, and the points of their boldly forked prongs were so deeply hooked we could discern their little curls at 150 yards.

But what we also discerned was that the big buck was in trouble. Two hundred yards is a distance to hear such a thing, but we could hear the sound of his breathing, a high-pitched rasping, and then we noticed his sides, the big white rectangular patches heaving so hard it looked like his heart was going to burst. The spindly buck had jogged jauntily to the west end of the field where he stood with the large group of does, but the big buck moved only haltingly eastward, in a series of starts and stops. Facing into the gaze of the smaller harem, he stood wheezing laboriously. Then he stretched his neck out straight and almost to the ground and in a fit of gasping and coughing lost all his elegance.

When he came upright again, though, he headed straight for the little bunch of does. He jerked his head up, high and stiff, and moved quickly and sharply, his effort forced but focused, to round up this remaining lot. For less than a minute they let him. Then while three stood fast, still acquiescing to his worthiness, the other five or six dodged south around him and took off toward the large group to the west.

The scrawny buck, lord of the group they ran to, had not so much as cocked a front leg. He just stood looking out as they came over to him, as he'd done earlier when all the scattered does had flowed in from afield, tightening the band around him as if to be close to his power. The big buck swerved back to catch the fleeing does, but they were long gone, and the instant they joined the large group, the little buck dashed out at him again.

It didn't last long this time. In not much more than a minute the big buck turned away huffing strenuously. Still, he wouldn't throw in the towel. He made a quick recoup of wind and then, ready to cut his losses and accept what was left, he darted eastward again toward the handful of does at that end of the field. He wasn't to have even that, though. The last three took off too, streaking to join the rest of the band, leaving the big buck behind in the empty end of the field.

He looked regal to us, but his inside no longer matched his outside, and if we couldn't see this, the does could. With his fine head, his bold bars, and the eloquent points of his horns, he might cut the same grand figure he had all the years all his does had entrusted themselves to him, but they knew something in him had changed. He'd passed out of the season of prowess for which they had known him. It was time to find home elsewhere.

Slowly, the compact, focused mass the band had formed while watching the fight began to spread out, as the does and fawns returned to their browsing. As they drifted westward away from him, the big buck made a few purposeful looking strides in their direction. He stopped, watched, then made a few more purposeful looking strides. The little buck glanced back over his shoulder at him once or twice, but that's all — he didn't even bother to threaten — and after another few steps, successively more tentative, big buck stopped. For what seemed a long while, he stood and watched as the band meandered back toward the badlands, till all you could see of them was a dotting of white rumps against red buttes. When he turned east again, I felt a pain beyond all reason. He blurred in my sight as he picked his solitary way through the field toward the sun.

. . . . .

Back in the jeep, as K spouted a flurry of reactions to what we'd just seen, I thought of another time, showing this country to another friend, Jan, then new to Wyoming as K was now. On our drive up the mountainside home her first evening here, the sky was a panorama of weathers. To the northeast, across the valley, it was nighttime, the sky black with storm and pulsing with lightning over the mountains there. More than fifty miles distant, their round peaks flashed hard-edged every matter of seconds against silver sky, and sheets of rain hung in grey smudges over the plain below. To the southeast it was still daytime, the air placid and temperate, the sky clear, and the rising moon looked insubstantial against it, translucent even, a frail white disk on pale blue. To the west the sun was descending, a half hour to go yet, in a pale glowing sky of indeterminate color, yellow with pink in it, yellow with green in it, peach / lemon-lime / tangerine — all of these colors yet none of them either, a color just outside the grasp of mind's knowing. Trying to label it got you right-on-the-edge-of-your-tongue frustrated. A color without a name.

When we rounded the switchback at eight thousand feet we could see all these weathers, these colors, these risings and fallings, all at once all these processes and effects of atmosphere. Jan jumped down from the jeep and stood at the edge of the gravel. A sage-covered slope dropped steeply before her and hills capped with stands of black trees rolled beyond. She stood watching the storm as it drifted along the horizon. She watched the distant black mountains slowly turn gold. She looked long at the storm and the moon and the pending sunset, turning and turning from one to another. "If you could grow up here —" she said from the road's edge. "It teaches you you can get through it," she said.

It teaches you you can get through it, if there's a way through it, I thought that morning of the antelope. But sometimes there's not a way through it, and when there's not, it teaches that too.

. . . . .

"Can you beat it!" K said. "That beautiful big creature had that whole herd stolen away by that little puny thing."

That was how we both felt it, although we had no grounds for feeling that way. We hadn't seen the fight from the beginning, didn't know how the does and fawns had been grouped at the start. It could have been that the little buck had his own harem to start with, maybe even the larger of the two, and coming upon the big buck with a harem of seven or eight decided to try to annex a couple more to his band. Given the size of the band it was much more likely, in fact, that it had been two bands at the start and not one as we had for some reason assumed. We were anthropomorphizing like crazy, projecting elements of human melodrama onto the scene. The "beautiful big creature" and the "little puny thing" were in fact not the handsome (and supposedly therefore deserving) hero and the worthless upstart we made them out to be, but instead an old buck, just going over the hill, and a healthy young comer, just starting out. And nobody'd "stolen" anything. They'd had a fair fight, and the does always picked the true winner, the one whose victory proved his worth. It didn't matter what he looked like. And it didn't matter that one ended up with nothing while the other got it all. That was how things kept going. A wildlife biologist might have had a good laugh over us. A couple of cornballs sucked in by the handsome hero stuff of old movies, imposing sentimental morality and trivial theatrics on a simple case of nature taking its course.

Still, I couldn't help thinking anthropomorphic thoughts about the old buck. And at bottom, it wasn't the handsome hero business that really got to me about him. All that was only a smoke screen to eclipse what really hurt. He'd followed a long path through this country, all that time in a certain role, things going along in a certain way. (I couldn't help it, groundless or not, I was sure that before the fight the whole hefty harem had been his.) Then suddenly today he'd been pushed out of that path. Would he try to get back on it again somewhere else, try to get himself another harem? Or did he know that the old path had become irrelevant for him, that he'd passed out of that phase? And if he knew that, if he didn't keep trying to make the old tricks work for him, what would he do now? What new path could he take, and how would he know it? Picking his way through that grass heading sunward, had he been forging a path or in search of one, or had one just suddenly declared itself to him? And was this path the journey's last leg?

I could have gone to books to look for answers to these questions. That's what the wildlife biologist part of me would have done. But the anthropomorphizing part of me was in ascendancy at that point, and at that point I didn't care about the biologist's view. I didn't want empirical facts presented by scientists. Even if the books could have offered them, I didn't want clear-cut answers to the questions the pronghorn's debacle had set in flow. At that point, I just wanted to ponder those questions, broadly and lavishly, following all forks in the path. I pondered the destiny of that pronghorn many times in the following weeks.

One morning some months later when I looked in the mirror, I noticed that something had changed. I'd stopped nagging at it. I could no longer deny I'd indeed turned a corner, and, at bottom, losing my looks was not what the corner was about. It was about a new path, and

I was on one. Like an arc of surf, after the wave has broken, sweeping unresisted over the face of the beach, an emptiness washed through me, hollowing my arms, my legs, all my body, of any tension or former strife. The peace of an inexorable sadness acknowledged spread throughout me.

. . . . .

That evening for the first time since the antelope fight I looked into the books. One writer reported that bucks sometimes formed harems of up to twenty does, boosting my theory that the entire band was initially the big buck's, but other than this, not one of the books stacked around me under the lamplight addressed the questions I'd pondered. I think I'd known down deep all along that they wouldn't, that the answers I sought lay outside their covers and beyond that circle of light.

Still, the books held their own hard and quite splendid facts. Not only was the old buck's species the fastest in the West, and wondrously hollow haired. The pronghorn's white rump was a semaphore, its shining hairs, erected in response to danger, sending a warning of mirrored sunlight even to its fellows two miles away, who in turn flared the alarm, on and on to the last antelope within reach. And in casting off its horn coverings each fall the pronghorn was thoroughly original, the only exception to the rule that antlers are shed yearly and horns are kept for life. Traced down from Middle Miocene fossils (aged about fourteen million, give or take a few million years) to a look-alike ancestor who roamed this continent two million years ago and on to its present-day form, this species was the only native American hoofed animal. All others — deer, elk, moose, mountain goats, you name it — were immigrants. And, singular among mammals on yet one more count, the pronghorn had no close relative here or on any other continent, nor had they ever had. The old buck belonged to a species more unique and strange than I'd realized.

No proper answers to my questions. Just these bizarre gorgeous facts. But they opened some kind of sluice gate for me that night. Coming upon them one after another, I felt the bigness of the world and the longness of time in the pronghorn's history. I felt how small even that long history is against the eons before it, and I felt how infinitesimal are the codes of life, which, ever changing, keep changing life's details, yielding such results as the pronghorn's uniqueness, its

strangenesses that serve it so well. And as for the old buck himself —
who probably never even lost his beauty, who very likely was taken
down before that — I felt how even the remains of his body the morning after, fed on by scavengers and decomposing back into the soil, are
part of that chain of prodigiously worked-out details. I saw the old
buck's fate inside pronghorn history, small as a pinprick but, like all the
teeming pinpricks in all the histories, part of that great, odd, illimitable
scheme.

And though my questions and the answers they threatened still
loomed in the darkness, and would continue to loom there, they
weren't the whole show out there past the lamplight anymore. Instead
they were in company with such details as these expressions of the
working out of the old buck's species' fate. Wacky, erratic, but always
a-weaving, fueled by the dissolution of old bucks and of everything
else, the illimitable details of life sprang forth continually, passing from
one far-fetched, utilitarian form to another all along the evolution trail,
and there on my new path that night under the lamplight I felt a shrewd,
obscure mercy in them.

. . . . .

That spring I was especially attentive to pronghorn. One day I seduced
a young doe by not walking. I stood on a low hill with my binocs and
watched her until the motionless sight of me drove her nuts and she
had to get up close for a look. What she did was kind of tricky. She began to circle me, each circle smaller, so that I had to keep pivoting as
imperceptibly as possible, trying to present the same bewildering image to her every time she looked. As long as I succeeded reasonably at
this she spiraled in closer. But then, of course, I failed.

This was fine, and so was a young buck dubbed Mozart. One night
I camped with a music-lover friend who is never without a tiny tape
recorder, spinning out the boy genius's music this time. The little buck
had to approach to investigate. He just couldn't help himself. He came
way closer than shooting distance, close enough for us to axe him if
we'd liked, and in the morning when we woke he was there once more,
just feet away from the tent, waiting to hear if we'd do it again.

This was fine too, but still not enough, and since out in the hills in
my part of the state you see pronghorn infrequently, and then solitary
more often than not, I took a trip east to the open plains. There, there

was a bounty of pronghorn. You saw strings of them along the tops of low ridges, silhouetted against the sky. Mostly then, it being late June, there were mothers and babies. Fawns with ears two times the length of their faces, a largess of fawns dotting the sagebrush, all with those bizarre, gorgeous details hard-wired inside them, one of them perhaps carrying the infinitesimal code for some far-fetched but salutary detail to come. You had only to move and in a flurry their miniature white rumps were zigzagging off toward the horizon along with the big ones. Wherever you looked, the plains were bobbing with them.

Note

1. Although *pronghorn* is the correct name for the species in question, among people who live where they're found, these animals are most often referred to as *antelope* and *pronghorn antelope*. It's for this reason that I've intermixed all three common names in this essay.

Cows, Arrogance, the Natures of Things

TO THE MEMORY OF JOHN FOX

We were driving a jeep trail through a wide velvet valley, a grey wall of the Absaroka mountains before us, when rounding a bend we were stopped by a cluster of cows. Ambling along the muddy ribbon of ruts that was the road, they'd heard our engine, and wondering what was here now, they'd turned to meet us with big impassive stares. The woman riding beside me did three things. She wrinkled up her face, stuck her tongue out, and putting her thumbs in her ears, waggled her fingers at the cows. "I hate you," she spat at them.

The woman was an environmentalist. She worked for a number of national organizations that were trying to save the Earth. In spite of myself, I bristled a little. Why would a woman who worked on behalf of the natural world stick her tongue out at a cow?

I was no rancher, and I too call myself an environmentalist. Still, I'd lived on a ranch once, and I'd had some vivid scenes of cow life burned into me. "If this woman thinks cows are just a heap of shit and flies with no brains, I have things to teach her," I thought, a few scattered hackles still rising. Not that I didn't appreciate the issues that prompted her. I knew the cows-are-the-enemy attitude she was wielding, its sources, its political expediencies. But comrade in arms or not, my passenger's gestures just didn't sit well with me.

. . . . .

The contingent of anti-cow environmentalists my passenger belongs to aren't the only ones to malign cows, of course. Many others with less righteous motives disparage cows in similar, sometimes more hostile, ways. Most of them aren't even aware that cows damage fragile land and water courses through overgrazing; they just think cows are dumb. "Stupidest goddamned things you could ever hope to see," they will say. As if thinking cows less-than-animal, sometimes even so-called animal lovers will do this. In the same breath they'll extol the virtues of the bison and trash the cow.

Maybe we think cows are stupid because they're such easy victims for us — something along the lines of Groucho Marx's quip that he wouldn't want to belong to any club that would take him: if these creatures submit so easily to our manipulation, they must be lowly indeed. (A cowboy might legitimately argue that, detail by detail, this manipulation isn't actually so easy. But when you consider how thoroughly we dominate cows' lives birth to death — tampering with their bodies, determining when they breed and with whom, appropriating their offspring, governing even the hour and manner of the young steers' death, and all this by the hundreds of millions — with all due respect to the rigors of cowboying, I think you can say overall we control cows with relative ease.) We manipulate other animals too, of course. But cows seem so passive. Whatever we do to them, much of the time cows more or less just stand there, pretty much just standing for it.

Or do they? In the case of many of the other animals we manipulate so thoroughly, we actually seem to get through to them. We succeed in "breaking" horses. We get dogs to acknowledge us as boss. We say this is a sign of their intelligence, and by a certain definition it may be — although the idea that responsiveness to our biddings is a measure of brain power seems pretty self-centered. The thing is, though, after a course of our training, the dogs and a lot of the horses offer us a kind of adulation. They don't just do what we want, they do it willingly, often even eagerly. But cows, while they tolerate us, just don't let us get through to them that way. They may not resist our efforts at manipulation so doggedly, but neither do they ever really give us the nod of assent. *Okay, so you're going to herd us. You've got us beat from the start on this one — it's our genes' orders to bunch — so we'll go along, but don't expect a show of enthusiasm over it*. They haven't much choice but to do what we want, but they don't flatter us that they've bought the idea as a good one.

Whenever we get animals to do what we want them to, what we're really doing is exploiting genetic predispositions; it's the dog's pack-animal nature, for example, that dictates his compliant behavior — as long as we manage to establish ourselves as a substitute for that alpha dog he's genetically ordered to submit to, that is. As for beef cows, most have a docile nature — they've had docility bred into them — and for our benefit (more flesh: more meat) they've had a certain cumbersomeness bred into them too, so at this point in their human-guided evolution they're no longer built, psychologically or physically, for effective rebellion or self-defense. Exploiting these traits we've fostered in them, along with their natural bunching behavior, we round them up fairly easily with our dogs and horses and bullwhips and crowd them into corrals, and once they're in there they're ours to do with as we wish. And to an uninitiated viewer much of what we do once we've got them there might very well seem not just fearsome, but probably diabolical, and maybe a little perverted too.

The herd is a serious security factor for bovids. Some wild cattle will collectively attack even a deadly predator — Cape buffalo, for example, will attack a lion — and even blind, lame, or otherwise handicapped individuals can thrive in such a herd. Although domestic cattle may not be aggressive enough to enjoy such solid defense as this, their reliance on the group is nevertheless very strong, and once we've exploited their bunching instinct by herding them into our stockades, we turn around and exploit their psychological dependence on it by isolating them. We run cattle through narrow chutes, separating them from the group they see as their protection. Then we pierce their ears with plastic earrings, Day-Glo tags with ID numbers on them and fly tags infused with pesticide. We immobilize them in webs of rope or in metal vises called calf tables and burn our symbols into their flesh. We cut off their horns, or "burn" them off with caustic, and if they're male we cut off their testicles. Segregated from the herd and confined in our contraptions, there's nothing much they can do about it. Given their nature, once they're released the most cows can do is run off bleeding and bawling, to band together again and hope for the best until the next time we come for them. And if we're talking in terms of intelligence, what's dumb about any of this? If they don't stand a chance against us, why fight a losing battle? But at the same time, why give us an inch more than they have to give? Maybe by human reckoning cows aren't as smart as dogs or horses in some ways, but on this count they seem to have pretty good sense. And a certain stolid, self-respecting integrity too.

What's more, whoever pays attention will notice that cows aren't less-than-animal at all. Let them loose and they'll find forage just about anywhere — from grasslands to desert to forest to tundra — which is part of the reason my environmentalist passenger stuck her tongue out at them. They're so "animal," so much a part of Nature, that they can get by eating the poorest, coarsest grasses, the most pitiful shrubs — even bark when all else fails. And cold weather has to be extraordinarily cold to be a problem for the right breed of cow. The cow has a multipart stomach and chews a cud, meaning it can store food only partially digested in the first stomach part — the rumen — bringing it up later at will to chew and prepare it for final digestion and assimilation in the other stomach parts. In some breeds the contents of the rumen ferments at 40 degrees Celsius, providing these cows with a central heating system so that they don't need to generate extra heat by shivering or eating more, despite temperatures as low as −18 degrees Celsius. And the calves of such breeds are astonishingly hardy. Even born in below-zero weather, the calf of a Hereford or an Angus is soon up and cavorting around like a fawn in the month of May. Other breeds (Brahman and Santa Gertrudis, to name two) do as well in extreme heat, relying on a fleshy hump, or a generous dewlap, or long drooping ears, or a flap of flesh beneath the belly known as the underline to radiate heat away. Some breeds work without fatigue even in extreme climatic conditions, and with little food. Not even lack of sleep need be a problem for cows: they sleep in bouts of two to eight minutes, often with a total of no more than one hour in twenty-four. They're tough customers, cows, with a physical endurance any animal would be proud to match.

So why do we think so little of cows?

Maybe it's because we eat them. It takes some introspection, a little spiritual digging and turning over of stones, to acknowledge the complex virtues of a creature you're going to kill for food. And juxtaposed with that other possible motive — that tinge of self-hatred, Groucho Marx style — maybe in part it's our vanity that leads us to sell cows short. On the one hand, we look down on cows because they're easy to manipulate. On the other, we scorn them because we can't get much of a rise out of them. If this bugs us a little, we rationalize it by saying they're stupid, not intelligent enough to feel much of anything: just look at that dumb blank stare. Once again this interpretation is anthropocentric, and it overlooks an interesting fact about the nature of cows. Cows have a rigid facial musculature that actually *prevents* a range of expressions. A dog can signal hostility or submission through its facial expression, but a bull can do so only through posture and movement. The cow's blank look doesn't necessarily denote affectlessness at all, but oblivious to the cow's proper nature, we interpret it as impassivity. Cows don't have the sensitivity of other animals, we say. Horses are high-strung, skittish, highly emotional in our eyes, and dogs quiver with love and the desire to please, but cows just stand there, as if (as we'd have it) they don't feel anything. But let me tell you a couple of stories about cows.

. . . . .

It should be just dusk, but the snowstorm has turned it dark early. The snow is falling thickly and the light of the pole lamp is only a lavender smear at the edge of the corral. Beneath it a cow lies on her side in the cow muck. Up to this point the heat of the muck has been melting the snow, as has the cow's body heat, but the snow has begun to stick now and the cow's red hide is covering over with a veil of white. She has been lying here for almost three hours with the tips of two little hooves and the swollen tongue of a calf sticking out her hind end.

When the rancher and his son gave up trying to pull it and called the vet, the cow was still struggling to get the calf out. At that point she'd been in this condition an hour. The vet was an hour from the ranch, but when they phoned him he was out on a call, and then there was the snow, so it's taken him twice the usual time to get here.

The cow is a little Hereford, a first-year heifer. One of the bulls on the ranch is a Charolais, and she accidentally got bred by him. Charolais are big white cows, one of the largest breeds, and they throw big calves, and you shouldn't breed a Charolais to a first-year heifer because she's too small. Last summer, though, the Charolais bull broke out of the bull pen and got to this little heifer, and now she isn't able to pass this calf. She appears just about out of whatever it takes to get through it, when the vet's headlights appear through the snow's whirl.

The three men bend above the cow, working. They try to get her to her feet, but no dice. They yank at her legs and shove at her swollen sides, finally wrestling her onto a tarp. Her feet are tied at this point, the two front ones lashed together and the two rear, and ropes are twined through the grommets of the tarp, and the men strain at these ropes. Her legs in the air, the cow moos in low moans, as the men, slipping in snow and mud against the weight of her, drag the cow-laden tarp through the door of a nearby log shed.

In the shed the cow lies upside down mooing weakly. The men hang droplights from the ridgepole, and keeping her on her back, they spread her front and hind legs in opposite directions, tying them to opposite walls so she can't kick. Kneeling over her swollen belly holding something that looks like a miniature fire extinguisher, the vet sprays her with antiseptic. The cow's eyes roll, the whites showing, and she lets out faint moans, ever dwindling protests of pain and fear.

The vet cuts through one layer of tissue, then another. Suddenly a huge slick grey balloon with veins running through it comes popping up out of the slit, part of her large intestine pushing out as the cow pushes to pass her calf. The vet presses down on the balloon the way you press down kneading bread, pushing stubbornly until he finally gets it back in. Eventually, he gets to the uterus and cuts that.

The vet drags a big white calf out of the cow's belly and flops it down onto a hay bale. The little bull's sides are heaving and in a few minutes he's trying to get to his feet, but no one pays any attention to him. The cow's mooing has stopped, her breathing is highly irregular, and for now all attention is on her.

Meanwhile, a tiny white heifer, just three days old herself, has been intruding periodically through the side door of the shed. When the men were binding and dragging the cow, the heifer and her mother were standing at the edge of the circle of the pole lamp's light watching, and since then, all through the birth one problem there's been to contend with has been keeping this little heifer from nosing in. Squatting at the head of the cow, watching to learn how the vet does the Caesarean, the rancher has had to interrupt his study many times to shoo the tiny heifer back out the door. Now that the birth is over, she has nosed back in again to catch the tail end of the commotion and to see the new calf.

Finally the cow is again breathing regularly, and the vet is finishing up his ministrations. The newborn lies shaking on his hay bale. "I'm just a limp little fella, ain't I?" says the rancher, standing over it. "Cain't get up, just a limp little fella," he says. Opposite him is the little white heifer, having finally made it through to where she wanted to be.

Across the hay bale from the rancher she stands, unimpeded, licking the little bull like a mama cow.

After the long hard delivery the Hereford was traumatized. She wasn't to get up for a couple of days, and as often happens with a traumatized first-year heifer, she wouldn't accept her calf. It was the little white heifer who took care of him. While the rancher's son helped the vet during the Caesarean, he was figuring he was going to have one more calf to bottle feed, but he got a welcome surprise. It turned out all he'd be responsible for was ensuring the calf got his colostrum, a substance in the mother's first milk that provides immunity against disease until the newborn produces its own antibodies. After that, when the little bull was up and wobbling around, the little white heifer coaxed him outside the shed to meet her mama, and from that day on he nursed from her.

Contrary to how this might sound, it didn't happen on Christmas, and this is not a little Christmas tale. This is a random, ranch-life event that happened one day in March, and the curiosity and generosity of the calf who took the abandoned newborn home to supper is pretty much run-of-the-mill calf nature; that is, this is part of the way cows are.

. . . . .

The cow issue's a problem, no doubt about it. I have no quarrel with anti-cow environmentalists on that. Look at all the questions surrounding the cow. In a world in which one-fifth of the people go to bed hungry each night, how can we justify eating beef when the grain used to feed one person an eight-ounce steak could provide forty people with a meal? And in a world of dwindling resources how can we afford the twenty-five hundred gallons of water used to produce a one-pound steak, and how can we afford the billions of tons of topsoil eroded in growing crops to feed livestock, the greatest consumer of which by far is the cow? And it's not just the water required to raise the cow, it's the water that's polluted and wasted through overgrazing of riparian areas. And it's not just the land devoted to crops that go to feed cows, it's the land that's eroded and rendered useless through overgrazing by cows. And in a world in which the number of plant and animal species is rapidly shrinking, it's what would grow on that land if it weren't overgrazed and eroded and what could live off that land if it didn't have to compete with the cow. "Biological diversity is the key to the maintenance of the world as we know it," says Edward O. Wilson, foremost expert internationally on biodiversity. He's not alone in his opinion. It's widely held that, working hand in hand with overpopulation, the accelerating extinction of species is the most serious threat to the healthy perpetuation of the biosphere. Like the car issue and the plastic container issue and the air conditioner issue, the cow issue's a problem, no doubt. But is the cow the real enemy?

The cow is a cause of the deterioration of our environment. That's one way of looking at it. But another way of looking at it is this: the cow is not a cause but an effect. Over eight thousand years ago we began to develop the cow as a resource, when we began to domesticate the wild aurochs in Europe and the Near East. These wild cattle were six to seven feet at the withers, lanky and fast and agile and fierce, a far cry from the modern cattle we've produced. Witness a traditional prize-winning Hereford. Thick-necked and broad-headed, deep-shouldered and so short-legged you wonder he's able to move, led around a ring on a rope with a ribbon at his temple, he's the result of a selective breeding process as old as domestication, but which has accelerated enormously since the development of modern breeds began in Europe and the British Isles in the 1600s, even more rapidly since the mid-eighteenth century. We've bred cows to grow faster and produce leaner meat (Charolais) and we've bred cows to withstand subtropical heat and ticks (Santa Gertrudis) and we've bred cows to withstand rigorous winter climate (Angus) and we've bred cows for easy manageability (Hereford), and on and on, not even to mention dairy breeds.

In short, taking advantage of attributes inherent in their nature, among them their natural hardiness and adaptability, we've bred cows so we could raise as many as possible, as easily as possible, to produce the greatest possible amount of meat, and we've deposited them all over the globe wherever they could possibly survive, which is just about anywhere — the easier and cheaper for us, the better. In doing so we've taken a neutral creation of Nature and made it a positive force for our survival (food, shoes, etc.); but at the same time, it turns out, we've made it into a negative force. At this point, cows are serious contributors to environmental degradation, yes. But we're their keepers and promoters, the overseers of their breeding (in the United States cows now outnumber people by more than four to one), and it's we who decide what they're given to gorge on in feedlots (twenty pounds of grain a day for ninety days), and it's we who determine where they graze (fragile public lands, among other places) and how long they're allowed to do so on any given stretch of range (traditionally, convenience to the rancher has been a chief determinant here). So in a sense, like the car issue and the plastic container issue and the air conditioner issue, the cow issue is man-made.

At the same time, however, the cow has its own Nature-given place in the biological scheme of things. And it has a Nature-given core that we haven't touched. We breed Anguses and Herefords, and we breed out fierceness and agility and breed in bulk and manageability, and we brand and castrate and de-horn to our hearts' content. Still cows depend on posture over countenance to express emotion. Still they seek refuge in the herd. If they suffer badly enough during calving, they're traumatized by the suffering and will reject their offspring. If the rejected offspring's lucky, another of his kind befriends him, another mother of his kind gives him nourishment. Despite our manipulations, a cow has its own essential nature, and it behaves, sometimes regardless of us, sometimes despite us, accordingly. And if we pay attention, we notice its nature exhibits a good deal of depth and complexity.

. . . . .

Let me tell you another story about cows:

In June, when calving was over, the rancher and his son moved the cows to summer pasture. Because their summer pasture was a good forty-five miles away and their only access to it for most of the way was along a highway, rather than drive the whole herd on horseback, the rancher and his son carted them there in the back of a truck. They'd round up twenty-five head and haul them away, then several hours later they'd come back and round up another twenty-five head, making trip after trip until the whole herd was moved. They took the cows as they happened to catch them, and cow-friends got separated, and many times cows got separated from their calves.

When a truckload arrived at summer pasture, the cows already there were scattered all over. They were up steep sagebrush hillsides, they were down by the stream in the cottonwood groves. As soon as they heard the truck, though, they came running. Splashing through streams and lumbering down hillsides, udders and underlines and dewlaps swinging, the cows came mooing, and the more nimble little calves came bawling all the way. They gathered around the truck to see who'd arrived this trip. A cow or calf would come skittering down the ramp and its mom or its kid or its buddy would lumber or cavort up to welcome it.

When unloading was finished, clusters of cows and calves still stood around the truck mooing and bawling, demanding to know where their mom was, or their kid or their buddy, complaining the truck hadn't brought her, calling her as if she were still inside the truck. And they came running to meet every subsequent truckload until whoever they were calling for, blood or buddy, had arrived.

Even if you liked cows all right, if you were human you probably couldn't help having been tinged with the old human attitude that cows are somehow less-than-animal, and so watching this scene you couldn't help being a little surprised by this show of camaraderie and loyalty of the cows reunited with friends and blood, and you couldn't help being struck by the plaintive mooing and bawling of the ones whose anticipation of such a reunion had been disappointed. This was so especially if you were ignorant of another essential fact of cow nature, or if, having once known it, you'd come to lose sight of that fact. Female cows spend their lives in small closed herds, "groups of stable composition organized on the basis of personal recognition," as one student of cow nature has put it, meaning that cows choose their friends. Especially if you didn't know this, or had forgotten, you couldn't help being struck pretty powerfully by the nature of the cows, and how there was a good deal more to it than you'd bothered to think about.

. . . . .

It wasn't just my passenger's particular attitude toward cows that didn't sit well with me that day in that valley below the Absarokas. Despite all her advocacy work, it seemed that in this particular case she'd lost sight of Nature, and this had me pondering. Brainwashed over time through human custom, maybe even an environmentalist can lose sight of the cow as a creature of Nature, lose sight of the Nature in things.

I think it starts with control. Controlling the cow, subverting it to our uses, we begin to ignore its nature. We simplify it in our minds to our own concept of it — a creature with just those traits that fulfill our purposes, nothing more — and we stop seeing the full, subtle nature of the cow. And the less we acknowledge its nature, the more control we believe we have over it — and the more right to control — and on in a spiral we go. For usually, it seems, the more we think we control something, the less we respect it, and the less we respect it, the less capable we are of seeing it truly and the more we see it as a tool/appurtenance/resource of ours. We de-nature it in our minds.

This may be the story in the case of the cow, and the story reminds me of a lot of others in the history of our dealings with the Earth. With the aid of our often splendid technology, we cleared forests, hauled boulders and stumps, plowed virgin soil, shored up waters, cut deep into rock to extract minerals, and when we were through, it seemed to us we'd tamed the Earth. Of course those who lived intimately with the mines or the fields or the dammed-up waters knew the constant vigilance required to *keep* the Earth "tamed." But to humanity at large — in most of what we call developed societies, at least — such elements as soil and water and vegetation seemed essentially conquered, where we wanted them forevermore. We saw the Earth then as pastoral and obedient, forgot for the most part the dynamic, unruly, extravagant body of activity that it was, except as a character in our old stories of subduing it. It had been that, and we had dealt with it, but now what it had been it was no more.

Still, the Earth continued to express and proclaim itself as it always had, dropping lots of clues of its activity along the way. When we dammed the big rivers, silting resulted (many United States reservoirs are now 50 percent or more filled with mud) and, denied their natural annual overflowing of banks by our levees, rivers responded with erratic, uncontrollable floods. In response to overgrazing by domesticated animals, the exposed soil increased Earth's albedo, and with more sunlight reflected away the land cooled, causing the air overhead to cool too so that it didn't rise as it once had, and so clouds didn't form as they once had, and so rainfall decreased, and as rainfall decreased there was still less plant cover, and greater albedo, and on and on toward desertification things went. In response to our pesticides the pest species we wanted to cancel mutated, developing hardier strains, or if those pests were in fact canceled, the species they'd once preyed upon then flourished unchecked, presenting new pestly problems to us. When we pumped our pollutants into the sky as if to float them up and away forever, they came back down to us in the rain, poisoning our community reservoirs and secluded mountain lakes, our backyard gardens and the wilderness forests, sickening us and remote fish and trees indiscriminately.

You can fill books with this stuff: example after example of humanity punching the lump out of one side of the pillow of Nature, only to find a new lump popping out on the other side. But although in Nature's time the Earth's expressions and proclamations are big and full of consequence, in time measured by human lifespans they're slow and small, the early intimations of their far-reaching impact often lost on us, and stuck thinking Nature is where we want it, we don't notice the new lumps for a long time. Or, who knows, maybe somewhere down deep in an old buried wisdom we *do* sense the hints Nature drops; but at the stirring of a faint, sickening awareness that we have never subdued Nature really, that we're not independent of her as we thought, we panic and stick our heads in the sand.

Whatever our reasons and motives, for a long time we've done the Earth as we've done the cow: de-natured it in our minds. We've focused just on what we've been doing to the Earth, and because we've failed to acknowledge what the Earth itself has been doing, in our minds it's seemed not to resist. And the longer we've managed to ignore its reactions, the more we've felt lords of the Earth, rightfully in dominion, and as we've felt our power more and more, we've felt the Earth's nature less and less. And the less we've felt *its* nature, the more divorced we've become from our own nature, and the more divorced we've become from Nature, the more justified we've felt in tampering heedlessly, and the circle goes on. But just as the cow acts and reacts whether we notice or not, so does the Earth, and in spades. And while the behavior of cows might go largely unheeded forever, the Earth's reactions have accumulated to the point that even if we would resist seeing them, we cannot.

. . . . .

One more cow story comes in October, after the cows have been hauled back down from summer pasture and gathered at the ranch where the rancher can put his finger on them for the winter, where he can truck them their hay every morning and tend to calving when it starts in mid-winter, if they need help. It comes after another bout of trucking cattle, this time loading up the little steers and some of the little heifers and hauling them away for good.

The cows stayed off in the fields on the ranch in question. You never caught them down around the corrals or the barns. They were lucky to have a nice-sized river flowing through their ranch, gravelly willow bottoms, cottonwood groves to meander through, and lots of flat, irrigated green pasture, and sagebrush hills to meander up and down when the fancy struck them, too. They stayed off in this bounteous varied land, never came down to the jumble of log sheds and pole barns where the corrals and humans were, except for when they were driven there — for branding and injections and de-balling and other indignities.

But the night after the little steers were hauled off to market was an exception. The area among the sheds and barns was filled with cows that night. We drove down after dark to check that some new water lines down there hadn't frozen, and cows filled the roadway and the turnaround, and all the packed-down spaces among the sheds and corrals and barns were filled with cows. They stood bawling in our headlights, relentlessly. They stuck their necks out at our oncoming truck, their mouths gaping at it, and until we were right upon them they stood their ground, not shrinking from the beams of electric light coming at them, undaunted by the engine sound they usually shied away from. All night off and on we would wake and hear them all down there bawling, calling their lost calves, protesting the loss of them.

. . . . .

"What if hell was that we had to endure the suffering we've inflicted on animals?" a friend once speculated to me. I recalled those cow faces that market-day night, eyes unblinking, necks extended, their bellowing mouths held out to the two rounds of light coming at them in the dark — mourning in the headlights, recklessly.

Ranchers can't afford to pay attention to the more complex sides of cows because they're going to slaughter them. The general public can't afford to pay too much attention to their living nature because we're going to chow down on them. Anti-cow environmentalists can't afford to pay too much attention to a cow's creaturely complexities because they're trying to abolish them. It's the way of Nature that one life-form sacrifices another to its own needs, and it makes it more bearable to do that if you de-nature the life-form to be sacrificed, make it less "living," less like you.

Probably the image of those cows in the headlights sums up as powerfully as you'd ever need to why we tend to de-nature what we would use and control. But it's an insidious tendency.

The environmental movement has come about in response to myriad acts of de-naturing, some vast, some minuscule. We've ignored, at best oversimplified, the physical and chemical properties of the abiotic elements of Nature, behaved to a great degree as if land, water, and air were static, nonreactive, as if they didn't have a dynamic nature of their own. We've numbed, sometimes even blocked, our awareness of the complexities of many of the living creatures of Nature, among those complexities their life-given dignities and their similarities and connections with us. If environmentalists are fighting to remedy the effects of these tendencies, shouldn't we strive to keep the natures of all things — cows as well as bison — steadily in view?

John Donne said no man is an island. As any biologist will tell us, neither is any other part of Nature. If we lose sight of the nature of any part of the Earth, we're inevitably losing sight of other parts of the web of Nature too, and when we lose sight of enough of the web, we lose sight of our own selves as well. If we lose sight of the nature of the cow enough to believe it's no more than our convenient idea of it, we're blind not just to the cow but to ourselves also. If we see the cow's nature fully enough to discover what we share with the cow, however, we have a better sense of both of us. We have a better sense of who we all are and where we all stand.

If not for the sake of the cow itself and the other living creatures and their life-given dignities; if not for the sake of the Earth itself and the elegant, intricate, prodigious systems that make it work; if for none of the compelling, enriching, enlightening, uplifting aspects of the things of Nature that are worth our attention in their own right, then for the reason that all these things are inexorably and quite consequentially *there*, sustaining the web that defines and sustains us ourselves, it seems we'd be wise to foster a worldview that takes note of the nature of the cow.

. . . . .

Nothing is ever simple. There are many proposed solutions to the car issue, the plastic container issue, the air conditioner issue, and to the cow issue, too. Even if we leave the question of food supply apart entirely, the question of cow-related land damage alone generates solution theories and subissues galore. Some put their faith in raising grazing fees to protect federal lands from the devastation of overgrazing. Some advocate measures to eliminate the cattle industry entirely. Allan Savory, an ecologist who has spent a lifetime with his eye on both the natures of cows and of semiarid ecosystems like certain ones in the American West, puts a paradoxical spin on things: he believes that, properly managed, cows are the way to restore those ecosystems to health.

Simplified, his reasoning is as follows: Such areas were traditionally populated by vast herds of plant-eating ungulates (bison, mule deer, bighorn sheep, pronghorn) that through their particular grazing habits and patterns promoted the biodiversity upon which the health of an ecosystem depends. When bunching to protect themselves from predators, these herds broke up the hard soil, working in nutritive plant litter, thereby promoting water retention and seed germination, which the concentration of their urine and dung then fertilized. The herd then moved on to avoid their own waste, not returning until it was absorbed, with the result that while the *area* got heavily grazed, *individual plants* didn't and so weren't killed but instead stimulated to grow. Cows are ungulates too, and if our cow herds were wild, their grazing behavior would be similar to that of traditional herds. But since they aren't wild, and since the large wild herds are gone now, Savory has developed a process for managing cattle to simulate traditional grazing patterns, including a method of bunching cattle without the use of predators. He says that in the semiarid ecosystems in question the difference between the heavy but short-term grazing of traditional herds and the light but prolonged grazing of today (where the cows *do* eat plants down to the roots) is the difference between trailing 365 cows along an area for one day and trailing one cow along the same area for 365 days. The former rejuvenates land; the latter reduces it to barren hardpan. Though in certain ecosystems (for instance, riparian zones and humid areas of uniform rainfall and climate) resting damaged land will restore it to health, in these semiarid ecosystems Savory says the land will *worsen* with rest — to ensure carbon cycling, it *needs* the action of herbivorous ungulates — and, at this point, cows are our best bet for restoring these ecosystems to health.

On the other hand, there are biologists who disagree with Savory, arguing that we don't know as much about these ecosystems as he thinks and that therefore his ideas aren't as solidly grounded as he makes out. Nothing is ever simple. There are enough theories on this issue and its solutions to make your head swim. The cow stories here, these reflections, offer no solutions to the man-made cow issue, and they are not intended to.

. . . . .

But it may not be beyond our nature to be able to keep the natures of things in view. It's not unprecedented. It's been a practice in primal cultures to honor the prey, the sacrifice/the thing used, to ask its forgiveness, to keep sight of a shared livingness with it, and — whether plant, animal, mineral, water, or sky — to keep sight of shared origins with it and of comparable if different places in a shared scheme. Maybe this capacity for respectful attention to Nature is muffled in us somewhere yet, gasping faintly but still not asphyxiated.

Maybe you'll say, Yes *but*: you can't expect us to think as primal peoples have. We have the whole vast buffer of our technology between us and the tooth-and-claw fight for survival; they had the wolf at the door. Well, yes, *but*: maybe in a way we've come full circle now. Maybe the wolf is at the door again, or has been all along, and as our technologies are backfiring — as our efforts, however splendid, are suddenly failing to camouflage from us one wolf after another — maybe we're beginning to notice its howl again.

It's the nature of things, yes, that we — environmentalists included — sacrifice others to our needs. But with managing this aspect of our nature, as with all things, there are ways and there are ways. The way of respect and attention will help keep the web functioning. The way of ignoring and unattended arrogance will disrupt the web. It's been disrupted before, of course, on a grand scale about a dozen times, the most recent disruption putting an end to the dinosaurs. Now we

have the power to do to our world the same thing that the giant meteor strike or the great volcanic eruption or whatever it was did to
theirs. But we don't have the ultimate power. Nature, which does, will
readjust the web again in the long run. In the long *long* run that human
minds can't really grasp.

. . . . .

Calves are cows' lot in life. There's always a new one on the way. Sometimes, in difficulty, a cow will have to have her calf pulled for her; usually she's a first-year heifer, green to the whole thing. She lies on her
swollen side not knowing what's happening to her, while some human
mucks around at her hind end with a thing that looks like a handyman
jack with a motorcycle chain attached. Then, maybe in a flash of red
pain, the pressure is broken and, the mechanical operation over, she's
escaped this mysterious martyrdom — if she wants, she can flee. One
heifer I remember, after such an experience, pulled herself up on her
feet so fast you wouldn't have believed it. She took one bewildered
look behind her at the wet bundle and the mess on the ground and ran
like hell the other way.

"Where's your damn maternal instinct," the cowboy said. "She
looks at the little sucker like it was no more'n a big shit she just took."

Her maternal instinct was inside her; further trauma excluded, it
might come out next time around. But thus far this first-year heifer had
had only a mysterious man-attended ordeal for experience with moth-
erhood, and for the moment she'd been divorced from an ingredient
of her nature by it.

In this final story there was once again a nursing mother nearby
who took the new calf. But this story is not as romantic as the earlier
one. No innocent little white intermediary, lacking experience of the
world and acting solely on instinct, intervened. Just an average cow,
in whom instinct was blended with a healthy exposure to the natures
of things via several years' calving experience. She knew how to recognize a creature of her own when she saw it, and although the little
wet heap wasn't that, she knew it was one of her kind. And seeing it
abandoned, and already having one of her own to feed anyway, she
came to lick the new calf, rescuing it from the peril a benighted mother
had exposed it to.

The Porcupine's Old Clothes

TO MARTHY McDONNELL

A t first it was a little blur in the woods. A blur in slow motion, the ground moving vaguely back among the trees. Ducking out from under the boughs of a big spruce I glimpsed it — just motion, no form — and pulling up short I glued my eyes to the spot.

Late spring, up near timberline. Isolated snow drifts eight feet tall still lingered in the subalpine park above the forest where I'd been hiking, mini mountain ranges of white scattered here and there on rivulet-veined, marsh marigold–bedotted meadow, which was tan still, yet to green. The forest snow, not having drifted to such heights, was gone for the most part, but the floor of the forest was still damp and drab too, the bright green leaves of arnica, geranium, and lupine to come still mere coiled potentials down in the soil, and it was hard to distinguish one form from another against the dark mottling of forest-floor debris. It took a long lot of hard staring to make that patch of ground configure into a large bespiked rodent. Against the ground's brownness he blended in well, my first porcupine.

Then too, once frozen by a sense of something awry, he knew how to be endlessly still. I moved, but I had my own kind of persistence. Step by slow, tentative step I closed the gap between us — fifty feet, twenty-five — but I never took my eyes from where the blur had been, and finally, as my visual cortex gradually decoded the subtle jumble of light images received by my retinae, yellow guard hairs began to differentiate themselves against the ground's brown. Then the body took shape there, round, squat, like a marmot's or a muskrat's, but big for a rodent, Rocky Mountain–porcupine big, a yard long. Closer, fifteen feet, the patch of face a dark clearing amid the sweep of long yellow guard hairs, snub at the muzzle, two tiny bright eyes. Even then, with the critter distinguished from his background, it was hard to make out parts of him, nose, mouth, and where were the limbs in that bristly ball? Thirteen feet, ten. There was a tremble in the guard hairs, a faint quiver with a beat. It was throbbing, the body of the porcupine. His little eyes looked toward me but not at me, unseeingly. His nose twitched continuously, in a constant question. The way it seemed, he suspected I was there but didn't know for sure.

I stood forever, supporting myself against a tree to quell my nerves' little jerks of rebellion at motionlessness. Minutes passed, three, five. He looked unseeingly. His nose twitched on. His guard hairs quivered to a steady throb beneath. Was it his regular heartbeat, or his own difficulties with motionlessness, or fear? Nine minutes. Twelve. Maybe he guessed he must have been wrong — nothing was there, it was all right — because all of a sudden he moved. He turned and waddled a few steps away, awkwardly, impossibly slowly, allowing me to see. There was a bowed hind leg, and the leathery sole of his foot made me think of a bear's foot. When he sat, forelegs drawn up to his chest, more or less like arms folded there, I saw the claws, long and curved like the claws of a bear. Half turned from me, he gave me a good view of the palette of fierce hard little white quills on his back, and the stubble of them erect on his tail.

. . . . .

The dogs on the ranch used to get into it with porcupines. Or Rufus did, anyway. The Norwegian Elkhound, Scooter, had his encounters with porcupines, but what he did with them couldn't be called getting into it, I guess, since he never got a single quill in him. The elkhound was what on the ranch they'd call "a mean little shit"— he'd bite you out of nowhere, passionlessly — but he was smart and shrewd and always came at things from some hitherto unnoticed place off to the side, so he could always take porcupines by cold surprise, flipping them, helpless, onto their backs, then going at the soft belly he knew so well how to expose.

Not Rufus. Twice as big as Scooter, twice as beautiful, and probably twice as dumb, Rufus was a travesty of his bloodlines. Half German Shepherd, half Doberman, he was sweet and blundering, completely incompetent. He fell out of a moving pickup on three different occasions trying to see if he could stand with all four feet on the cover of the wheel well, got half run over the second time and lived not just to walk but to try the same trick again. He was so congenial toward the chickens that a prankish wrangler put him in the henhouse "to protect them" one night when there'd been sign of a fox around the pen, and though all the chickens were still there the next morning, everybody chalked it up to the fox's caution rather than to "bonehead" Rufie's prowess in holding him off. Around the ranch, word was that all Rufus was good for was a laugh, though he had lots of heart. He came home once whimpering and dragging his haunches, appeared not to have a mark on him till the vet found a fang puncture under the fur either side of his spine at the shoulders and said he must have been jumped by a mountain lion. (From a big boulder overhead maybe, Rufus wandering along aimlessly below sniffing the yellow cuplike flowers on the prickly pears, the cat's weight coming down on the dog's hindquarters. . . . Did Rufus twist his own powerful jaws just right and by accident get the cat in the jugular? How did the big oaf ever get away, I wonder — it must have been a young cat, still in training probably; mysteriously there weren't even any gashes on the shoulders where a cat would grip with its claws.) But that's another story. The point here, if a little long in coming, is that unlike the skilled wily Scooter, Rufus got into it with porcupines over and over, never learned. Came home with a muzzle full of spines many a time, providing me my first encounters with porcupines, once removed.

I can't say Rufus introduced me to the idea that porcupines throw their spines. It comes out of common folklore, after all, and is ingrained in the culture despite its contradiction by science. But though I knew very well what science said, I still couldn't believe Rufus would put his tender nose close enough to those quills to take a swat with them — despite how bunglingly and affably curious he was — not after the first time, at least. So if he came home with a pincushion nose over and over, it must be that the critters got him from a distance, was the heretical feeling that over the course of Rufie's porcupine adventures began to creep up in me. In my affectionate regard for old Rufus, I just couldn't conceive the magnitude of his bumbling, and so his repeated appearances as a pincushion had made inroads on my faith in the scientific facts.

. . . . .

Fourteen minutes. fifteen. The porcupine returned to his foraging as if he'd decided the coast was clear. He took a pace forward, one lethargic step of a bandy leg, and I caught a good look at the sole of his foot again, noticed with amazement the covering of little round bumps. How weird he was, I thought. Familiar to us in the United States, as an image at least, accepted pretty much without wonder, but really as weird as the animals we consider exotic: penguins, pangolins, kangaroos. How could such a strange creature exist? How had the species survived a day? It couldn't see, for all intents and purposes. Despite its purported good sense of hearing and smell it seemed not to be able to rely on them with certainty: the porcupine never seemed sure I was there in the first place, and now that I'd just kept still for fifteen minutes or so, it seemed to think I wasn't there at all. And what difference would good vision or a good sense of hearing or smell make in protecting him anyway, when the creature could barely move? Little forelegs curled on his chest dangling long curving claws like a Mandarin's nails; soft, spike-covered ball of a body bristling a patch of little barbed needles at you from his back; waddling along, body throbbing, nose twitching, beady eyes about the right size for a large bird — poor thing, he was ridiculous.

How in the world could such a body as his ever have come into being? On a mission to prove that the question *Why?* is irrelevant? Though parts of his body might have their logic, overall it seemed an illogical, inefficient mix. Why soft with a spiky coat when the porcupine could be like a human, an elk, a heron, a trout? Why not just good old standard skeletal protection for innards, instead of this elaborate, unwieldy apparatus of needles and spikes? Or, more practical still, why not at least just a decent range of vision and sensible legs that would carry him along at a reasonable rate? Why not just have him able to *see* and *run*? If I'd dared to move, I'd have been shaking my head in incredulity. My smile was at the bursting point; and it was all I could do not to break into a laugh.

But he had the upper hand on me. As I said, this was my first porcupine. Not the first I'd ever seen, not the first who'd touched upon the world I lived in, but this was the first time I'd gotten hard up against a porcupine, one on one. Here was a chance for good close curiosity-satisfying examination, but though I might find him ridiculous, foolishly and ineptly made, he had me hanging back. For old Rufus had worked on the superstitious part of me, and although I knew very well that porcupines don't throw their quills, I didn't quite believe it anymore.

Yet that wasn't the whole of it. True, if it had not been for Rufus, I'd have ventured a few feet closer; but Rufus or not, I wouldn't have gone all the way. On a black hole's periphery, there's a set of points that physicists call the event horizon, the boundary around the collapsed star beyond which nothing, not even light, escapes its raging gravity. The danger zone, you might call it for simplicity's sake if you were traveling anywhere near such a thing. Had it not been for Rufus I'd have ventured considerably closer to the porcupine, no doubt about it, but even then I would have stopped just short of his event horizon, the boundary beyond which a swat of that bristling tail or a bump with that patch of quills on his back could reach me.

So I watched till I'd seen all I could from that distance and then left him to forage in solitude, his rear end swinging from side to side as he lumbered along. I could laugh at the way the porcupine had come out at this point in his evolution, at the jokes it seemed to me Nature had played on him. But though I was dying for a closer look at those funny bumps on his soles, those funny quills were keeping me from it, and so I couldn't laugh too hard.

. . . . .

The second porcupine, it was all different. I was driving a logging road out of the forest a half hour or so before sunset. The limestone wall of a little canyon down to my left was still yellow with light, but a ridge at my back blocked the sun's rays from the road, and plodding his way across it before me in the lowering light he looked like a lumpy shadow. "Now you've done it," I called gleefully out the window, and breaking into a clumsy gallop, he disappeared over the berm of dirt-and-rock pudding that edged the rough-hewn road. "No use, I've got your number this time," I called after him.

(Calling the porcupine a "he" in both cases is an educated guess. My encounter with the first one, in June, was just a little past birthing time for *Erethizon dorsatum epixanthum*, the subspecies of the yellow-haired western porcupine found in our pocket of the Rockies, and if it had been a female she would have had the kid along. Unless, of course, she were younger than two years, the age of sexual maturity of most girl porcupines, and therefore still childless. But porcupines don't reach full adult size till they've passed three or four of their fifteen or so possible years, and my specimen had been way too large to be such a young femme. And as for this second porcupine, I came upon it in October, when odds are a mother might still have the young one in tow. And again, this was a good-sized fellow, bigger than you'd expect a young female to be.)

I left the jeep tilted up along the slope at the roadside and set off after him. He hadn't made it into the forest proper, had instead taken refuge in a little grove of lodgepole pine just past the berm. I was intrepid this time, merciless. I'd read the books. I'd double-checked on the quill-throwing issue, canceled my Rufus-instilled superstition, and this time I knew just how close I could get.

It was dark in his little grove. He huddled there among a jumble of big trunks and little saplings like a shadowy rock at the base of a tree — I never would have seen him if I hadn't already known he was there. He hunched over himself facing me, little forelegs drawn up to his chest, and this time I know he saw me because I was *close*. I saw the glittery little round eyes in his dark face, no question about it: fixed on me. I saw the blunt dark nose, the long yellow quills and guard hairs sweeping back from the dark patch of face gracefully. He didn't swerve or budge a centimeter, though the old throbbing was there.

I hadn't hit the event horizon yet, but I was getting there, and then there was a movement of more than guard hairs trembling. The quills were rising slowly, all over his body, high on his back and out on his sides and in a mighty lionish mane around his face. And then he himself was moving. Clumsy, sluggish, like pahoehoe lava creeping out through a crevice in some Hawaiian basalt flow, he reminded me also of someone who's been bedridden for months, weak and shaky, taking their first steps. He lowered his front legs, and pivoting around them ponderously with his rear legs, he turned his back and presented me with his thickest thatch of quills. Take a look at this, he said. He turned his head to look back over his shoulder. You getting the message? he said. I poised myself for comfort and didn't move. I held it a long time, and finally it seemed he just couldn't help it (Doesn't she get it?): he had to turn toward me again. We faced each other some more in the languishing light.

. . . . .

A long time ago when we were teenagers, our parents having gone off to bed hours before, my brother and I sat Indian style on the oval rag rug in the kitchen, stoned, and he said to me, "What if an ear suddenly started growing out of your thigh?"

"Ugh! Gross! But jesus, *anything*. If anything started growing out of your thigh it'd be gross as shit. Ugh!"

"Yeah, I know, but *an ear*."

I caught the glint in his eye then, that get-it? glint of silliness, and I caught the wavelength (gotcha), and joined him in giggling at the foolishness of our auditory members: "Yeah, right. An ear. Yeah, I know."

"Especially if you'd never seen one before, right? If you didn't have a clue what it was? Especially if we didn't have ears and you didn' know what it was for and one started growing somewhere?"

"Ick," I said, "how weird."

But then, time slowed and details heightened by the cannabis, we focused on each other's ears, seeing them as if we'd never seen them before, the convoluted hard folds and curls and ridges, the shine of skin tight on bone in the basin, the fuzzy hole leading into your head where wax formed, the cartilage would-be trapdoor of a flap protruding before it, and the funny limp droplet of flesh dangling down. We saw our ears as they looked only, without a thought of what they were there for, how they worked, and we giggled and snorted and hiccoughed with laughter for a couple of pot-time eons just at the look of them. Perhaps somewhere mixed up in it all the laughter was a response to a certain discomfort, a nervous reflex triggered by faint flickers of horror and disgust at the notion of such a thing as an ear growing out on your thigh. But if it was, that discomfort hovered only nebulously in the wings of consciousness, pushed off there by the comicalness of the subject that filled center stage: the ear seen in isolation, and its preposterousness.

. . . . .

Maybe a fundamental aspect of humor is seeing something separate from its proper context. Seeing it in no context at all, or perhaps, like the ear on the thigh, placed in an alien one. Maybe seeing a thing disassociated from its proper role relative to other things can make it look ridiculous.

And maybe in the novelty of the experience during my first close encounter with a porcupine, that's how I'd seen him, as an isolated object, out of context, the way my brother and I had seen our ears that night. But then, after that, maybe the pages I'd kept on reading once I'd done my fact-checking on the quill-throwing issue had amplified my view of things somewhat, had helped me see the porcupine's odd features in their proper context.

Whatever, this time, hunched up in the little grove, the porcupine looked different to me. Such a presence of guard hairs. Such a fixedness of eyes. Such a stillness of porcupine. Such a staunchness of him. He made me smile again, yes, but . . . What a fine face he had. It seemed suddenly wise. What wonderful paws he had, such elegant claws. Suddenly he brought to mind a king on a throne, somehow — crowned as he was, by that mane of guard hairs and quills. Those prodigiously curving claws poised at his belly somehow put me in mind of a portly deliberator, clasped around his girth as he held court.

. . . . .

I have a friend with a hearing problem who is part of a group that's testing a new hearing aid, a thing tiny as a kidney bean, that fits right inside the canal of the ear. Unlike the standard hearing aid with the little flesh-colored plastic receptacle that fills the basin between the canal and those hard ridges and folds of the ear, this one leaves the ear open, preserves its natural structure, and what a difference this makes, my friend says. With either hearing aid he comprehends sounds clearly, makes all the distinctions necessary to know what he's listening to and to accurately interpret the sound. But with the kidney bean he gets not just the precise articulation of the words being spoken, but the timbre of the voice speaking them as well; not just a sound boost and increased discrimination of one sound from another, but the distinctive resonance of each, its undertones and overtones. With the kidney bean he gets the full subtle texture of sound that the ear's convolution of ridges and folds and basins provides, as if there were no "aid" at all.

The claws of the porcupine were ludicrous when I saw them as Mandarin nails. The quills were preposterous when I imagined that they'd stab their bearer in his sleep, that they'd puncture a suitor, or that the quills of the baby would torture the mother giving birth. The bowed legs were ridiculous when I focused on them as organs of running. The bumps on the bottoms of the feet were comical when I associated them with pimples and warts. But now that I'd learned that the porcupine's claws are shaped just right for tree work, for climbing and for ripping through bark, a staple of his diet; that the porcupine's muscle control in retracting her quills is exquisite, that her offspring is born in a membranous sac, and that even in the case of an accidental stabbing, infection is deterred by an antibiotic grease coating the quills; that the bowed legs of the porcupine are perfectly formed for hugging tree trunks and that the nubbles on the soles not only provide traction but have even been dignified with a name, albeit rather an odd one — tubercles, they're called . . .

I could go on, but the point is I'd gotten the point now. He's got natural selection on his side, the little porcupine, and he's a ne plus ultra emblem for it. The question *Why?* *is* irrelevant, declares Emblem Porky, no plan in this odd conglomeration of features I'm sporting, no preordained purpose, and why must your species want to contrive one de post facto — why must you at all costs impose logic on things? No plan behind the specifics, goes on Emblem Porky, nothing that banal, but something more elegant, a ubiquitous, inexorable, never-ending impetus toward becoming, whose only slogan reads, Let it all happen every which way, let whatever can possibly materialize come forth, and once in a while — by sheer accident — some of it, however crazy, will work. And whatever works works, however it does it, no getting around that.

Real proof of that dish of pudding, the old porcupine, and of another dish of pudding as well. "For a highly successful species . . . we should expect stability," Stephen Jay Gould says. "Large, successful species don't change for long periods of time." We've found porcupine fossils dating back to the Oligocene, the epoch in which the first advanced mammals appeared. That was somewhere between twenty-five and thirty-five million years ago and many of those first advanced mammals have long been extinct, but the porcupine's still around (found on every continent but the ice continent, in fact), in much the same crazy form he appeared in originally. Some drastic mutations must have occurred in his species over the ages, but no better adapted to the past five epochs' pageant of environmental transformations than that first blueprint which the porcupine's architecture still pretty much obeys, those mutations weren't rewarded by being kept around.

. . . . .

And so this time I was impressed not so much by the porcupine's weak eyes and trembling, or his bumps and quills, as by what they stood for. And that wasn't the whole of it. As we crouched face to face in the grove with the light dwindling around us — or perhaps to put it more accurately: as in an ungainly, uncomfortable posture, I hulked before him while, pretty much unruffled, he stood his ground — I was impressed most of all by the inner porcupine, his slow sureness, his confidence.

When my first porcupine had returned to his foraging, I'd wondered about his intelligence. The way I saw it then, I'd just kept still for a while and he'd decided whatever had spooked him was a false alarm and dumbly dismissed the whole thing. Later, after a little reflection, I'd reconsidered, thought that maybe he wasn't so stupid, that maybe he *had been* aware of my presence but maybe somehow — by some pheromonelike clue or something — had divined my intentions weren't bad. Confronting *this* porcupine, however, I knew it had been neither stupidity nor prescience. That first porcupine had known I was there. He'd intuited nothing of my intentions, probably. What he did know was himself, what he couldn't do and could. Not with his little quill-tufted head maybe (though to give him his due, the porcupine has a big brain and an excellent memory), but in a visceral way, in the core of him, he knew who he was. He knew he couldn't run or fight worth a damn with those little bowed legs, and he knew those chiseling teeth, so perfect for sawing twigs off cleanly, held little threat for me. But he also knew he had an event horizon, a point I wouldn't cross with him. Or that if I did, I'd pull back in a hurry, and while I was jumping and crying in pain he'd just waddle off along his way.

The stillness of this porcupine before me had at first seemed a big act of courage, but it was just an act of self-knowledge, really. No, not just: he must have been afraid. Though he has few enemies, those he has would try to flip him; some, like his archenemy the fisher, would invariably succeed — he has that Achilles heel of a belly, soft, no spines. No, it wasn't only self-knowledge, things weren't ever certain, he faced into risk. But, fear aside, courage aside, the porcupine knew the advantages of his combined apparatus, whatever its drawbacks, and he knew the odds were that things should go all right for him.

. . . . .

It was easy enough to find the dog Rufus ridiculous. Daily he made quizzical overtures to the cat, and daily he was rebuffed with a scratch on the nose; still, time and again, tail a-thumping, he welcomed her to share his place before the woodstove in the cold hours of the night. Out exploring the world, he got jumped by a cougar, but though, hind end bruised and muscle-torn, he quite literally had to haul ass home, he was soon out gathering olfactory pictures again, in, of all places, the old yellow canyon, where from the rim I spotted him below me, trailing blithely along under the ledges and stout cottonwood boughs of cougar country. He got whacked time and again by porcupines, but the pain never deterred him from subsequent attempts to investigate porcupines or anything else, as if despite its handicaps his unabashed curiosity was somehow its own reward. He kept falling into undignified mishaps like these over and over, as if he never learned a lesson anything had to teach, and you could say he was dumb — I've said it myself. But however inexpedient, this unflagging spirit of a puppy was Rufus's essence; and though at his age it might better have been replaced by some semblance of dog maturity, it was the nature he'd been given, and he was so true to it that in its own funny roundabout way it seemed to work for him. For all the comical affronts he suffered to his dignity, for the paucity of respect and the abundance of abuse, good-natured and otherwise, that he got from humans and animals alike, Rufus had these beauties, part and parcel with his foolishness.

. . . . .

And yet, how odd a thing an ear is. Despite the lessons of the kidney bean, I still can't help feeling that. Even with all of us having ears, I've often been embarrassed by mine — as if someone might suddenly stop before me on the street and, pointing at one of my ears, dissolve into uncontrollable, side-splitting hysterics. I've even been embarrassed for others by theirs, and somehow I suspect my brother and I aren't the only ones ever to have felt this preposterousness of our ears. How much more so then, if we didn't know what a miracle they are. But still, look at them. How could such a thing ever have come to be? They're ridiculous.

Though you might say that by that very fact they're one of our shots at dignity.

. . . . .

For an unbearably long time for the muscles of both of us I imagine, I crouched in the little grove mesmerized by the porcupine just a few feet before me. And then, in rebellion, a nerve in my leg twitched and I bobbed suddenly in my crouch. The porcupine swiveled, lightning quick this time ("I never knew what hit me," Rufus would have said, if he could talk), and showed me his tail. "Showed me it" is an understatement; he flaunted it, flailed it, jerked it side to side, flapped it up and down. If I'd been a foot closer I'd have had it, would have emerged with a patch of quills sticking out somewhere on me. As it was, I was lucky. The porcupine just pulled me up short, scared the hell out of me, and gave me an excuse to make some quick moves myself, back out of the little lodgepole grove, finally stretching those muscles that stillness had stressed to intolerance.

Darkness was all but upon us. The canyon wall that had shone like butter beyond the road was a dun shadow now. I headed toward the jeep, but turning back I got a last look at the porcupine, just emerged himself from the little grove. He was still in the larger-than-life state, expanded by the erection of thirty thousand needles and spikes, but for all the apparent unwieldiness of his goofy ancient costume, he was comfortable with the fit. "Know the power in your funniness and you don't have to run," says Emblem Porky. "Know what you are and you'll be able to be what you are outright and felicitously, despite ludicrousness latent and blatant, no apologies." In the wan haze of the afterglow the porcupine waddled off in his prickly suit toward the forest proper, hind end swinging side to side in disjointed little arcs.

Moose

TO LAURIE GUDIM

t was early May and the woman was out saying a final good-bye to winter. She'd gone up into the high country where the snow was still firm, snowshoeing one last time. She crossed a little meadow and was tromping along not too far from the edge of the forest. It was very bright and hot in this meadow high up in the sun, and she'd just stopped to take off her jacket and tie it around her waist, when suddenly she noticed a cow moose some fifty feet ahead, at the edge of the trees.

The woman saw no sign of a calf, but it's likely that somewhere nearby there was one, because the cow was coming at her. Though she saw this, such details as the flailing forelegs, the boot-sized hoofs flashing down through the air at her, did not really register — it all happened too fast — and when the moose suddenly jerked to a halt and swerved away, she had no idea why. All the woman knew was that at that moment her feet were swept out from under her. She was ploughing through open snow for some seconds and then she was ploughing along through the trees. Fortunately the blanket of snow was still fairly thick, because by the time the moose got its leg free of the webbing of her snowshoe, the woman had been dragged a good distance. She was scraped and lacerated on all her exposed parts, and she had two broken bones.

You hear stories like these in every barroom in moose country. You hear them told in the morning gatherings of cronies in the local cafés. There are stories of bull moose in rutting season charging head-on into cars, trains, and bulldozers. There are stories of moose in no particular season at all turning on a dime and driving someone up a tree. Sometimes there's a warning: the ears flatten, the mane goes up, the moose does a thing that looks like he's sticking his tongue out at you. Other times there's nothing; the moose just comes. Anyone who spends much time in moose country hears lots of these stories. Though there's often a comical edge to them, they always involve a good bit of damage, and anyone who hears enough of them learns to be circumspect.

. . . . .

One crisp morning in rutting season I see a bull moose in the willows with a rack as wide as a redtail's wingspread. In an instant he's pricked his ears up, and with that giant rack bouncing in the air above him he's taking one of those big one-two-three kind of trots toward me. One-two-three, he stops, looks, and I'm off into the trees, scanning hard for one I can climb.

Late one afternoon in the forest in summer I'm lost and retracing my steps to a fork in the trail where I suspect I went wrong, when I see a big cow and her calf up ahead just where the crucial fork ought to be, and she's watching me. When the calf tries to nurse, she jerks away from him, head tossing, and backstepping respectfully, I show her emphatically that I'm off. The light's lowering, I'm not sure where I am, and to figure that out I *need* to check the very spot she stands on, but instead I migrate right back off the trail and go floundering off through the trees.

Another time, emerging spider fashion from a steep climb through deadfall, I come face to face with a moose on a mountaintop, his rump two feet from my destination, the door of my jeep. And still another time, a moose blocks my way on a granite trail, wide enough at his end for him to turn comfortably, but at my end a tad too narrow for me to turn with my pack on — a cliff wall jutting up inches away on one side of me, on the other a precipitous drop. These moose don't threaten, but neither do they make haste to yield. In both cases all I can do is wait for them to get bored and vacate the only path I can take, but I'm spared the boredom that usually accompanies idle waiting by one hearty spritz after another of anxiety.

Moose can be difficult. You try to give them wide berth. At the same time, they're unpredictable — there's no standard m.o. with a moose. Despite all the bar and café stories, and despite those few times when I've felt I was about to be grist for one of those stories myself, in the gamut of moose ways the moments of bluster are far less rule than exception, and almost all my encounters with moose have been very different from what the stories depict. They'll surprise you by what they will do, but what they won't do can surprise you more. A moose is enigmatic. A moose is, at times, a bottomless thing.

. . . . .

Of course on many counts a moose is a perfectly fathomable thing, no enigma, but quite explicable in terms of its adaptations to its environment. Many of these adaptations are extraordinarily apt and resourceful, prime emblems of how cunning nature's workings can be. And they're all the more prime perhaps, and all the more cunning, because they're frequently effected through features that at first seem so awkward and nonsensical, even comical sometimes.

No need to go further than the moose's physique, for an example. People who live in moose country have a particularly keen sense of the animal's drollness, and to borrow one local depiction, a moose looks like it got caught in a crusher and smooshed end to end. Its head and neck escaped the crusher, but the big compression pads of the crusher caught it right at the chest and right smack on the rear and squeezed hard, and when the moose came out he had a short little body humped up at the shoulders, his head much too big for it, his legs way too long. In contrast to his black chocolate trunk, these legs are often grizzled like an old dog's muzzle, and his neck has a thing called a "bell" hanging from it, a clapperlike furry flap dangling down. The nose end of his face looks too big for the rest of it — his face is nose-heavy, wide and huge-nostriled, finished off below with a pendulous upper lip — and against the bigness of the nose end of the face, the smallness of his eyes way up back off the muzzle is unsettling. He looks disproportioned and ungainly, a ragtag mix of a lot of things, none of them fully realized — the head an early attempt at something equine; the slope of the back from butt up to shoulder hump suggesting a start on a giraffe, abandoned early, before the designer had the courage to take the design all the way.

But a moose body is far from the work of a crusher, and there's method in the madness of these oddities. The modified giraffe aspect of his physique angles the neck well for eating from trees. The rangy legs help here too, for rising on its hind legs, a moose can reach branches twelve feet up, and it can straddle saplings, riding them down between its long forelegs to get at the top shoots and leaves. And these 4½-foot-high moose legs maneuver easily in all sorts of elements and conditions. Moose can run soundlessly over a littered forest floor at thirty-five miles an hour; they can move with little effort in snow nearly two feet deep; they can plod over quaking muskegs where other large animals would flounder, swim sixteen-mile stretches of Lake Superior at a clip, and they've been seen crossing mud holes submerged almost to the withers in soupy mire.

As for the big head, long faces are a standard adaptation of large herbivores, providing space for large grinding teeth to deal with the silica and cellulose of plants, and the moose's extra-long jaws enable him to include in his diet not just the tender, herbaceous forbs and grasses and aquatics, but the tough woody plants as well. Then too, the pendulous muzzle, being nearly all muscle, enables him casually to strip shoots of their leaves, and the long snout contains phenomenal numbers of nerve endings, enabling him to detect the faintest smells. And though a moose isn't averse to sticking his head under water (they've reportedly uprooted aquatic plants from eighteen feet deep) the long face lets him browse much underwater vegetation while keeping his eyes on what's going on around him, if he likes. Although his vision isn't reputed to be the best at midday, it's good in dim light, and he can rotate his eyes independently to front and rear, so he can even watch behind him without turning his head. Even the strange "bell" or dewlap has a beneficial function, for in addition to being a visual status symbol for males (the bigger the better), it's also thought to be a retainer for a special saliva containing sex pheromones.

It's always a little startling, the moose's oddness, the comicalness of his disproportions, as if nature had played a joke on him, but all these idiosyncrasies give the moose flexibility — they expand his ecological niche — so as curious as they are, you can get to the bottom of them. But though these oddities, once deciphered as deft adaptations, explain the moose rather nicely, they don't cover all the ground for me. You can see a moose every day and not fail to be struck by these oddnesses, these comicalities, even once they've been explained; but eternally striking or not, they're not enough to account for the discomposure I feel whenever I notice a moose watching me.

. . . . .

Whenever, during my rambles, a dark place in the landscape materializes into a moose, what really startles me is the way he just stands there, looking. There's a thicket of willows up ahead, or a little pool choked with water plants, or a shadowy jumble of evergreen trunks, and suddenly the image of a moose coalesces within it, and I'm unnerved by the exotic stillness of him. Some would attribute his composure at these moments to bad eyesight. He's not just standing looking at you, they'd say; he doesn't see you at all. But in every one of these cases, whether he's seen me or not, he's heard me, he's smelled me — whatever. For who knows how long, he's known I was there. In all such cases, a deer would have frozen, then bolted. Ears sharp, an elk would have focused intently for an instant, and then he'd have been just a rusty flash among the trees. Other members of the family Cervidae are always nervously vigilant, but a moose just stands there, looking. He's focused enough, sometimes quite alert; he's even stirred up sometimes. But most often he's merely casual, not frozen as if hoping for camouflage, but fidgeting nonchalantly, nipping buds or munching aquatics as he watches you, chewing cud, flicking his ears at flies. His stillness is not lack of motion so much as cool silence and calm — and it unsettles me.

It's as if moose have a big still place in them, like a deep lake whose surface is never ruffled, its waters dark, cold, shining, and smooth. Like the rocks in the landscape, the cliffs, the outcroppings, they seem outside the frenzy of living, as if somehow they had transcended the perpetual dash and dither of mind and body that fetter us to the moment — the action and reaction of biology. It sets a jolt in my blood, this quality, so alien in a wild animal. It triggers an eerie thrill.

Of course, you might chalk this quality up to a position of sureness. Only wolves and bears are their enemies — bears only when they're wounded, and in this country there are no more wolves. But in the fall I see the trucks go through town with moose dead in the back, long grizzled legs jutting up out from under the tarps, big palmate antlers jutting out just beside them, their heads now where their butts should be. And so the position-of-sureness theory doesn't quite work for me.

A moose can be dangerous, I know that. But when all's said and done the moose rarely threatens, rarely uses his formidable store of fierceness on anyone; and as if this were some kind of Eden — as if god were in his heaven and all was right with the world — when faced with a gun a moose many times just stands there, looking on. It's as if moose were victims of a kind of innocence, cruelly exploited. It's as if they were informed with a simplicity so pristine that they don't grasp life's dark complexities. In the face of disruptions and signs of disruptions that would set other creatures dashing off signaling alarm, as often as not moose simply stand placid, with a seeming detachment that seems to go against nature, as if (though who knows how to explain such behavior) . . . as if taking it all as it comes.

. . . . .

On the coldest of days, in a very cold time, a moose came to my doorstep. He came in a dream. It was not a sleeping dream, and not a daydream either, but a waking dream that was focused, although I, the dreamer, had no idea on what. But there was a focusing, a searching on the part of the dreamer, a stretching of all the invisible insides of the dreamer toward something. It was a focusing not on a thing, but of a thing: the dreamer's heart.

I was in my cabin, a dark speck on a bare knoll more than eight thousand feet up the leeward slope of the Wind River Mountains, not far from the pass that traverses the western end of the range. Through the fine snow sifting down outside the windows you could see no farther than a few feet. Without sensory clue, I knew there was a visitor. I opened the door. He stood close by the doorstep, a huge dark form suspended in an ether of snow.

He didn't speak, but I heard him. He said to follow him and I did. Down the knoll and over the bench to the river bottom. Across the river and up through the trees. Over the ribbon of white that in summer is the road to the pass, and into the trees beyond it, climbing through them up sharp-planed slopes and down their nether sides, then up and down again, over wave upon wave of trees. Climbing and impossibly climbing, effortlessly, the moose form just ahead of me slow and indifferent and steady, like the constant procession of the planets traveling their ellipses, the perpetual spinning of the atoms in their orbitals.

Then we were at the top of Union Peak, on the crest of the highest slab of all the raw jagged slabs of granite that protrude from that mountain's top like massive knife blades standing on edge. And suddenly, as if I were two people, observer and observed, I saw myself from a long distance, as if through a telescope back in the cabin I'd left behind. I saw myself there on the slab at the moose's side, the two of us distant and tiny yet oversized in proportion to our surroundings, and despite all the snow sifting down through the miles between observed and observer, silhouetted sharply against the sky.

Standing beside him, I touched the moose's neck. I didn't stroke it, but simply laid my hand upon the side of it, flat. He stood motionless, made no reaction, but his lack of reaction itself was a kind of response. He was a moose and he let me touch him, and I felt the life of him.

He never betrayed the faintest awareness of me. You would have thought he was alone. It didn't matter; alone or not, he guided me. He stood at the top of an undistinguished peak in the storm of winter and looked out from it, and I followed his gaze and saw what he saw.

For a few moments the land was rushing before us, like a fast-forward of terrain photographed from an airplane, and us flying in it, our eyes the camera's eye. We stood stationary on our mountaintop and the land rushed south to north at us, as we scanned down the southwestern slope of the Wind River Mountains, into the plains below, on down over their vast sweeps to Rock Springs and past, toward the southern border of the state. We scanned south or it rushed north, one or the other, all of it snow, all of it empty landscape, bleak and cold and lifeless with snow.

And then the rushing had stopped and there was the huge white curve of the top of the world, not south any longer, but the cold arc of ice that held the North Pole. Then that curve of ice lengthened, we saw a vast arc of the globe, many degrees, and then we had a still more distant view. We saw down past the vast cap of ice to where the landforms started, the Scandinavian peninsula, its great lobes flat and edged with intricate indentations, sharp-edged as a saw blade and totally white. Beyond, a vast expanse of Eurasia, cold and still and white. A third of the globe white and inert and silent encompassed in our view, even as we stood on the rock blades of the mountain looking out over ridges of forest behind vast veils of falling snow.

White and white, nearly the whole eastern part of the Northern Hemisphere, every peninsula of it, its coastlines hard-edged and sharp white against winter grey sea. I kept peering hard, expecting something, a bit of motion, a spot of color, something to hook onto that might suggest the friction of life, but all the way down, as the curve lengthened, as the expanse grew, revealing more and more of the world, there was nothing but still, snow-covered continent and grey water all the way down.

It lulled me, that dream. There was a peace in it. All still, all white.

Beautiful. But cold. So cold and still it frightened me that this should be my vision, that when I called out for a truth, this was what the moose showed me.

. . . . .

There's a theory that evolution is based on a struggle among genes, not bodies. It represents a twist on the traditional Darwinian view. In the competition for fitness (that is, to leave more offspring), natural selection rewards individual bodies with variations best adapted to the environment, with the result that as their descendants increase in numbers, their species evolves into one that embodies these particular adaptations universally. Individuals are the basic unit of selection, say traditional Darwinians, while genes, which furnish the ingredients of variation, are just outfitters, as it were. But biologist Richard Dawkins's theory of *genes* as the agent of Darwinian processes would have us recognize that the gene is the true replicator on this planet, not the moose, not the fruit fly, not us. After all, in sexual reproduction an organism doesn't make a precise copy of itself, a gene does. And whereas the particular organism is relatively short-lived, the tiny bit of hereditary material Dawkins defines as a gene is long-lived, as it (or the information encoded within it) passes intact not only through generations of a species, but often beyond species, sometimes even throughout all the five kingdoms of life, informing everything from humans to willows to morels to kelp to streptococci. The bodies genes pass through are just vehicles, says this theory, each a unique and temporary combination of genes; but the genes (unless zapped by mutation) are constant, reproduced unaltered again and again. And since the true replicator is the gene, not the organism, says the theory, it's not the organism, but the gene that's the contender in the struggle for fitness, while bodies like us, moose and humans, are secondary.

Ultimately, the gene works not for individuals or species or any other taxonomic division, but for itself. "Natural selection favors those genes that manipulate their own propagation," says Dawkins, and so the gene programs us organisms, its vehicles, to do whatever is necessary to increase its numbers in the gene pool. And if we humans have deceived ourselves in this matter, thinking that we bodies are the ones with the stake in the struggle, it's because in organisms as complex as we are, the most effective programming plan hit upon by genes so far in the course of their evolution is to help us cope with limitless unpredictable environments by endowing us with an enormous plasticity of mind. Subject as our intelligence makes us to countless combinations of circumstances, it behooves our gene passengers, in short, to provide us with a consciousness so sophisticated that as decision makers — at many levels of action, at least — we're emancipated from our master genes. That we're deluded in this matter is to be expected. It's hard to detect that we're mastered, when we are also master. Hard to detect that we're vehicles when we also have a big share of free will.

I didn't yet know of this theory the day I had my moose dream, but many of its implications go hand in hand with intimations that raked my soul that day, and it may well have been the tip of some such iceberg that I was intuiting when the moose showed me the picture of a winterbound globe. The theory has its critics, and being no more than a casual student of such things, I can make no claims for its validity other than to note that some fine scientific minds (among them Francis Crick of the double helix) have received it enthusiastically enough to build upon it. All I can say is that here and now, many moons past the day of the moose dream, I find the paradoxical logic of it all quite compelling, even rather lovely. But if it's true, the world is a colder place.

And we are cold in it, if it's true; and not just in what openly passes as our darker side — we've been inexorably forced to acknowledge the predatory protoreptilian parts of ourselves; their work is everywhere and hard to escape — but even by virtue of what we call our goodness, we are cold. For "natural selection favors those genes that manipulate the world to ensure their own propagation" and if a "superficially selfless" gene (as another writer has called it) will do better at getting its information passed on, then even altruism rears a selfish head.

All sorts of animal behaviors involve altruism. Mice, for example, engage in grooming each other, and it seems a benevolent thing for them to do. But mice separated from other mice develop nasty sores on parts of their heads that they can't reach, and so when one grooms another it's likely not out of goodwill alone. Support is offered in exchange for support. Altruism is reciprocal. Myriad examples of such behavior have been the focus of extensive, distinguished research. A lot of this behavior occurs among kin (ground squirrels screaming to warn relatives of danger); but a lot of it extends beyond kin, occurring among kind, as in the case of the mice mentioned above; and some extends beyond kind, across species (one ant species protects aphids in exchange for sugar they harvest), and even across kingdoms sometimes (another ant species living in the bull's horn acacia attacks all that tree's enemies in exchange for nutrients the tree produces, and even clips surrounding vegetation competing with the acacia for growing space and light). Throughout the web of living creatures, one after the other is doing something for another in expectation that the favor will be paid back.

I think of an acquaintance who was always flattering others, very effectively generally, but if you took close note, suspiciously much. "She's a compliment junky," a friend said, explaining her. "She puts out as much of it as she can in an effort to get as much as possible of the same thing back." Richard Dawkins wouldn't extrapolate from the evidence of reciprocal altruism in animals to human beings, but some of the biologists whose work he draws on would, and so would a number of evolutionary psychologists. According to them, we've evolved a stake in good reputations on this sort of basis: if you do good to others, they'll do you good back. At some point in the labyrinthine course of human evolution, they say, via some subtle turn it became important not just to *be* good, but to *appear* to be good; just leaving the impression of goodness could gain the desired "reciprocation" for us. And the subtle adaptive adjustments didn't stop there. For as humans developed in astuteness, it came about that if we tried knowingly to deceive others we showed our hand in small ways — the others just might see through our ruse — and so it became adaptive behavior to mime our concept of goodness to our own selves, deceiving ourselves about our goodness in order to do a better job of deceiving others about it. Ground-breaking researcher R. L. Trivers has related his genetic model of *reciprocal altruism* (the term is his coinage) to many of our overtly fine moral sentiments, suggesting that sympathy, gratitude, generosity, guilt, righteousness, and others are not as purely virtuous as we've thought all these centuries, but instead have been targeted by natural selection for improving our ability to deceive, to discern deceivers, and to escape having our own deceptions discerned. And all of this is related to getting our genes to the next generation — or, as Dawkins would have it, to the genes getting themselves there.

In spite of myself (and the anguish that invoked the dream moose), when I read of this research and the hypotheses it generates, my intellectual excitement is exquisite. My mind takes in these theories with bated breath. It's all so amazing, this business of the gene that shapes us to shape ourselves for the good of its survival — if valid, it's another gigantic strike for the elegance of the workings of nature — but it's a cold world. With the immense flexibility of our natures we're given the choice of goodness, unselfishness. And yet even our unselfishness is selfish. And even our choice isn't a choice.

You can flip that back on itself, of course. If the choice isn't our choice, you can say, the selfishness isn't our selfishness. It's the gene that's selfish, not the carrier of the gene. If I'm deviously supportive, only superficially altruistic, if I'm too hotly engaged in this struggle for fitness to achieve the disinterest necessary to qualify even my highest feelings as true love, it's not me but the genes in me that are behind it, and I'm off the hook . . .

. . . . .

The arctic tern, though indigenous to the coldest latitudes, flies ten thousand miles to avoid the hibernal extremes of its native habitat. Some bats drop their body temperatures to as low as 29 degrees Fahrenheit and hang themselves up for the winter just about dead. Other mammals increase their body heat. Some tiny ones raise it considerably, insulating themselves underground or undersnow right at the onset of cold weather, but the arctic fox needn't do so until the outside temperature drops below −40 degrees Fahrenheit, and even then, with only a minimal increase in body temperature he can sleep safely on open snow at −80 degrees Fahrenheit for up to an hour, so well insulated is he, fur covering even the pads of his feet. Some amphibians burrow down into the mud all winter so as not to freeze, managing minimal respiration through their cloacas, even through their skin, while the wood frog buries himself in the shallow soil of the forest and, by a miracle of biochemistry, freezes till spring. Although as the water in the spaces between his cells freezes he gets hard as a board, as long as the glucose his cells are packed with keeps the living matter of those cells free of ice, when he thaws out in spring he will start jumping again. As for plants, many species begin to dehydrate their cells as the days grow shorter. Consequently, although water by necessity freezes inside the plant, as in the wood frog it does so only in the spaces between the living cells, and so the plant, like the frog, goes on living in the frozen state. In some cases even the nature of the freezing within plants is different from usual; in a process called vitrification, ice forms without crystallizing, so there are no sharp edges to puncture and destroy the cells. And some plants, like spring beauties and snowbank buttercups, even manage to develop while deep within snowdrifts, utilizing the meager light that penetrates snowpack to do some minimal photosynthesis.

Dealing with cold isn't easy. It requires ingenious biological plans. But even the cleverest accommodations of winter fail to exempt the plant or animal from the rigors of cold. There's always a sacrifice; winter exacts a harsh toll. It inflicts brutal physical hardship. Sometimes it dictates total suspension of activity, even of consciousness; the very life of some organisms is in abeyance for months at a time. Even then, winter kill is a fact of the season; whatever plan a species follows, there is always a percentage of the population that doesn't make it through. But tough on the world as it is, winter is not evil. It has nothing to do with morality. It's just a neutral coldness, part of the cycle of things. While one pole of the Earth has its turn tilting toward the sun, the other tilts away from it, that's all.

. . . . .

The moose pays his winter dues like everyone. He makes a modest migration, not far south generally, mostly just down from the mountaintops, though because of his long, flexibly jointed legs he needn't even make the trip very early, deferring departure from subalpine bogs and creek bottoms, if he wishes, till the snowpack is close to two feet. He makes a dietary adjustment, switching from nutritious pond weeds, sedges, and tender leafy shrubs to woody shrubs and trees, and this requires increased fermentation time in his rumen to deal with the heavy cellulose load. As his dry weight consumption reduces by half, he metabolizes body fat stored during the summer, losing weight slowly but steadily till spring. To compensate for lowered nutrition, he sheds the weighty antlers that would drain his energy (seventy to eighty-five pounds of calcium grown in one four-month season, exceeding the antler growth of all other species), and without going into torpor, he lowers his body temperature, reducing his basal metabolism and thus the energy demand on his food. He starves in bad seasons, if snow is too high; if he's weakened by too poor nutrition, he's susceptible to pneumonia, parasites, other disease, wolves.

Most of his adaptations aren't spectacular, but more often than not they cut the mustard. He has ten-inch guard hairs and a dense woolly underfur — in the wintertime an inch or more thickness of it on the inch-thick hide of his back — insulation to suit him for life in some of the coldest places, the high places in altitude and latitude, boreal forests of circumpolar lands. When the grasses and ferns and low shrubs of summer are many feet under in winter, he rips the bark off aspens with his lower incisors (like all cervids, he has no front teeth in his upper jaw), and straddling aspens weighed down by ice, he bends them down farther, to get at the finer twigs at the top of the tree. With his long, loose-hinged legs he moves fast even through deep snow, and when the snow surpasses the comfortable limit, moose, like deer, do a thing called yarding, several of them staying in a small area, or yard, and continually packing the snow down in a number of criss-crossing trails. Snow, in fact, is his winter comforter; when things are at their roughest, he burrows down and insulates himself with a covering of it.

It's said that in the Middle Ages European moose were sometimes used as draft animals in Scandinavia, drawing sleds long distances through deep snow much faster than relays of horses could. It's even been reported that American moose were occasionally broken to harness. I don't have too much trouble believing it. Until not long ago some miles west of me there was a couple who hosted gatherings of moose every winter for years. All they did was put out plenty of hay and the moose came back and stayed every winter, munching around in their yard from November to April, clomping around on the hay-bestrewn wooden deck that belted their house, and if the couple had wished it, I bet at least some of their moose guests would have stood for being harnessed up.

The moose is as winter a creature as just about any. His adaptations aren't as dramatic as those of some organisms, but in their understated way they're about as effective — in fact, in allowing him to go about the business of living almost as freely and fully in winter as in summer, they're more effective than most. When winter comes, the moose doesn't go around it or away from it, he doesn't switch to a whole new game plan, he doesn't shut down; he just lives in it, taking it as it comes as straightforwardly as he takes summer. He does more than survive the cold world; he makes it his home. Like the dream moose that showed me that white arc of ice with such equanimity, he moves through it with something very like the sangfroid and disinterest that characterize nature itself.

. . . . .

Last spring I stood on a rise at the border of forest. The pink petals of least lewisias hid beneath the new blades of grass at my feet. At the bottom of the long, steep slope below me there was a trickle of a stream and a deep stream bank, eroded. An expanse of watery mud, black and textured with pocks. I saw something moving, and then he materialized, as usual. It was a bull moose in velvet, submerged in mud over his knees. He was stuck, and even those long, loose-hinged legs wouldn't get him out of it. He plunged and plunged, and it was to no avail. His feet were tangled in submerged roots perhaps, or perhaps due to illness or age he was simply too weak to defeat the suction's drag. But the moose showed no signs of panic. He worked for a while and then rested with complete unconcern. I'd once read an account of something similar, but hadn't quite believed it. The writer was a high-level national parks official who'd watched a moose plunging in a quicksand of volcanic ash, and that's how he'd put it: between times he "rested with complete unconcern."

I stayed for a long time and watched him. But I was far from camp, and finally I had to leave. Still, I stayed for close to two hours and watched him, as he plunged and rested and plunged and rested, and when I left he didn't look any closer to getting out. Perhaps when the temperature dropped that night the mud would firm up and, the suction reduced, he'd get a foothold. If a grizzly didn't happen upon him first. I left reassuring myself with that rather strained notion. Perhaps the coldness he knew so well how to live with would save him here.

. . . . .

I philosophize on the neutrality of winter. On the beauty of the cold world the moose showed me. But when a bear surges over the top of the hill before me and, in his rolling gait, pours down its side toward the trees where I stand, it's all I can do to keep my wits about me. My heart can soar at the notion of the vast indifferent plan of nature, I can theorize what I theorize, I can know what I know, but when even just the metaphor for death comes, my heart freezes in me. I'm as far from the peace of that dispassionate power as I can be in those moments. Is the rest all delusion, hypocrisy?

The image of the moose in the mud says it isn't. Even the bones on the porch of my cabin this bitter fall morning say no. I went up to look before the snow should be final and found a profusion of them helter skelter in the willows around that stream, some flecked with matter, dried gut like scraps of rawhide. A long jawbone, a large femur, but I couldn't find a skull. I'd left the jeep on the log road and hiked in on impulse, no pack on, no water. While I was searching, I got more and more nervous as a strange leaden sky filled the east. By the time I got back down to the jeep my whole body was shaking. A fall blizzard on the mountain is beautiful as long as you're not caught in it.

I'd gathered the large ones, the whitest. Back home, the books seemed to confirm that some were moose bones. I've spread them in a line under the porch rail. That way, most of the day they catch the sun.

Going to Rainbow . . . .

TO JAN EISENMAN SHODA AND YUICHI SHODA

The first time I saw a double rainbow was in Leadville, Colorado. I still have a photograph of it taken from inside the house I was renting there, through a long bright window that spanned the top of the kitchen wall. Since this was back when Leadville was authentic and shabby — before tourism hit and they pranked the place up with pseudoantiquities — through the windowpanes in the photograph you see the crumbling cornice of a tall, brick, Victorian building. You see an old electric pole and some wires. Leadville is the highest town in the country, and since at ten thousand–plus feet above sea level the leaves aren't out yet even in mid-June, the aspen branches you see out the window — though knobby with buds — are still bare.

Above the cornice and the wires and the naked branches, in a sky so dark it's maybe just two shades from black, a double rainbow curves into the picture. Two arcs of light — all the colors we know repeated twice. The photograph is actually a slide, so I can project the rainbow, big, on a white wall whenever I want to. On a midwinter night I can feast my eyes on a double rainbow, life-size.

The slide was taken by a boyfriend from back East, come to visit. A gun strapped inside his pant leg, he consorted with drug lords in big-city housing projects for a living, pulling his badge and arresting them when he'd nailed them, confiscating their Cadillacs. Yet when I took him up Dry Union Gulch, east of town, he said, "This place gives me the creeps." A bristlecone pine twisted out of a rocky ledge there. The oldest living things on Earth are bristlecones — at least one living specimen has been found that sprouted before the pyramids were built — and I was eager to show this one to him. He laughed at its contortions, called it "a helluva looking Christmas tree." He saw the silver-veined peaks of the Sawatch Range across the valley below us as generic mountains from old Westerns, not specific or real. Even the tumble of smooth-skinned boulders and the incandescent red willow canes along the stream, white with glacial flour, sparked his suspicion: a place where inbred mountain crazies might lurk in sinister wait. Our shared penchant for the wild had announced itself as forked during his visit: what thrilled a sense of the wild in him and what thrilled a sense of it in me were down separate paths.

But the rainbow, in its doubleness, caught both of us the same that evening. "I'll never forget this," he said. The primary bow was solid and stark in its brilliance. Then the secondary bow slid arching above it, ethereal. The primary was violet at bottom, red at top, going from cool to hot. The secondary was red at bottom, violet at top, hot to cool. He stood in the dark kitchen taking pictures of it until it faded. Then, quick, it was nearly dark. We leaned on the counters, the shadowy cupboards around us, still watching the pale rectangle where the rainbow had been, as the knobbed branches, the pole and its wires, and the erstwhile solid brick building dissolved into the night.

Although stirred together we'd been a wild brew, we'd settled out in different places. I would stay West, he'd return East, in more ways than one. But though we had no future, we had feeling for each other, and so his stay had been bittersweet. Days, we drank wine warm from the bottle along the roadsides. Nights as we slept, ice formed on the water glass.

That night when we woke in the cold bedroom it was as if the ice were ringing. The ringing had split the walls and a rainbow had shot through the night. There was a pungency to him I'd never tasted, calluses on his palms it seemed had never grazed my skin, little hollows of his body I'd never explored before, and a curve to his soul I'd never felt. These things weren't new — they'd always been there — but I only took in the joy of him fully the night before I would never see him again. Our bodies arched, concentric. Strident blue top and bottom. Humming red within.

. . . . .

In the sixth century B.C., Anaximenes of Greece proposed that rainbows were caused by the collision of clouds and sunlight. He thought that when the sun's rays couldn't penetrate a cloud's blackness their light was bent back toward the eye and a rainbow was seen. He was on the right track, but it seems he hadn't taken into account the skins of fishes. He hadn't considered the similarity between the iridescence of rainbows and the iridescence of some species of fish. Hung up on the pier after you've caught it, a sailfish is black; but when, fighting the line, it breaks the ocean's surface — its sides still running with water — it's an eruption of blue. In talking about the simple grayling of Rocky Mountain stream waters, David Quammen says that swimming in a creek it is "the most exquisitely colorful bit of living matter to be found in the state of Montana," dotted and streaked with turquoise and orange, aquamarine, mauve, and rose. But once the fish is lifted from the water "the bright spots and iridescence drain away instantaneously," he tells us. The fish, out of water, is drab.

The colors of the rainbow are probably the brightest you'll see except maybe for those on the skins of some fishes, and in both cases light going in and out of water is what makes it so.[1] Within a couple of centuries after Anaximenes, Greek philosophers began to catch on to that, and in the third century B.C. Aristotle devised the first systematic theory of rainbows, founded on the essential role of the raindrop. Subsequently expanded upon and calibrated repeatedly over more than a millennium, the theory eventually yielded a fundamental explanation of the interaction of light rays and raindrops that still circulates as the basic explanation of the rainbow even today.

One way to put it is to say that a raindrop bends the light that penetrates it. And not only does the raindrop bend the light once; even in the simplest raindrop-light interactions, it bends it a number of times. When the light ray first pierces the front of a raindrop, it bends slightly. Then, instead of passing out through the rear of the raindrop as you might expect, the light bounces off the inside of the back wall, bending more sharply this time, and heads toward the front again. Finally, passing back out through the front of the raindrop it bends once more, ever so slightly. The obtuse first and last anglings, when the light passes the air-water boundary, are called refractions; the bouncing off, a more acute angling, is called reflection.

In bending the light that passes through them, raindrops alter it. The light emerges colored now, not white. Each raindrop refracts a spectrum of colors, and if someone is standing in the right position — such that the angle of the raindrops relative to his eye is somewhere between forty and forty-two degrees — he sees the colored light. The rainbow is an optical phenomenon. Because each viewer sees a different set of refracting raindrops at a slightly different angle, everyone sees a slightly different rainbow — even people watching at the very same moment and standing side by side.

This is the basic-science explanation of the rainbow found in most schoolbooks. Although you'll find that things are a good deal more complicated if you delve deeper, this is what anyone looking in general sources finds. But the way the rainbow is commonly thought of in human cultures often has very little to do with the scientific explanation, however basic. Instead of conjuring up thoughts about light interacting with raindrops, the rainbow is usually thought of metaphorically.

In Arawak myth, the rainbow had a double meaning. If seen above the sea it was good luck for the viewer, but it was an evil spirit if seen above land. Many ancient myths have taken the rainbow as both a good and bad omen, but in today's popular culture its symbolism seems less complex. Often it merely invokes a kind of sentimentality: you see rainbows on greeting cards; there's a rainbow on the backdrop behind my nephew's face in his nursery-school photograph; you can buy rainbows in souvenir shops in the form of stained-glass doodads to hang in windows, or of ceramic mementos inscribed with saccharine platitudes. Perhaps due to a popular take on the myth of the pot of gold at the end of the rainbow (which, neglecting to note that you can never get to the end of a rainbow, mistakenly infers that you will find something wonderful there), the rainbow has widely become associated with a facile brand of cheerfulness and hope.

However myopic his theory, it seems that Anaximenes had a better handle on the rainbow than current popular culture does. He made a substantial error in identifying the cloud rather than the rain as one of its two key elements, but rain does come from clouds, after all, and in positing that a rainbow was somehow about the meeting of light with darkness, he touched on an essential quality. A real-life rainbow is more complicated than the image on school lunch boxes and gift cards. It's more in the realm of the story of St. Teresa of Avila than of Sesame Street.

. . . . .

I subscribe to none of the organized religions, but I'm interested in their stories, so many of them exquisite embodiments of the mysteries of being alive. In the story of Teresa of Avila, an angel appeared to her in a dream and pierced her heart with a flaming arrow. "The pain was so great that it made me moan; and yet so surpassing was the sweetness of this excessive pain that I could not wish to be rid of it," she wrote. "It was not physical but psychic pain, although it affected the body as well to some degree. It was the sweetest caressing of the soul by God." That is St. Teresa's verbal summation of the experience.

In a niche in the transept of the church of Santa Maria della Vittoria in Rome you can see another kind of summation of it, by the Baroque artist Gian Lorenzo Bernini. There, a multi-ton marble sculpture floats, fluttering, in a wide column of light. It is St. Teresa swooning on a cloud, an angel standing above her grasping the shaft of an arrow that he seems just to have withdrawn from her breast. Or it may be that he's poised to thrust it. Or maybe he's between two acts, and having already thrust it, he's preparing to thrust it again. The angel is beautiful and young; he is mild and dreamy and detached. Something is blowing his drapery, molding it to his lower body, while tearing it from his upper body and exposing his breast. Head tilted, he gazes at Teresa of Avila's face, smiling as he grasps just the border of her robe between the thumb and forefinger of a delicately poised hand. His smile and the tilt of his head are simultaneously soothing and titillating. The expression of his gaze is an ineffable blend of adoration and power. His hold on her garment is both fastidious and suggestive. He is at the same time erotic and dispassionate.

Teresa herself is half collapsed before him. Hanging from the border of cloth that the angel holds her by, she seems light as air despite the voluminous heavy vestment that envelopes her. All we see of her body is her face, one hand, and one naked foot. Her hooded head is thrown back, and her lips are parted — her mouth just open, gasping, or perhaps uttering a cry. Her eyelids are closed, but just loosely. Her hand dangles slack from her sleeve. Except for her bare foot, rigid below her hem, she hangs limp, dangling smoothly from his two fingers. But her draperies are anything but smooth or limp. While the ripples of the angel's thin raiment are sinuous and rhythmic — wafted, it seems, by a steady breeze — Teresa's heavy robes are swept into frenzied, jagged angles, as if lashed by a wind of every which way blowing in full turbulence.

This thing happening to her, it's supposed to be a good thing. But this thing is having an arrow run through her heart. This thing hap-

pening is supposed to be a heavenly thing, incorporeal. But her draperies have gone crazy wild. And the angel above her is shocking:
dreamy and rapt, beatific maybe, but such an earthly boy. Such downy
feathers of a swan on those wings unfurled behind him. Such lips he
has. Such curls.

Of course, we're not talking precisely about Teresa here, but about
a sculpture of Teresa. More precisely we're talking about my interpretation of Bernini's interpretation of Teresa's interpretation of a vision
she had. But how focused was Bernini on Teresa specifically, and how
focused on a sculptural problem — the problem of the human body as
a medium for holiness to refract through, revealing in the process a peculiar alloy of flesh and spirit epitomizing saintliness? A glimpse into
the life of Teresa suggests that his interest in one was inseparable from
his interest in the other. For even as Bernini's sculpture expresses the
intangible alchemy of sainthood, at the same time it renders precisely
certain specifics testifying that he was well-versed in Teresa's account
of her life.

No biographical source fails to mention at least once how very attractive Teresa was. We know she was a romantic who even in childhood ran away in secret to die for her faith at the hands of the Moors.
She read romances, even tried to write them herself. We know from
her autobiography that in her youth she had begun "to imitate the fash-
ions, to take delight in being well-dressed, to have great care of my
hands, to make use of perfumes, and to affect all the vain trimmings
which my position in the world allowed." In those days when she first
was a nun at the Carmelite convent outside of Avila, it was a custom in
Spain for monastics to receive and mix with secular visitors of all
kinds, and it's reported that Teresa was so involved in social inter-
course in the monastery parlor that she neglected her meditations and
prayers.

Eventually she quit the parlor, but that didn't free her mind of
worldly temptation. She entered a period of great inner struggle,
hounded by yearnings the nature of which she perhaps was not even
able to acknowledge — her writings on the unworthiness that so tormented her in this period are curiously and uncharacteristically vague.
She made endless attempts at penitence, always harboring a recalci-
trant desire she did not know what to do with. And then one day in a
meditation she heard the words, "I will not have you hold conversa-

tion with men, but with angels." Thereafter, she describes sometimes being lifted in the air, saying that God "seems not content with drawing the soul to Himself, but He must needs draw up the very body too, even whilst it is mortal and compounded of so unclean a clay as we have made it by our sins."

It was around this time that the angel with the arrow tipped with flame appeared. He left her "all on fire with a great love of God," she said, and she wanted to die to be speedily united with Him. Later, all over Spain, Teresa founded convents of the order of the Discalced Carmelites, so called because they wore no shoes. These nuns (and monks, in two of the foundations) remained forever within their convents, constrained to almost perpetual silence, abstinence, and strict poverty.

In the transept of the church of Santa Maria della Vittoria in Rome, Teresa is solid flesh — solid marble — but she's suspended. And (from a window hidden above) she's illuminated in such a way that she's dematerialized. Marble-cold, marble-heavy, and yet animated, dynamic, flesh-warm. Massive and buoyant, static and fluid; substance and shadow, flickering with light and dark. Floating in Bernini's *St. Teresa in Ecstasy*, this image of Teresa of Avila may express even better than her words do this confluence, this contradiction, this mystery.

. . . . .

The combined role of reflection and refraction in creating a rainbow was first explained correctly by a Teutonic philosopher named Theodoric in the early fourteenth century. He studied the behavior of light rays as he passed them through a magnified, simulated raindrop that was actually a water-filled globe. Although Theodoric was the first to do this, Descartes usually gets the credit — partly because he experimented more thoroughly. He passed light rays through globes full of water more times than you would imagine possible. In the process he arrived independently at Theodoric's findings and established a good deal more.

Theodoric had observed that a light ray moving through a raindrop bends three times — refract, reflect, refract — as explained earlier. But it was Descartes who noted that light rays following this pattern ended up projected at an angle of forty to forty-two degrees from an observer's eye.[2] All this applied to the single, primary rainbow and occurred only when the light ray entered the raindrop near the top and exited near the bottom. But when a lightwave entered a raindrop near the bottom, Descartes discovered, it bent *four* times: after refracting once (upward) as it pierced the front wall, it reflected *twice* off the back wall, before refracting the second time as it passed back out into the air near the raindrop's top. Light rays following this pattern ended up projected at an angle around fifty-two degrees from the eye of an observer, Descartes noted, forming the secondary rainbow. In so discovering the cause of the double arc and determining the apparent diameters of each, Descartes explained the skeleton, the basic structure of the rainbow. But he didn't get the elusive part, the soul of it, the colors of the light.

Newton did, for all intents and purposes — or made a damn good start on it. As Alexander Pope has expressed it, "God said, 'Let there be Newton,' and all was light." Descartes had established intricately and beyond a doubt that, when traversing the boundary between mediums of different density, a beam of white light refracted; but Newton established that that white light was not what it seemed. It was not a unity, for one thing; it was not pure, and it was not white. By passing a beam of white light through a series of prisms and lenses, Newton found that the seeming unity of the beam was instead a composite of rays of many different colors. As it turned out, each ray of a given color had its characteristic index of refraction, so when light passed from air to glass or glass to air, refracting, the different colored rays that made up the white beam bent at slightly different angles and separated, showing their colors and dispersing along different paths. The implications of this for a rainbow? When sunlight passed from air to the denser medium of the raindrop and vice versa, refracting, the colors were winnowed out, dispersed by the drops, and projected into different bands at different angles from the viewer's eye.

And so after Newton we had more than an expanded understanding of how water and light interact to produce a rainbow; we had a better sense of the elegance of these interactions. Light without water is always light, as a folded fan is always a fan. But mixed with raindrops, light suddenly manifests itself in "all the colors of the rainbow." Like a fan unfolding, it exposes its scope.

. . . . .

Once, for an instant in the middle of a funeral, I envisioned myself standing by my own grave watching the grey box descend. The sense of deprivation was devastating: I would not be there for my own interment. Later, after I'd moved West, the slash of loss I felt during phone calls back East was oddly similar. "It's been raining straight down all day here," they might say, or, "Last night an owl hooted outside the north gable off and on for hours," and despite my love for the scruff and roll of the sagebrush hill out my window, and the gleam of the mountains beyond, I'd want to be there. But on visits back East, despite silver strings of rain off the porch roof and the owl outside the window by my bed, a picture would sometimes flash in my head of the ragged cutouts of fir spires rimming the hilltops in the evening, or of a grey water ouzel bobbing among the creek stones through a veil of September snow, and suddenly I'd be bereft. Not being in both places at once was like death somehow, like a glimpse at the meaning of death.

Times come when the fear of death weighs on the heart like a lead apron. Not Death as in the inevitable closure that comes after climax and denouement, not natural withering, but death as in being yanked up when the roots are still tight in the soil, replete with a rich fuzz of root hairs sucking nutrients through their sieve cells with vigor — ripped out in medias res. The fear of mutinous cells dividing in the head stealthily as you brush your teeth and empty the garbage and walk the hill in the evening slapping mosquitoes, your boots wetting up in the grass. The fear of the MRI in the morning, of what the tests will tell but perversely, too, of what they won't tell — that they will remain inconclusive, the source of strange symptoms unknown.

When the first MRI was still three days away, I went the night without sleeping. The pain in my head distorted my vision. When I looked to the golden pine purlins overhead, they seemed to zoom back from me; one eye saw them red, while the other saw them blue-green. The window frame was pulled out of shape, the table edge drooped like taffy. The world's meaning was disintegrating, and though eventually the pain left no room even for fear, it wouldn't stop thought. I thought of the mountains out the windows of my cabin and the streams threading down them that I hadn't followed yet. I saw vibrant pictures of my childhood. I had an urge to climb down from my loft to the telephone at three o'clock in the morning and call up people from the past whom I've wronged. I would have, I think, but when I tried to move, I couldn't lift my head.

Then through the vortex of pain and tormented notions came a photograph I'd just seen in the magazine *Natural History*, of a fox stretched out on the crossbar at the top of a telephone pole. The image was like a stone plopped in pond water, pushing silver-rimmed circles of energy rocking through its soupy dark. Against an even blue sky, the fox lay sunning himself in the morning, casting a crazy fox smile down at the photographer and dangling a hind foot lazily; and despite my illness — as if I were adrift in sun-soaked tropical water — I suddenly seemed to float warm, almost drunkenly happy, honey-rich in accord with all that was or would be.

There were eight more high-tech scans before the search was finished. Hard as I conjured, I could never get the fox to come again. Still, over and over in those weeks I'd suddenly feel the peace of dailiness. Of sitting on the porch with my feet on the newly painted white railing, and the smell of the boxwoods across the mossy brick path. Of the maple's trunk dark and shiny with ivy before me, and through its branches a glimpse of the red dollops of seed leaves in the crown of the Tree-of-Heaven, waving against the white sky.

. . . . .

There have been lots of discoveries about color and light since Newton's: Thomas Young's, for example, that color equals not only angle of refraction but also frequency;[3] and James Clerk Maxwell's, that light is transverse undulations of the same medium that causes magnetism and electricity; and Max Planck's, that radiation is divided into quanta, which establishes that in some circumstances light can be thought of as particles as well as waves. These and other more esoteric discoveries continue to this day to expand and complicate rainbow theory. But a simple way to understand the rainbow may be to think of it loosely as a case of light changing state.

A classic example of a substance changing state is hydrogen monoxide. Energized or deenergized by an increase or decrease in heat, H_2O molecules arrange themselves differently: all bonded together in a rigid crystalline structure, they form ice; flowing freely around one another in small unstructured clusters, they form water; and zipping around independently — every man for himself — they form vapor or steam. Generally H_2O changes state step by step, from vapor to water to ice or vice versa. But sometimes, in a process called sublimation, you might say that H_2O goes directly to jail without passing go: when enough heat is added or removed quickly enough, ice evaporates, vapor becomes frost or snowflakes, as H_2O jumps from solid to gas, gas to solid, without passing through the intermediate liquid state. Since hydrogen monoxide is the only compound that exists in all three states at the Earth's surface, it's sometimes surprising to learn that other elements and compounds also change state. I, at least, was flabbergasted when I learned that, at 3,470 degrees Celsius, solid carbon actually turns straight into gas. Metamorphosis of rock is another instance of state change, as with the appropriate increase of heat and/or pressure, preexisting rock changes to new rock — without melting — as its atoms rearrange into new molecules. In limestone subject to extreme heat and/or pressure, for example, a given proportion of calcium, carbon, and oxygen atoms rearrange to form marble — just as, via a similar rearrangement of the atoms of their constituent elements, granite becomes gneiss, shale becomes slate.

These cases of transmutation are remarkable, particularly those where a gas or solid catapults past the liquid state and, in effect, calls its own opposite into being. But in each of these cases, despite often drastic alterations in form, all that happens really is that with a change in circumstances (that is, in the presence of the appropriate set of variables) the components of a substance are reordered; the substance remains always the same. In this sense, sunshine becoming rainbow may be considered simply another case of something changing state.[4] The common essence of sunshine and rainbows is radiation within a certain range of the electromagnetic spectrum known as lightwaves;[5] and just as varying amounts of heat cause different arrangements of H_2O molecules, or varying amounts of heat and/or pressure cause different arrangements of the atoms in rocks, so varying amounts of moisture in the air cause different arrangements of lightwaves. In the presence of minimal atmospheric moisture, lightwaves of different frequencies are mixed randomly and you have sunshine: light is manifested as white. In the presence of enough atmospheric moisture so that water droplets form, the prismatic effect of the drops focuses all lightwaves of the same frequency, isolating like waves into groups, and you have a rainbow: light is manifested as multicolored.[6] In the same way that changes of state like sublimation and metamorphism help us to see the multiple nature of elements and compounds, the prismatic effect of raindrops helps us to see the multiple nature of light.

Just as discoveries like those of Young and Maxwell once increased our knowledge about light, other more recent discoveries have revealed more about raindrops, increasing our knowledge about their prismatic effect. We now know that an intensely colored rainbow depends on drops one to three millimeters in diameter (which, though round, are flattened, like hamburger buns). We know that if the drops are smaller (and consequently almost perfectly spherical) the color bands of the rainbow are wider and overlapping. (If they're small enough, the bands are superimposed, creating an almost pure white fogbow.) We also know now that the size of the raindrops determines the spacing of the arcs in a double rainbow, and that the radius of the primary bow itself varies with their magnitude. Other factors abound to account for the endless variability in width, spacing, brightness, and purity of colors from one rainbow to another, as well as in which colors are present or absent in certain rainbows. As science has advanced, our understanding of the rainbow has been readjusted accordingly. Eventually research findings proved so intricate that even calculus wouldn't suffice to describe the rainbow. Since that point the development of rainbow theory has become inextricably interwoven with the development of mathematics — a complex affair indeed — which is why, in explaining the rainbow, most textbooks stop with Descartes.

Despite its deep simplicity, nature always proves more complicated than expected. We may be forever chasing the definitive explanation of the rainbow. But for all the revisions in rainbow theory over the past two and a half millennia, the essence of the thing resides in the amalgam of storm and sunshine — wet and dry, cold and heat, water and fire, and even (as Anaximenes would have it) dark and light. Vibrant bands of color arranged in specific order in sweeping impalpable arcs, the rainbow is a whole greater than the sum of its parts. But like some of the transmutations mentioned above, where one aspect of a thing seems to call its opposite into play, this greater whole at the same time throws its parts into penetrating relief. The rainbow is light made more visible by rain, if only fleetingly: light revealed in precise detail. The light is there without the storm, but we don't see it so truly. And water's capacity for shining is lost on us without light.

. . . . .

Running out the door, I snatched the blanket from the chair back and grabbed my oilskin cowboy hat. Fat, widely dispersed, arrhythmic raindrops pelleted the hat and soaked in widening splotches into the wool of the blanket as I wrapped it around me. The screams had come from far off, but they were so loud that even from inside I'd heard them: horses in a frenzy. As I clambered over the rim of the hill, my cabin sank out of sight behind me, and the last rays of the sun fanned out over the western ridges, drenching the hilltop in coppery light.

The top of the hill seemed wider and flatter than usual in the thick intense light. The lodgepole pines along the east edge were detailed almost painfully in its burnish, their bark like red stucco, the needles in their bottlebrush clusters metal-sharp. The air was caustic with ions. While beams of light wheeled in the west, in the east the sky roiled with cloud. All around that hill the horizon is jagged with mountains, and the high thin whinnies coming one after another seemed to bounce off of them. As if even the echoes were echoing, they pierced the electric wet air again and again.

Above the almost unbearably specific lodgepoles the closest mountains were glowing: two steep forested mounds, Warm Spring Mountain and its companion, with a windswept saddle between. The sky was that rich, deep galena. Against it, Warm Spring looked incandescent, as if from some sly light brooding within. The belt of grassland that winds up its side glowed green-gold in the sunset, and the bristling sea of black conifers it divides was tinged with brass. The shrill volleys of whinnies kept redounding, as if surging from one end of a whole herd of horses to the other and back again.

Where were the whinnies coming from? From the corridor of sedge in the swale beyond the lodgepoles? From the aspen grove on the shank of the mountain? Down on the river bottom, near the stream? And who on Earth had set a whole herd out to graze way up here? The whinnying volleyed, shrilled, echoed. The horses were in trouble, I was sure. Wounded, lightning-struck, struck with terror? Slashed by the fangs of coyotes, jumped by a lion?

Wrapped in the blanket, I ran to where the flat stops and the hill slopes down to the floodplain. I looked down on the willows, where the creek winds unseen. Although I knew it was impossible, I expected to see a hundred horses, freewheeling and crazy, frantic and rapid, under the turbid sky. But there was nothing. No black hulk of a lumbering bear. No horses running. Just the sage glowing silver in the charged grey air.

I ran farther, to the easternmost crest of the hill, where I could see all of Warm Spring and its sister mountain. Spanning both mountains and the saddle between was a rainbow, one perfect arc, with another one building above it at a rapid pace. Clearly it had been there some minutes, but my attention had been on the mysterious business of the voices of horses, on the enigma of their presence and whereabouts, their prompting and multitudinousness. Besides, there's a double rainbow in that sky lots of evenings, and I've become a bit used to them. Nevertheless, for a moment I strained automatically to see the ends of the thing, puzzling at where the colors start. They seemed to be coalescing just above a dip below Warm Spring Mountain, where I know the canyon cuts. If I were down in there, I wondered in spite of myself, would I see the rainbow's end, hovering just above the water roaring on the canyon floor? The whinnying filled the air in every direction. Expecting a hundred horses, I saw nothing on the mountainside; then, at the foot, I saw two.

Around and around they ran at the base of Warm Spring Mountain. Manes flying, as if screaming their hearts out, they tore through the waterlogged sedge below the monster bow, itself shrieking its luminous arcs of color against the churning dark. What was it? *What was it?* Was it just the tingling of their flesh in the ionized air? Had they caught the smell of nitrate from higher reaches? Was it the unnatural darkness? The unnatural light? Was it the rainbow that had spooked them, the uncomprehended appearance of that sheen on the sky setting their nerves haywire, sending them reeling and shrieking like a hundred of themselves? Peering down into the harshly gilt little swale, I looked for danger in some bodied form.

An open swath runs from the foot of Warm Spring's sister mountain up to the saddle. It's striped at one edge by a pair of wheel ruts and a wire fence that runs alongside like a fine black line. As I scanned the base of the mountain for causes, the horses down in the swale were still racing around madly. They were tiny, half a mile from me maybe, but in my mind's eye I could see them in detail — the curve of their flanks, their legs' taut tendons, the muscled swell of their chests — as they circled erratically. Then suddenly, from their indecipherable panic — which had perhaps been incited only by the hovering beams and electric air — they exploded in exhilaration straight up the mountainside. The side of that mountain is half again steeper than a staircase, and it slopes at that angle for a quarter of a mile, but they ascended it steadily. Flowing like leaves carried on rapids, jittering a little side to side, ever up they went, almost vertically it seemed in that dim light, following the fence line. They were really moving — their whinnying still echoing in the gathering dark, though fainter and fainter — as the rainbow they headed toward became fainter and fainter, just one arc, and then only parts of an arc.

Behind me the wheel spokes of sunset had vanished. It was grey all around, and just a smudge of the bow remained on the eastern sky. Straining, I followed the two dots moving side by side up the mountain. I lost them behind an outcropping, a clump of trees, then finally picked them up again — the tiniest specks now — my mind filling in their forms. When the last bit of arc was nearly gone, they were well over a mile from me, but still I could hear them. They were whinnying in ecstasy, I was sure.

Animal behaviorists would say I have no business assigning emotions here. Without the strictures of experiment, they'd say, I have no proof. All I know is that the horses suddenly broke loose from the treadmill of circling and shot straight up the mountain. As for the feelings behind that, behaviorists could be right: in this case, too, I might have been filling in forms. But the way it looked to me, the running just suddenly took over. Whatever had caused it to start with was gone, and the energy had become all. Scared shitless, they had run themselves bodiless. Run themselves bodiless. It was as if they had sublimed.

. . . . .

One detail about rainbows I've neglected to mention: a rainbow is actually a circle, not a bow. Earthbound, you can't see it; you see just an arch because the horizon cuts the rest from view. How much of the arch you see depends on the sun's altitude — and your latitude. The higher the sun, the less you see of the arch, until a couple of hours after sunrise, you can't see it at all, except at high northern lattitudes. (Nor can you see it again until close to sunset — except at high northern latitudes.) But when the sun is low, as it was that night of the horses up the mountain (and that night in Leadville), its rays strike such that the arch rises highest, and you see a full semicircle. Sometimes you even see a bit more than a semicircle, but never much more, for the perfect circle is cut off by the Earth you stand on.

But some birds — like the blackpoll warbler, which flies as high as twenty thousand feet — will have seen an iridescent ring from time to time in their migrations. And if you're in a plane just before sunset or just after sunrise, as the plane flies between the sun and a rain cloud — and if you're in a window seat on the rain side of the plane as this occurs — you might see such an iridescent multihued ring out your window with the shadow of the plane in the center of it. And so there are circumstances in which creatures can see the rainbow whole after all. It's called a glory, when seen in full circumference like that.

Notes

1. The fundamental cause of the lustrous, changing colors that we describe as iridescent is a phenomenon called interference. A lightwave reflecting off two surfaces a very tiny distance apart may produce two rays traveling in step, with the result that the rays "interfere constructively," adding together and creating bright, shifting colors. If the rays are out of step, they "interfere destructively," canceling each other out, so no color is seen. In the case of the iridescence of some fishes, water is a factor in this phenomenon.

2. Willebrord Snell first discovered the law of refraction (the characteristic ratio between the angle of a given light beam before bending and its angle after bending, and the fact that every substance has a characteristic refractive index), but he didn't publish it. It was first published by Descartes in *La Dioptrique*. Other scientists, among them Ptolemy and Alhazen, had been experimenting with refraction for centuries before Snell or Descartes made their codifications.

3. Actually, Young's theory was that each color corresponded to lightwaves of both a specific wavelength and frequency. However, nowadays — because light of a given color has the same frequency in air and water, but has different wavelengths in these different mediums — a pure color is technically described by its frequency, not wavelength.

4. Albeit the "something" is a form of radiation and not a substance.

5. Visible light is constituted of electromagnetic radiation with wavelengths measuring between 400 and 750 nanometers. But there's more to the rainbow than meets the eye. Along with visible lightwaves it is composed of infrared and ultraviolet waves too, with wavelengths longer and shorter, respectively, than those in the visible range.

6. Besides water droplets, other requisites for a rainbow are the appropriate latitude of the viewer and the appropriate location of the sun in the sky, as explained at the end of this essay.

Paedomorph Pools and Other Blighted Bounties

TO PETER KENT NUNEZ

think it may have already been true when I was still walking back and forth over the top of the buck-and-rail fence on snowshoes. Back when the snow was still up to my armpits and the snow midges that pepper its crust when spring's about due had yet to appear. Even at eight thousand feet, on the south slopes I found sage buttercups in March — six weeks early — and not just a sprinkling of one here and one there as they often grow, but little crescent-shaped patches of them punching through windthinned snow around the bases of rocks. A thousand feet lower and a few miles down the valley where the hills were snow-free, a day or so later riots of birdsong rose from a hillside below me. To the naked eye the Doug firs there looked stolid and still enough, but when I scanned down through the fuzz of their needles with binoculars, I saw their branches swarming with crossbills — red-orange young males and bright olive females perched upside down and every which way in the acrobatics of prying seeds from cones — while at my back the dried grass twitched everywhere with throngs of horned larks. Looking back it seems it was already true even at the last fringe of winter: life teemed lavishly from the start last year. But it wasn't until one day in July that the uncanny lengths such swarming increase could go to was brought home to me.

Every year on my birthday I go off alone for the day, to start my own personal new year by exploring a place I've never been before. It needn't be a whole new valley or mountain range; an unscouted pocket of a familiar area will always do. Last year, in the great sweep of subalpine forest above my cabin, I went off on a rocky two-track I'd never taken before and within the first mile glimpsed a little glacial pond back in the forest. Bristling with black-green reeds around its border, it was flat as a mirror on that rare day of no wind, and I set off to hike around it.

Rounding a brushy bend of the shore I saw there was another pond beyond this one, and then there were others, a proliferation of bright pans in the sun, filling a whole string of glacially scraped hollows where snow had piled deepest and where all the melt from surrounding snow drained. On every side they were surrounded by lodgepole forest, its floor also liberally scooped out in wide bowls, some of them just bare mud holes on their way to drying up for the summer, some still holding vernal pools. Pond led to pond and I followed, reveling in the sheen of the reeds in the sunlight, the ring-necked ducks' dividings, the pools' sinuous contours, and that old feeling that just around the bend there was something new and strange that I'd never seen.

When I hit the last pond in the string, I rounded it, for variety's sake heading back on its nether side. The shores on this side eventually opened into broad willow bottoms, and though the willows were barely waist high their twigs were like wire, and I had on shorts. The mosquitoes in the thickets were ignoring my bug dope, and my legs were giving up blood to the twigs as well, and since the glacial pools were shallow I decided I'd take my boots off, put on Tevas, and wade back through the ponds.

But just as my foot was about to break the pond's surface, I yanked it back in a flash. Down through the clear water, flush with the mud just where I'd been about to step, I saw a little snout. The snout was a surprise in itself, but what was more jolting, and eerie, was the shape of it — a snout with the same ancient profile I'd seen in a glass case at the American Museum of Natural History, on a gloriously intact fossil called *Acanthostega gunnari* and an artist's rendition of what it might have looked like in the flesh.[1] A snout shaped like a perfectly round-toed shoe, this one bright green. Next, either side of the neck, I saw the feathery gills protruding. Then the laterally compressed tail, and the tail fin that, not confined to the tail, extended up the creature's back almost to its head. Finally — peering — I made out the little round toes on the forelimbs. *Acanthostega* had eight while this had just four, but the little lobed tips looked the same.

Then another round-snouted creature, this one brownish, stirred the sediment next to the green one. Then another, and another, and another, and more. Some faintly spotted, some olive, some almost chartreuse. Some tiny, the length of my little finger, some amazingly close to the length of my foot.

Given that I'm living in the geological period known as the Quaternary, some three hundred million years after the Mississippian when *A. gunnari* roamed, the creatures were, of course, salamanders. Which meant they had to be tiger salamanders, *Ambystoma tigrinum*— the only salamander species found in these parts, although the description didn't fit. The subspecies of tiger salamander in my part of the world is dark brown or blackish, with yellowish splotches that sometimes fuse to stripes — it is not bright green. And it does not have gills protruding from its neck or a fin up its back or such a perfectly round-toed-shoe snout — it is not so *Acanthostega-gunnari*–esque. Still, these had to be tiger salamanders, and if they looked so much more like their ancient ancestor than like the modern-day tiger salamander you see in the books, it was because they weren't full-blown editions, but rather *Ambystoma tigrinum* larvae, and, as is the case with the embryos of many species, in various stages of its development *A. tigrinum* repeats various aspects of the ancestral form.

I hovered over them, studying. I sketched and scribbled in my notebook. Then I moved on, back into the scratching willows, lest in the water I might step on one.

Every twenty feet or so a little rope of water flowed through the willows to drain into the pond, and stepping over one of them I noticed that this glinting rivulet was writhing with life. More salamanders. And in the next snowmelt rivulet, too, and the next. I followed one to the water's edge to look: the pond was jammed with salamanders. Like cobbles on the oldest London street, they paved the bottom as far out as I could see. Everywhere I stopped at the water's edge this was so, and in all the rivulets. There had to have been a thousand salamanders in that single pond alone.

And then there were all the other ponds in this string of glacial depressions to consider. And all the pools in the scattered hollows back in among the lodgepoles. If the strange jolt of déjà vu at the sight of the first little snout had set my juices flowing, this unbridled profusion had them gushing. I was electrified, my senses, my spirit a-dance. At the same time, though, there was something unnerving about such rifeness. As if somewhere back beyond the dance music there was the faint sporadic jangling of a chord being played out of key.

. . . . .

As I said, this was the kind of year it was. The salamander pools were a spectacle, no question about it, but in their teeming bounty these pools weren't alone. For hundreds of square miles around them, the meadows pocking the forest were congested with flowers. Almost every genus went rampant, almost everywhere. The sticky geraniums grew pinker, as if more densely pigmented; they grew fleshier-leaved and -flowered. At an inch and a half their corollas were half again their usual diameter, their leaves brighter green and big as my palms, the plants sometimes elbow high. Usually their blossoms are sprinkled, a dotting of pink circles over a miniature green understory, inclined to nod and wave from fine stalks; but this year they sat firm and steady on fat turgid stems — clumps of geraniums in thick far-flung juicy pink carpets, the blossoms impenetrable, not a single thread-sized interstice between them through which to see the green below. Along the road-sides there were squadrons of scarlet gilia, their trumpet-shaped flow-ers fat and bristling at right angles all up their stems. Usually runs of these measured in inches, but last year one patch I saw ran three hun-dred feet. Their color more vulnerable to ultraviolet rays than those of other flowers, they revised the hue of the slopes along the highway from day to day, starting out as startlingly red as Carmen Miranda's toenails, then muting to orange, and finally to sun-faded pink. And up in the foothills, there was that tiny *Oxytropis* I've tried to key out to its species so many times without success.[2] Every year it grows scattered about on that high open ground like a fine fuzz, but this year it coated all the bald hills and their saddles, showing through the frail subalpine grasses like thick blue smoke. Lush, lascivious drifts of fireweed, paint-brush, elephantheads, bluebells — painting the passes, stippling the river bottoms, smearing the parks. Species of plants on all sides were nuts and hollering color, besotting the retinae, shameless and wanton and hussyish as could be. "Come get it, big boy," they called out to in-sects, moths, hummingbirds. "Come see if you can handle me."

And amidst all the vegetation, other life-forms commanded atten-tion for their numbers as well. The Richardson's ground squirrels around my cabin, for example. Through my window on an average summer morning I always glimpse one or two of these little "picket pins" (so-nicknamed because sitting up they're the size of a stake you'd tether your horse to, and just as erect). But last year at each glance I'd see nine or ten of them, perching on rocks or fence poles, scurrying through the grasses and forbs, stretching up through the lacy leaves of the prairie smoke to pull the seed heads of flowers to their mouths with little sharp-clawed paws. The average summer afternoon, a picket pin or two may climb into the sage and call out from the highest branches; but last year the sage tops were alive with them, ditting and trilling on all sides, and every daylight hour there was one perched at the top of the woodpile, while sometimes as many as seven or eight at a time fidgeted in and out among the logs all up and down its sides.

I saw badgers a handful of times on the hill where I'm lucky to see one a summer. There were more yellow-rumped warblers in the willows than ever, more sandhill cranes in the high marshes, more horned toads in the mudstone draws. It was even a cicada year, and back in the badlands almost everywhere, their crisp, amber shells littered the ground. The salamanders were a shocker and a thriller, no doubt about it. But they were just one of a hundred manifestations of the fecundity raging over the landscape last year.

It played havoc with the spirit, that rage of bounty. From the end of one winter to the start of the next, the deluge of life kindled a heady sense of well-being that ranged from a hazy satiated reverie to bright jags of *joie de vivre*. It was glorious, and yet — as I began to sense that day of the salamanders — there was something suspect in it, a nagging unease, a sense of warning, hidden in the thick stream. There was something merciless about it, an inkling of being at something's mercy. As if something had you around the throat by silken bands or was smothering you with billows of velvet — killing you softly, as they say . . .

. . . . .

One day in my twenty-fourth summer, I sat in a white gazebo on a hilltop, looking out over tilting green fields ringed by stretches of woodland and a string of luxuriant ponds. It was the farm I'd grown up on, and that day the memories of my life there were thick and vivid all through me, visceral and rolling, like technicolor movies projected all over my insides. The red-sand-bottomed brooks through oak-hickory forest that I'd rambled along almost daily in childhood. The black swamp waters I'd sloshed through, winding among swamp mallows and elders and hopping from hummock to grassy hummock in the company of muskrats and black snakes and redwing blackbirds. The spaces among the red barns where I'd ridden imaginary horses, and vanquished imaginary enemies with my rusted railroad spike of a sword. The low-ceilinged rooms of the big old farmhouse in the distance, their morning walls dancing with reflections of sunlight bounced off the pond's waters, their suppertime windows flecked with candle flames and the blurred reflections of our faces glowing in their steamy glass. The winter evenings sprawling by the fire before bedtime with my brother, mesmerized by the lick of its gleam on the carved legs of tables and chairs, dreaming our lives as our parents' voices floated above us proclaiming all our good fortune, affirming the benevolence of the world. Years later, summer afternoons in the garden, reading the great books. Summer evenings on the porch with my friends home from college, our laughter drifting in riffs out over the dark, dewed lawn. Summer nights in my canopied bed with the rich, humid air wafting through the windows, drifting toward sleep as the voices of bullfrogs boomed up from the ponds assuringly, as if proclaiming all our good fortune and the benevolence of the world.

I was going away soon, and so that day in the gazebo the nostalgia was pumping, but the future looked bright as the past. Though I'd been brought up in coddled innocence, all the advantages I'd been given had convinced me that I knew the world. Already I'd lived in three major cities, traveled the backwaters of much of the country, had lots of adventures with boys. I'd had a fine education, navigated with some distinction, and the past year I'd done my first work in the world, teaching the power of words to people who needed their power, helping humanity (as I saw it) while plying the discipline I loved. As I felt it then in my twenty-fourth summer, I was rich in every direction — not just in material, but in experience and history, rich in body, mind, and soul. And with such a base I would of course create a rich future, on and on. That fall I was going off on a journey, equipped with a vision and a year's worth of plans: to see the great art of the Western world, to do some writing, to ride a motorcycle through Spain and Morocco, and then to come back and marry my soulmate of seven years. I felt so rich it was exhilarating. Sometimes I could hardly stand the feeling's pitch.

But there were also times that summer before the big journey when I'd get a creeping feeling that there was something not right in my lavish good fortune. Something false at its core. I felt surfeited, disgusted — and why would good fortune prompt feelings like that? I felt a hint of something obscene in my bounty. I was spoiled, I told myself in explanation: I had way too much. But though this appeased logic, a vague, indecipherable shame chafed on unappeased, and in those obscure, sickening moments I felt a guilty suspicion that I was out of step in the world somehow, oddly barren, inane, unfit.

. . . . .

Until that July day I'd savored the year's fecundity unconditionally. As I savored the fecundity of those glacial pools at first sight. Scanning the stretches of salamanders paving their bottoms like cobblestones, I had the old childhood feeling of taut springs in you just ready to snap, to set you running off in a mad, gleeful frenzy, blurting out an excitement you can't contain. At the same time, though, that little out-of-tune chord kept intermittently jangling, and eventually it damped down the springs' tension and demanded a thought. Why this strange inner jangling, when this glut of salamanders was merely in keeping with the rest of the gushing world?

But, in fact, it wasn't. And that was the thing. Because unlike the floods of flowers and picket pins, this glut was a matter of more than just body count — it was a matter of body kind, as well. Most salamanders hatch as aquatic larvae, which become terrestrial adults only through metamorphosis. (Starting as tiny tadpole-like creatures with frilly external gills, they gradually develop forelimbs, then hindlimbs, and finally, having undergone several other profound if less conspicuous changes, they emerge as adults, their tail fins lost and their gills resorbed.[3]) Many species comprise these two forms only, but in some species — for instance, *Ambystoma tigrinum* — as many as three different types of larvae may occur: those that routinely metamorphose to the adult form, those that metamorphose only under certain genetic and environmental conditions, and those that live their whole lives in the larval form. The first type are standard larvae, but the second and third larval forms are paedomorphs, sometimes called axolotls, salamanders that grow to full size and become sexually mature while retaining larval characteristics deriving from their evolutionary fish ancestors: a lateral line system, lidless eyes, gills. And the thing was, not only were the majority of the salamanders I saw that day larvae, but the majority of those larvae, I was pretty sure, had to be paedomorphs.

The way I figured it was this. Breeding can't take place until snow and ice are gone, and at the altitude of those ponds (about ninety-five hundred feet) they hadn't gone until early June. In these parts, once eggs are laid, they require a two- to four-week incubation, and even with the shortest incubation possible, this year's crop couldn't have hatched more than a few weeks before I happened upon those ponds. Hatchlings are about a half inch long, and they don't even develop forelimbs before they're about three weeks old; but although in one isolated little pool I saw a smattering of tiny larvae — some tadpoleishly legless, some a bit further along — the majority of larvae I noticed cheek by jowl on the muddy bottoms of those ponds were *big*— eight or nine inches long, fully-legged, with wide-arcing mouths — a state of development they couldn't possibly have reached yet if they'd hatched only that year. As I reckoned it, these larvae had to have overwintered, and so were paedomorphs.

The thing about the three-larval-form plan is that by providing flexibility in adjusting to the vagaries of the environment, it allows many more salamanders to survive. The glut of paedomorphs I discovered in those pools had presumably been occasioned by a season of particularly lush and lucky conditions — the previous summer had been uncharacteristically wet — but more than just a colonization during a favorable season, a population of paedomorphs is a built-in insurance policy for future colonizations, even in seasons not favorable at all. When eggs hatch in vernal pools destined to dry up in summer, the three-larval-form plan provides larvae that quickly metamorphose and disperse to better habitat. When eggs hatch in permanent waters, it provides larvae that can postpone metamorphosis, taking advantage of the hospitable "island" of water in which they find themselves to develop more slowly and to larger sizes, so that when they finally do metamorphose they're better-endowed to cope with conditions beyond the pool. And the fact that some salamanders can live their whole lives as larvae — while propagating the species, to boot — permits a population to persist indefinitely in the water when conditions on land pre-

clude the survival of metamorphosed adults. And so, if the majority of
the larvae in those glacial pools could reproduce now as juveniles,
as well as later as adults, then this preponderance of paedomorphs
represented an even more extraordinary fecundity than did just their
large numbers per se. In effect, you could consider the population
of salamanders before me — already so large in itself — compounded
exponentially.

At first, this proliferation of life seemed to call for celebration. If I
was wishing for a fruitful new birthday-to-birthday year, I thought to
myself, I couldn't have asked for a more auspicious sign. But then the
dissonant chord in the background jangled a little louder, and the nagging unease articulated into an equally nagging question: for the bulk
of these *A. tigrinum* larvae, what was to be the outcome of all this burgeoning?

. . . . .

Two things about that journey I went off on at the end of my twenty-
fourth summer: (1) I saw and did everything I'd planned to and more,
but I wasn't enriched by any of it. Instead, as I went, whatever I saw or
did, I seemed to feel always progressively emptier, for in a curious way,
nothing seemed real. (2) In the course of that journey, I broke my en-
gagement to my soulmate of seven years.

These things seemed inexplicable to me at the time, as if they'd
come out of nowhere. But that wasn't exactly so.

I recall vividly now the day my first college roommate — a girl I saw
as my most cherished friend — confided a secret anguish to me. What
she told me was convoluted and dark, ugly like little else I've heard
since, and looking back I shrivel at the realization of the hopelessness
she must have felt for her life. But back then, as I listened to her, I felt
only as if the two of us were characters in a novel. And when I spoke
to her — in the character of the loyal, compassionate friend — I melo-
dramatized her pain, making it gaudy, like a sunset, and glorifying. I
made of her situation a romantic abstraction, the way the intestines-
hanging-out reality of war can sometimes be made noble when eulo-
gized through the distance of art. In short, I couldn't really hear her. I
didn't know what she was talking about. Instead of acknowledging the
terrible thing she told me and trying to bear it with her, I turned it into

some kind of grim fairy tale, making of her some monumental emblem of The Afflicted bearing up with remarkable grace. Afterwards, she must have felt she betrayed herself by telling me. She must have felt even more hopelessly alone.

Although this story is pretty much representative of my opacity to trouble and pain during those years, once or twice the knifeblade reality of someone's desperation did strike to the real heart of me. Like when a boy I'd made blood pacts with in childhood wrote me a tortured letter from boot camp, after impetuously enlisting in the Marines. He'd come as a foster child to a family up the road from us when he and I were both ten, and in all the years I'd known him he'd never once talked about the life he'd led before that day, but in that letter he unleashed it all. As he wrote, all the misery and horror of his orphaned young life were detonating in him, all the hatred and shame, and he feared for his sanity. Though his raving was bizarre — raw and naked and unprecedented in my life — somehow I recognized it. I got it, but I couldn't take it. I was revolted as I read his letter, and afraid — afraid for myself, of all things — and mysteriously ashamed. I never answered that letter. I never wrote to him again. I had no other resource for dealing with such naked desperation but to recoil.

In short, I was never as rich as my prolific good fortune suggested. That summer of my twenty-fourth year when I'd had inklings of something obscene in my bounty, I'd explained it by telling myself it was because I was spoiled, had more than my share; but as things developed, it wasn't what I had that was obscene, but what I didn't have — what having all that I did have made it easier for me not to have.

It's true that much of the bounty of my young life — the forests and swamps, for example, the years of good books — was soul-enriching. But it's also true that the soul can be stunted by what bounty permits and promotes. In our family what it permitted and promoted was an attitude that all could be right with the world for us always — that our lives could be safe, perfect, best — and that there was no need to pay any mind to the world beyond our own borders, that even if it held threats for others, those threats did not hold for us. We made of our bounty an island — where anything lost was quickly replaced, anything hurtful was barred or explained away — and, pampered and protected on that island, we so entrenched ourselves in the belief in our luckiness, that life was one-sided, a good half of it hidden or unconfronted, masked or kept at bay.

Being alive, I was of course subject to some slings and arrows. But I was wearing a bullet-proof vest. What few falls I took were cushioned, as if someone were always running ahead spreading big pillows in my path. What few losses I suffered were made up for, as if some generic tooth fairy were always slipping something under my pillow in recompense. No damage seemed irreparable. Good fortune flowed in a thick, endless stream. But bounty is a tricky thing. It seems like a flourishing, but to flourish is to thrive; and bounty often swamps and smothers, chokes the grass down to its roots, until there's not enough to thrive upon.

. . . . .

Pools of paedomorphs. Elation at life bursting at the seams. But if these salamander larvae were packed thousands to a pool now — most of them capable of producing hundreds to thousands of eggs — what did that mean for their offspring? For that matter, what did it mean henceforward even for them? However high, this was dry country, the east side of the Rockies. Even if half of these paedomorphs — and all of their hatchlings, when their time arrived — should metamorphose in short order to full-blown adulthood and make tracks for new habitat in the terrestrial realm, the moist sites they required were few and far between up here, even in the wettest of years. The dissonant chord in the background jangled a little louder. For the specific lobe-toed creatures at the toe of my Teva as I'd gone to step in the water — this chartreuse one, that olive one with spots — what good did this fecundity bode in the end?

It may seem odd that I should dwell on the destiny of the paedomorphs in those glacial pools. It may seem odd that I should identify with such an alien life-form as a larval population of tiger salamanders, much less feel my fate resonate with theirs. But mine is a story of how too much can lead to too little. The crux of the thing is that.

Population biologists are well-versed in the too-much-to-too-little story. And basing their forecast on nothing more than their knowledge of reproductive strategies, they'd tell you that for the bulk of those individual paedomorphs, this season's rich teeming didn't bode well.

Populations of those species more vulnerable to environmental vagaries tend to fluctuate dramatically. Such species (most of the arthropods, most plants classified as annuals, and many reptiles and amphibians, to name a few groups) are called opportunistic, because to make up for their vulnerability they blanket the place with huge numbers of offspring, releasing them to waft, crawl, or float on air and/or land and/or water, ensuring via dispersal through the widest possible range of environmental opportunities that at least some will manage to survive. Under ideal conditions, opportunistic species experience immense population booms, flooding open or disturbed habitats — or new habitats devoid of natural enemies — with legions of dandelions, locusts, brown tree snakes.[4] But, even so, at every spawning and hatching, sowing and sprouting, the fecundity of opportunistic species is responsible for the death of thousands, because in order to be begotten in such abundance, not only do their offspring come into the world tiny and undeveloped, but unattended as well. Their progenitors' role stopped at the production of gametes, and with no parents at hand to guide and protect them, these scattering legions must fend for themselves.

But though the offspring of opportunistic populations are particularly vulnerable to disaster, they don't have a monopoly on it. At the other end of the continuum of reproductive strategies are the equilibrial species, ourselves among them. Although some equilibrial species are small (think: hummingbird), most of us are relatively large vertebrates that sustain small broods of slow-to-mature offspring via extensive parental care. Thanks to this, as our modest numbers of offspring realize a proportionately high and consistent survival rate, our populations tend to stabilize near the carrying capacity of our habitat — that is, to hover around an equilibrium. Still, sheer fecundity can be the root of the collapse of whole populations, even of highly adaptive equilibrial species, even when the organisms comprising that species are large, fully developed, healthy, strong.[5]

The direct mechanism of ruin can be any of a number of what biologists call density-dependent factors. Shortage of food is the most obvious: the more individuals, the less there is to eat. And in many cases, as the food supply dwindles, not only do many die of starvation, but those who survive produce fewer offspring — the remaining birds produce fewer eggs; the remaining plants, fewer seeds. But sometimes a booming population of herbivores will crash despite a sufficient food supply, for although vegetation may remain ample, its quality has been compromised by them. The case of the snowshoe hare is an example. We once thought that periodic crashes in their populations resulted from predation by lynx, but the fact that hare populations follow the same cycle on lynxless islands suggested a different cause. It turns out that when a booming population of hares stresses their main forage plant, the result is not a shortage of plants but a decrease in their nutrient content — and an increase in their production of defensive (that is, toxic) chemicals, as well — so despite lush enough herbage, many hares starve. Overpopulation itself causes environmental degradation — in this case deterioration in the quality of food — and it's now hypothesized that hare population cycles determine cycles in lynx populations, rather than conversely.

Other density-dependent factors have nothing to do with food. In some species a booming population will crash even when food is not only abundant but also of good quality. In white-footed mice, for example, high population density causes hormonal changes that inhibit reproduction. In some species hormonal alterations caused by over-crowding increase aggression, and individuals kill each other off. Other species — for instance, certain fungi and bacteria — can be poisoned by their own metabolic by-products, which swamp the environment as their population grows. And sometimes booming populations of prey species crash at the teeth and claws of even a scanty population of predators, as those predators switch from pursuing their usual variety of prey and focus exclusively on this single, now very common species.

And so, although the burst of fecundity that leads to the teeming pool serves a purpose, its ultimate goal (so to speak) is not that teeming pool. Its proximate effect is to provide enough individuals to ensure immediate perpetuation of the species. Its distal effect is to provide winnowing pools for evolution, from which emerge ultimately only those whose genes provide optimal adaptation to environmental change. And so this fecundity is an insurance policy for the species. But for the individual salamander or geranium or picket pin — and the future of their particular genes — too much can lead to too little. Indeed, too much can lead to doom.

. . . . .

Biologically speaking, normal development is due to the switching on of genes in a predetermined order: a switch is "flicked" (biochemically speaking) and gills develop, another is flicked and a tail fin appears; then, as it may be, still later more switches are flicked and the very same features are resorbed. When some genes are switched on according to schedule and others are delayed (or permanently checked), the result is neoteny, the retention of certain juvenile somatic features beyond the normal stage in an organism's maturation process. Because of lush circumstances that suspended the usual pressures to forge ahead into less hospitable terrestrial habitat, this is what was going on in the case of those paedomorphs in their little islands of water last summer — another word for paedomorphic is neotenic. And, metaphorically speaking, you might say this was what went on for a long time in my own case, too. Facilitated, at least in part, by my own island of bounty — and the ethos and expectations fostered by it — I was in some sense neotenic, adrift in hospitable circumstances with some part of my development held in abeyance, not altogether unlike those larval salamanders.

Casting a cursory glance from a distance, you might chalk up my opacity where trouble and pain were concerned to youthfulness merely — to a cavalier attitude toward disaster not atypical of youth. But if that's what it started as, the cavalier attitude of youth went on in me long past its time. You might say I was like the man of privilege Edith Wharton mentions in one of her letters, whose family had always "united before him in a smoothing way." Having the means to do so, they "kept him out of the struggle of life, and consequently out of its experiences"— the tougher, character-developing ones, anyway — with the result that he remained boyish long after boyhood, an effect that, although appealing enough at the outset, rendered him pathetic ultimately.

Paedomorphic salamanders are found in constant waters, for where pools are transient, larvae must metamorphose punctually to terrestrial adults or die. And as Edith Wharton describes him, this man's waters were nothing if not constant — as were my waters, too. Unlike most of my friends who had to get out and experience the hard truths of things, I was able to linger in a state of arrested development, lolling around on my island with certain switches indefinitely jammed. As a paedomorph hasn't developed the traits necessary to cope with the world beyond the medium it's been born into, neither had I; and even as I advanced well into womanhood, nay on toward middle age, my island was a drug that stimulated me with illusions, while at the same time, in lots of ways, rendering me insensible to the world at hand.

That day in the gazebo I saw my life as a rich field that would produce ad infinitum. But even during that journey I embarked on shortly thereafter, in ways I would not soon detect much less decipher, the delusions of bounty began catching up with me. Even as bounty was feeding me with illusions of fulfillment, it was stunting my growth, chewing my inner resources down to nubbins — keeping them at the level of just meristems, undifferentiated cells, no chance for stalks, leaves, fruits to develop — and so bounty itself slowly created its own shortage, until it had to crash. Essentially unversed in consequence and obtuse to the intricacies of suffering — including, ultimately, my own — I took everything lightly, and let everything go lightly, too, as if I treasured nothing, as if anything I let go of were sure to be replaced from life's endless stores, until in the end I abandoned even my true love with no more effort than the writing of a letter from two continents away. "I'm with a man here," I wrote. "I don't want to get married anymore."

. . . . .

Fecundity can be the root of the collapse of whole populations. Even of equilibrial species whose members are large, fully developed, healthy, strong. Even when those species are extraordinarily adaptive, like we are. And in our case, at least, maybe even because of this.

Or more precisely, maybe because, blessed with such high adaptability, we've developed an attitude. Maybe we've made of our adaptability an island, of safe, perfect, best. And maybe lulled by this notion, we've indulged in delusion. Telling ourselves that though the world past our island might hold threats for others, those threats do not hold for us.

In 1999 the Population Division of the United Nations Department of Economic and Social Affairs projected that if fertility continues at the growth rate then current, by 2050 our population will increase from the current 6-billion-some to 14.4 billion people. Such estimates vary depending on the fertility rate used in the calculations, but even the lowest growth rate realistically possible results in a projection of close to 9 billion. Although population growth rate is declining in many countries, population increase continues, reflecting high birth rates in past decades.

Sometimes it looks as if we humans think we're not on the evolutionary tree with other species. We carry on as if, despite geometric progressions of billions, we can somehow circumvent that too-much-leads-to-too-little doom. But are we really immune to density-dependent factors, exempt from ecological laws?

Whereas other species have to contend with their predators, we say we've deposed ours. But what about microbial disease organisms? Even those microbes we thought we'd ousted are swiftly evolving resistance to our pharmaceutical controls; and scientists predict that as our exploding numbers drive us to probe parts of nature previously uninvaded by humans, our rummagings will unleash new species of microbes, perhaps of heretofore unimagined virulence or ingenuity (think: HIV). Although in many species population booms are reversed by toxins secreted by the crowded organisms themselves, we assume there are no such checks on us. But in the pollution that proliferates along with our numbers we have our own brand of poisons, some with the potential to trim back our numbers royally (think: nuclear contrivances and their ever-accumulating waste). And though we presume we can sidestep resource depletion via technology, expanding our niche to include every nook and cranny of the planet, that niche ultimately has limits, too. We may envision the dubious solution of eventually going off-planet, but at the rate things are going — namely, with the possibility of our population more than doubling in the next fifty years — you can't help but wonder whether we won't reach our limits before we manage that. Of course, there's another solution that sometimes comes into play in nature when there's not enough to go around: after famine and disease, there's war — as the haves and the have-nots turn on each other, killing each other off. We're subject to the same basic laws as the rest of life, no question — except, perhaps, for this difference: we have the power to recognize it.

Responsibility for overpopulation and overconsumption belongs to humanity in general — haves and have-nots, the developed and the developing world. But in certain respects, responsibility lies more with a segment of humanity than with the whole. Some may point out that it's those least susceptible to delusions of safe, perfect, best who are the biggest culprits in the problem of overpopulation, and consequently in the overconsumption of certain resources, too. But when it comes to the failure to do all we can to address these problems, for the simple reason that we decline to grasp their applicability to us; and when it comes to the attitude that come what may our adaptability will save us, that our technology will exempt us from ecological controls — when it comes, in short, to complacency regarding overpopulation and overconsumption — responsibility lies most with the segment of humanity that controls a big enough share of resources (human and/or natural) to count itself lucky, blessed. And this complacency can be so great that, whereas many developing nations gobble up resources in a struggle for subsistence, some developed nations gorge themselves equally in the pursuit of luxury. Among the latter it may be that the most complacent is the United States of America, which snubs international environmental conferences, declining to sign on to their treaties, and which with only some 5 percent of the world's population consumes some 25 percent of the world's resources[6] — carrying on as if the twin threats of a burgeoning world population and dwindling resources do not apply to us.

There's a rationale for designating nations as developed based on the magnitude of their technology and living standards. But there can be an irony, too, in labeling as developed a nation thus blessed. For buffered by our blessings, we can make of our bounty an island, where we so entrench ourselves in the belief in our luckiness that life is one-sided, a good half of it hidden or unconfronted, masked or kept at bay. And lolling around on such an island, we're subject to remain what I'll again call neotenic — as yet partially undeveloped, at least in that faculty so crucial for coping with conditions fast encroaching upon us: our consciousness. We in the developed world have the time, energy, and resources to make significant inroads on the problems of overpopulation and overconsumption. But if this very advantage promotes in us a false sense of security, retarding our consciousness where the problems of abundance and scarcity are concerned, then we're no more effectual at coping with those problems than the poorest nation is.

We pride ourselves on the notion that we're more adaptive than other species, thus more in control of our fate. But an adaptation that might *truly* be useful in our gathering predicament would be a further evolution of our equilibrial characteristic of parenting — an expansion of the solicitude we shower on our immediate offspring to include the projected progeny of our species as a whole. If natural selection — or better yet, a boost in our consciousness — were by chance to provide *that* adaptation, it alone could help us adjust a multitude of other behaviors to the darker lessons of bounty.

Meanwhile, so close is our pond to being overcrowded that I sometimes imagine we might appear to an outside observer the way those salamanders in those pools last summer, upon some reflection, appeared to me: an opportunistic population in a pre-crash stage. Opportunistic in the sense that, though we may attend to the needs of our personal biological issue, we're not providing for our posterity — on the contrary. In light of the environmental degradation proliferating as our population mushrooms, to an outside observer it might easily look as if we're just carelessly blanketing the place with our issue with no thought to their future — as if, like the opportunistic dandelion, we're just releasing them like seeds on the winds of pollution, of overpopulation, to waft helplessly by the millions toward doom.

. . . . .

I never saw my true love again after my twenty-fourth summer. And none of the loves that followed turned out to be true. As why should they have, when I was too callow of heart to know how to love? It took decades for me to realize the full extent of my poverty. Because I kept being buoyed by delusions of bounty, it was a long-winded crash. One day, though, I woke to discover my island had submerged beneath me. Adrift in the pellucid, dead waters of a pool gone anaerobic, I woke to a lifetime of loss.

But as it turns out, it looks as if I've had some *true* luck. For although the blooms of bounty choked back the shoots of my soul till they withered, it seems a bit of meristem managed to survive. Which is to say that as I lost the insulation my bounty had always vouchsafed me, the capacity for self-awareness so long squelched in me began to revive some. And in its wake came a more grounded consciousness of the world.

To sum up, you might say that when my life was purged of the last blooms of bounty, a few native shoots sprouted in the clearing.

Shoots with their roots in firmer and deeper, in closer participation and struggle with the soil—shoots better adapted to this world. These days, if a friend confides a secret anguish, I can hear her. I can answer tortured letters, unafraid, unashamed. Things are precious. It hurts to lose them. To sum up, you might say I've joined the human race.

. . . . .

Because a bout of illness prevented me from going back to check them, I don't know how long those hordes of paedomorphs persisted in those pools last summer. This year I checked the area often and saw only what I've seen over the years customarily — just a few salamanders here and there in a pond. Most of them had round finless tails, yellow splotches, no external gills — adults, in the ponds temporarily, fishing for freshwater shrimp. I barely saw a paedomorph — much less anything vaguely resembling last year's teeming pools. And so, though I've done no serious study, I have a hunch that last year was a rare year for salamanders, probably one I won't see the likes of again.

Were there simply too many of them to make it? Had environmental conditions a bit more lush and "lucky" than usual led to an unsustainable boom? Did those hordes of paedomorphs strip their habitat of resources until their population crashed, or did they make it — metamorphosing and moving on beyond the pools? Three or four migrations of adult tiger salamanders numbering in the thousands have been reported in this region, all of them occurring at night. Though the reports were decades apart, maybe such migrations are actually more common, but since they take place in the wilderness, in the darkness, we rarely witness them. Maybe those multitudes of larvae I saw last summer survived perfectly easily, graduating to some massive adult migration, crossing those high sagebrush flats after a thunderstorm in the dusk, far from human eyes. Maybe that bounty was not blighted, but blessed. But it's hard to believe.

Amassed on those pond bottoms like so many cobblestones, those salamanders had so much against them. And recently I've learned of one hazard more. Salamanders are carnivorous, usually eating insects and small aquatic animals, but under crowded conditions, the big paedomorphs so plentiful in those pools last summer — those eight- or nine-inchers with the extra-wide mouths — become what scientists call cannibal morphs. Experiments show that when there's another salamander species available, cannibal morphs will eat those instead of their own kind, at least most of the time. But in all the vast forest above my cabin, *Ambystoma tigrinum* is the only species of salamander to be found. So beyond food scarcity and the scarcity of moist habitat in an arid country, each individual in those bright teeming pools last summer had yet another density-dependent factor to contend with. The prospects for cheek-to-jowl masses never look good.

Notes

1. The discovery of fossils of this 360-million-year-old tetrapod is significant because they suggest that, contrary to previous belief, rather well-developed limbs evolved in water-dwelling creatures long before our ancestors crawled onto the land.

2. Serious bontanical field guides provide a means of identifying plant species called the dichotomous key. This is an organized list of characteristics that you work through, checking the plant under consideration against them one by one, until by a process of elimination you arrive at the precise set of features belonging to the plant—thus keying out its identity at various taxonomic levels, that is, class, order, family, genus, species.

3. As a group, amphibians have the greatest variety of respiratory structures of all vertebrates. There are both lungless and pulmonate species of salamanders, but even those species that metamorphose to have lungs breathe through their skin a good deal of the time.

4. It's believed that the first brown tree snake was carried into Guam in the 1940s on a ship. With no natural population controls and plenty of prey, this exotic species has reproduced unchecked, until it's now estimated that there are between thirteen thousand and twenty-six thousand snakes per square mile in some forested areas of Guam. They've caused serious economic and ecological damage, perhaps the worst of which is that they've wiped out virtually all native forest birds.

5. Actually, the distinction between *equilibrial* and *opportunistic* is an oversimplification. These categories are usually not cut-and-dried, but shade into each other along an opportunistic-equilibrial continuum. Not only do the life histories of many species fall somewhere between the two extremes, but sometimes different populations of the very same species will exhibit different life history characteristics in different environments.

6. The litany of limits is well-known by now. To give just one example, the excessive clearing of forest alone (whether by industries of the developed world or by poverty-stricken hordes of the developing world looking for firewood and farmland) leads to erosion, loss of fertile soil, flooding, siltation of water bodies, threatened

water supplies, albedo and climate disruption, desertification — that is, to a decline of resources in all sorts of directions beyond just the loss of the forests themselves, and thus to more hunger and poverty among humans, and to the continued depletion of biodiversity in nature at large (which in turn leads to a further decline of resources in all sorts of directions, and on and on in a spiral we go).

Cache

TO R.B.P.

found the deer not long before I got his first call, the first Sunday in October. Before that it had been just letters, since I'd met him back in June. It was mid-week preceding his call, Wednesday or Thursday. I'd been hiking back along Wildcat Creek, and just as it was coming on twilight I found the body, cached. It was all but covered with a heap of spruce cone scales, but I saw a tawny bit of it, and I bent down and touched it and it was a fresh-cached deer.

I went back Saturday to see if it was still there, and it was, but it was snowing, and the deer was covering up with snow. I uncovered it some to look for a wound — maybe a hunter had shot it and it had dragged itself here, and then maybe some scavenger had cached it after it died. But why had it stopped here in this cramped little crook of the creek among the tangled hard spruce roots? Its neck was twisted back as if broken, its head lying stretched along its spine facing its tail.

I'd met him in June in the Tetons, where we were all studying plants together. When he came up behind me that day in the woods I could feel him all along the skin of my shoulder and side. I'd found a place to eat my lunch apart from the group, and I could feel him in my skin as he approached even before I heard him, although I didn't know him at all.

The deer wasn't frozen yet and her head lolled when I lifted it. There was a mountain of spruce cone scales over her, spruce cone scales galore. Death had dropped her in this crumpled pile, ungainly. As if she were an intimate friend or relative, I found myself thinking, She would never have allowed herself to be seen this way in life.

He was a wildlife ecologist and I told him in the phone call about the cache. For a moment he let go of science and his voice tinged with the hush of significance: "A lion." In a letter, I'd recommended that he read Charles Bowden's "Love among the Lion Killers," and then he'd recommended that I read *Soul among Lions* by Harley Shaw, and so I knew lions cached and he knew I knew it. Then right away he got his science back and asked if there was a wound near the anus, like a puncture, because coyotes would do that, and they might cache too. He spoke in a soft drawl, reserved, diffident: he thought he'd like to accept my invitation to come see this country I'd talked so much about.

Coyotes would attack the rear, safer from hooves, antlers; a sensitive, vulnerable spot. In my mind's eye I see her halt, stumble, pulled down by teeth at her private parts. The day after his phone call, in the sunless cleft where Wildcat Creek flows I scraped off the snow for a second time, this time melting and soggy, exposing her sodden hide. I lifted her tail, her legs, privy to her privacy, nothing she could do about it because she was dead. In life she wouldn't have been seen this way, I once again caught myself thinking; she would have kept herself up, and if mangled would have gone off to hide where no one would have seen the indignity. But she was dead and I could examine all of her at will.

After, I was guilty at the awful intimacy. In the night something in me foundered in sorrow and shame. I had no right, and I wanted to apologize to her for demeaning her with those liberties. Such intimacy with a creature who in life would have bolted if I just looked at her. Reason said she was dead and it didn't matter. But what right is the right death gives you? I had violated her dignity. Examining her fine muscles, now flaccid and powerless. Hefting her floppy head. Wrenching at her delicate limbs (crosshatched with little scars), snatching up her tail from purple puckers, prying as if toward the very inside of her, and even, as an afterthought, aimlessly fingering the little scratched hooves.

Her anus was intact, no punctures on her rump. Nor on her flank or shoulder either, where a lion would likely have planted its foreclaws. I could find no wound on her anywhere, although I hadn't managed to flip her and look at her other side.

. . . . .

He came the weekend of mid-October. I'd prepped good dinners, made up the cot in my office for myself and put him in my big bed up in the loft. He came unpresuming, his cooler stocked with food, expecting to sleep in the back of his truck. He received my routine hospitality as gracious luxury, embarrassed, appreciative.

We hiked along a bare stony ridge that looked over creation. Lying casually in the scree of a parallel ridge, a bighorn sheep watched us with grey-yellow eyes. He'd worked with U.S. Fish and Wildlife catching bighorn, shooting them with tranquilizers and transporting them in nets. How did you feel doing it? I asked. He didn't answer, and I thought I'd embarrassed him, that he'd taken my question as a kind of reproach. But he was only thinking, perhaps debating whether he knew me well enough yet to say such a thing to me. "I felt privileged to touch them," he finally put it.

We hiked up into a high meadow in the breccia mountains, the past week's snow blinding in the blue morning and deepening as we climbed, until when we got up on top we had to posthole to the ledge that looks over the world. Despite the snow, though, most of the way up the trail had been heavily used by animals and in many spots was melted open to black mud. He was exceedingly attentive to the tracks, and when I asked about the little ones that always confuse me, he knew all of them. But it wasn't until a couple of miles after we'd both started seeing the prints of a grizzly that he said anything about those.

From the moment they appeared everything was, of course, heightened. The allure, the danger, the chance of a bear just ahead in the trees. You wanted it to be there. But if it was, how would you protect yourself? He lived down more in desert country where there were no more grizzlies, and he was deeply excited by the tracks. It showed in the fix and wonder of his attention, even if he didn't say it. Even when we'd come down out of there, the chance of that encounter behind us, he still had the glow of it on him.

He was demure with his knowledge, temperate with his assessments, respectful of facts. At the same time there was an intensity, magma pushing under cooled granite, and a kind of bluntness about him, side by side with the demure. Both mornings he came down from the loft bare-chested, his hair falling around his face, and looked at me like it was nothing. I was stunned at the look of him, and had to turn away. Saturday night when we'd showered and changed and opened beer bottles and I stood with my back to him, sautéing yams at the stove, he asked me: How long have you been alone? I felt the allure, the danger. For him too, he said, it had been a good while. He went off on ecological restoration assignments, often alone, for months at a time. No one, as he put it, understood. Do you think you'd ever want to be with someone again? he asked.

I didn't dare hope to trust the sense I had, the feeling. But what if my sensing was right? I said I didn't know, to answer his question. For his part, he didn't think he wanted to. It was too hard, he said.

Later, the only light was from the oil lamps. I caught him looking when I was bringing the plate of fruit. A certain fix and wonder in his attention, unselfconscious, appreciative.

. . . . .

The weekend of the end of October, I went down to see him. I jogged southwest some three hundred miles on my annual drive back East. As I climbed the steps to his house, I saw him through the door in there waiting for me, in a chair reading, his hair still wet from the shower. We ate his cooking, the beans steeped all day carefully. We drank a special wine. In two chairs bathed in the sepia glow of a single old lamp, we talked the evening away with charged demureness, and went to bed in adjacent rooms.

In the canyon next day he pointed out mountain mahogany, *Cerco-carpus ledifolius*, because we didn't have it in my country and I wanted to see it. On our hike to the top of the eleven-thousand-foot ridge we came upon what we thought was the print of a mountain lion. He looked at me, the circles of his wire-rimmed glasses significant. It was round, clawless, huge, in a patch of snow off to the side of the trail.

The thing about a lion is that you never see it. Or at least you didn't until recent times, when by pervasively invading its habitat we've given it no choice but to show itself now and then. But once, unless you were a skilled lion hunter, you never saw it. If anything, you saw only its sign. A detail from Harley Shaw's book, that Charles Bowden repeats in his essay, is stunning: a single twig left on a kill by a lion. A lion is a creature of hiding. It secludes itself, it caches its prey. It seems, no matter how hard-pressed, it can't override that hiding instinct. Even in a boulder field with no caching materials available, this lion found a way, however minimal, to honor it.

But though you never see a lion, you always want to. It's dangerous, but it's alluring, and in spite of yourself you want to see it. Sometimes the desire to see it is impudent. It would feel like a prize—a conquest—to break through the secrecy and snatch some whiff of this creature's private essence; to own it a little; by breaking its power a little, to make a trace of this power your own. Then again, sometimes the desire is not impudent, but enthralled. You are drawn by a yearning, a hunger for intimacy with the greater ground of being, by the intimation you might feel more complete by touching that other, wild life. But except for the necessary interlude of mating (a brief companioning, then parting again to wariness) and except for the necessary predation (a brief grappling of a stranger's body, then the ripping and consuming of it), the lion's every habit preserves it from contact with others, averts the threat of another's familiarity. Because we don't get to observe even the most routine of its daily functions, to penetrate any creaturely detail that might betray its vulnerability—because we have not a shred of intimacy with it—it has a special dignity. And so there's a special aura to an event even remotely connected with a lion. Being privy to such an event feels like a privilege.

All day he listened as I talked way too much. The times he talked his stories were pithy, lucid, fun, and I kept trying to stop myself talking because I wanted to hear more from him. But he just laughed and said he thought he'd probably talk the same amount whether I talked a little or a lot. I talked about everything, even old lovers, and once he reciprocated slightly. But whereas I prated frivolously and dismissively of many, he spoke with elusive momentousness of just one.

On the drive out of the canyon, things went quiet. The last light of daylight saving time shone yellow around the truck. I noted his profile as he drove, his eyes forward. He had one of those beards they have now, just around the mouth. The rest of his jaw was clean-shaven back to the ear. The line of the bone was graceful, smooth under the skin, and the beard just coming in was prickles of gold. Time seemed to slow in a pitch of intimacy, all absorbed by that stretch of skin over bone, and I was lost in a yellow buzzing, all other details of the drive receding, fading away at the edges of a hazy libidinous trance.

Back at his house we hosed down our boots, took showers, played John Lee Hooker. We shared the meal preparations, went around his house in bare feet. We sat drinking wine and scrutinizing pages of large round paw prints under the time-ambered lampshade. We ate ice cream, looking at slides of a deserted island he'd worked alone on for five months once. Bald and rolling and fiercely blowing, it shone to life on the wall before us, and for a while I felt it with him as if I'd been there myself. Afterwards, we stretched and put our feet up. We turned the lights off to see the moon out the window over the yellow leaves. We carried our coffee cups to the kitchen and washed them. Again, we retired to adjacent rooms.

When I came in from brushing my teeth in the long white cotton nightgown (high-necked, long-sleeved) that I'd bought before his visit to my cabin, his door was still open. He was standing in his room bare-chested, hair falling down, his sweatpants rolled up to the middle of his calves. I looked at him. He looked at me. He looked at me longer and something was in his face. I turned away from him, definite and final. He didn't know how old I was, and I couldn't face it.

When he'd come up to my country, I'd very carefully chosen the places to take him. They were back and away and wild, but not so arduous to get to that they'd show up the flagging of endurance I'd begun suffering in recent years. We'd been able to take the jeep a good part of the way into the places I'd taken him; but there was no jeeping to the places he'd taken me, all steep and jagged, no access to them but to climb. Even as we labored through the high snow, postholing, he was looking off longingly at a steep little bowl sunk in the ridge beyond us, dreaming of telemarking to come, but it was all I could do to keep up with him on that rugged mountain he'd chosen, and sometimes I lagged behind purposely to hide my breathlessness, the tremble of my legs after grappling a crag. The next day, heading east, I stopped to sleep three times in the parking lots of truck stops on the interstate. Five years earlier, I'd have moved as easily as he did on that mountain. My face still belied it, but the rest of my body was betraying me.

. . . . .

In November he sent me *Cercocarpus ledifolius* pressed in a letter. Then he went off to spend the winter alone on a remote island (now abandoned but previously used by the military) to study the effect of domestic animals gone feral on the native wildlife.

In the spring, I went back again as soon as I could get in there, to look for the deer. I figured she would have frozen up, and so not decomposed, nothing would have been able to eat her. Absurdly, I figured she would have been preserved. In the little cleft the creek flowed shaded all day from the sun, and its banks were still mostly under snow. I wavered along, unsure of the spot, and then at the edge of a melting drift there was a bone, then another, ribs, both of them. Then there was the hump of land where the creek curved around, the place where the deer had been, for sure. I rooted in the rotting snow, no bones. But then nestled in a hook of the creek, through glassy swirls I spotted part of the skull, the hind part, the bony cup that holds the brain.

I wondered when she'd been eaten, scattered. Had she thawed that warm last week of October, becoming edible, or had they managed to gnaw her apart even frozen? I put the bone cup in a plastic sack and put it in my backpack. No face skeleton that someone might pick up and stick on their porch or their fence pole, but that very specific, unglamorous-looking part of the skull that's most intimate with the brain.

I was prying again, taking ungranted intimacy. But why this sorrow and guilt for it, and this fascination, unable to help myself? What is this body thing? You live in harmony so long with it, it feels you are it, it is you. Then suddenly it is different, while you feel still the same. I apologized to the deer again, but this time hypocritical, having done it a second time. A violator, taking advantage of her ultimate vulnerability — underscoring it — the vulnerability of the body, flaunting its betrayal. Flesh heir to predation, deterioration — weakness, illness, aging, ugliness — laying us open to indignity.

That May he sent me another letter. It was written on the back of a biological tally form, from the desert where he'd gone straight from the island to do a herpetological survey. There was a sprig of creosote bush, *Larrea tridentata*, pungent yellow blossoms flattened in the pages, because we didn't have it in my country and I might want to see it. He said the weeks on the island had been harsh and had "pressed him to it," but he loved the raw, wild emptiness. He said he hoped to tell me more about the island when he got back home, maybe "'force'" me (as he put it) "to endure another slide show."

A second chance. The temptation. The one time in my life I'd come across someone who might like it the way I'd like it: solitary work and letters and occasional trips to each other across the miles.

I had the bone cup of the deer's skull nestled on the shelf with other relics of my rummagings through the landscape. I thought how even death, in the form of a lion, had tried to hide her from view. I had swept off the piles of cone scales, even ferreted out her bones. But the lion, if only for its own selfish reasons, had covered her, in effect honoring her dignity even as (I kept so inexorably feeling) she herself would have tried to do.

. . . . .

I didn't answer the wildlife ecologist's letter. In the thing we shared most — ventures into the landscape — my scope was narrowing. It was a simple fact, I could not have kept up, mortifying to try; and if he'd indeed been fixing to put himself on the line after such a long time, it was best he do it with someone more his age. And then, too, he was not so all-fired decided, really, about putting himself on the line.

In his book on wolves, Barry Lopez talks about how tricky it is to get to see one. He cites an eminent wolf expert who, except when clued to their whereabouts by radio collar signals, saw wolves only a handful of times in more than two decades of researching them in the wild. "Elusiveness is defense," says Barry Lopez. It is a simple matter of fact, elemental — they know where the danger lies and they keep away from it — and Lopez declares this fact matter-of-factly, without cynicism or qualms.

Barry Lopez is, of course, talking about wild animals. But voices that talk about people (whatever we are) tend to be less accepting, more suspicious of the defenses in us. Specialists in analyzing the behavior of people often tag these defenses with sterile-sounding, clinical labels — "fear of commitment," "approach-avoidance mechanism"; they ponder the neurosis of keeping our feelings "repressed." Not a few such voices, I imagine, would say that the wildlife ecologist and I did it wrong, that we should have owned our fears and been open with each other about them, that we should have behaved with each other another way. I hear the psychological savvy here, the spiritual wisdom even — acceptance of oneself, of life's passages, simple acceptance uncomplicated by fear and shame. But still, even as they would question us, I question these voices. They would, it feels, deny my hiding any dignity.

But what is this concern with dignity? What is this thing I did with the deer, the lion — construing their behavior as stemming from a concern for dignity, when they are fighting for their lives? What was I doing going back and back to the deer that may have been cached by a lion? Putting my face down to her sheenless eye, touching the hide tough and tight on the stone of her body, fingering her cold hooves. On the surface, it was a naturalist's curiosity I pretended to: you study them alive, and it's just an extension of that to study them dead. But my delving was suspiciously driven. And I had too many notions from who knows where, and I was too haunted by these notions in the night.

E.g., the notion that the deer went off to hide where no one would see the indignity of her vulnerability and suffering. E.g., the notion that in scrutinizing her I had violated the dignity she sought. In actuality, a deer would hide simply for safety. Wounded, she would go off to protect herself. We see these wild animals — we see our own pets — wounded or sick, going off, and we say they're going off to die, but it's more likely they're taking themselves out of the fray simply to await healing — going off not to die, but to live. Where did I get this notion that a deer's hiding would have anything to do with a concern for dignity?

From somewhere in the convolutions of the human psyche, it looks like. For it seems that, somewhere along the way, somewhere in me avoiding indignity has somehow come to equate with safety. As per-haps somewhere in the wildlife ecologist, holding himself just outside the boundary of intimacy seems to have gotten bound up with the guarding and healing of wounds.

. . . . .

This spring, two years after that forsaken invitation, a friend and I passed a porcupine lying dead at the roadside. When she said she'd never seen one, I swung a U-turn and pulled off next to it. Over the years I've studied porcupines on the ground before me and in the branches above me. I've studied them through binoculars in the tops of distant trees. I've had a good look at such details as their reddened incisors, the tubercles on the soles of their feet. But until that day I'd never had the chance to touch one, or to intimately peruse the body of one as yet unaltered by the pillage of death.

This one lay on its stomach with one rear foot extended behind it, as if while walking it had suddenly just stopped short. I touched the sole of that foot first, felt those nubbles, explored them systematically.

The feet were so warm I thought the porcupine might still be living. I turned it gently with a little shovel, held my hands flat on the soft underbelly, but there was no tremor of a pulse.

On its back, with its undersides exposed, we saw that it was a female. My friend minced around it with her camera, hovering over the thatches of quills, the curved claws, the holes in the dark snubbed snout, the tubular genital pouch. Then, standing back to take a shot of the whole of it, she blurted, "My God," and let her camera dangle. "It's just like a little person," she said. "A little person in a parka of fur."

The porcupine lay there on her back, as if looking up at us. One foreleg lay across her breast and the other was curled by the side of her face. It did seem, in fact, that she wore a parka of guard hairs, yellow around her body. A shining hood of them circling her face. Her hind feet curled toward the earth, the golden hairs curving over them like little fur boots.

There were no wounds on the outside of her. She must have been butted from the road by a vehicle's bumper, blindsided as she was making her way to the cover of the trees.

Then, in spite of ourselves, in the grip of some frantic fascination we fell to investigating her again. My friend snapped close-ups of her claws, her genital purse, her nostrils. I palpated and prodded, kneading for a firsthand sense of the famous vulnerability of the porcupine belly, pulling her lips back to see if the other teeth were also stained red. We covered every inch of her, as if she were nothing — and had always been nothing — but a lump of senseless clay. And though I knew this was not so, even as I forged ahead with my prodding I felt the old guilt and sorrow — as if by these intimacies we had reduced her to that.

. . . . .

When my friend's photographs came in the mail, I at first was confused by them. I couldn't make out the porcupine, couldn't distinguish her from the ground. The lines of her yellow guard hairs and the grizzled brown underfur blended in with the grizzled streaks of the dried grass she lay on, browned by cold and flattened by a season of snow.

And then in an instant — as in one of those puzzles where the foreground is at first the background and then the background comes to the fore — I saw her. I saw her sharper this second time than the first time, penetrating and clear. Lying open to us as she never would have in life, her life was so present and vivid. The life she'd lived that no one had seen. Her armored meanderings, her feastings and scentings, her takings in of suitors and issuings forth of facsimiles of herself—all her solitary intimacies lived out within impassive rock crevices, among thousands of anonymous trees.

The fact of these comings and goings was impervious to the dissipation now upon her. And even as she lay exposed to the world, the essence of those comings and goings was beyond violation, impudent or enthralled. We'd had the privilege of her, but that made no inroads. Even in ignominious death, she had all her inscrutable life upon her, and whether or not she'd given a fig for such a notion, she was the very shape and gist of dignity.

. . . . .

For a big chunk of my life, I had lots of what my mother might prefer to call "boyfriends." One after another, facilely. Such wide ranging in sex, so much quick, ruthless, and unsustained intimacy often struck my mother's generation as undignified. But many women of my generation turned that view, if sometimes rather crookedly, on its head. Speaking for myself, the having of "boyfriends" was a kind of protective self-aggrandizement, a little like the trick of the puff adder, bloating itself almost double to blind you to the serpently disgrace of its vulnerable venomlessness. Blunt affairs of the body and the brash confessions attendant upon them were some queer kind of defense, safety—brazen intimacy a kind of shield, my body a kind of rampart to keep them away from the core. For years this was how it was, and then suddenly all this was turned on its head (albeit crookedly), and I found that my body, which had seemed a rampart, had betrayed me. It had become, it seemed, the very portal to the guarded core.

And so I eschewed the old brazen intimacy. To do so seemed a matter of dignity.

But you always leave your track. Claw pricks in black mud. A round depression in the snow. The body of a deer cached in a mound of cone scales. And even with the most elusive of creatures, a tracker in the landscape can achieve a certain priviness and privilege. Even at a distance, if a certain fix and wonder of attention is there.

Without so much as a finger on the body, without one candid word, the core can be infiltrated. In an oblique way, a certain intimacy achieved. The intimacy of the hider and the seeker, the hunter and the hunted. Especially when each plays both roles. Secrets intermingled despite screens and evasions. Fear, desire — whatever buried vulner-ability — exposed in its simple dignity.

. . . . .

Ready to fall on my face in the snow, I hung back to keep to myself in my huffing and trembling. I wore the high-collared gown with long sleeves. Did I think I ever wanted to be with someone again? he asked me. For his part, he didn't think he wanted to. I hid my age, pretend-ing I could go with him. He hid his desire, pretending he did not want to go with me.

Eluding and luring, luring and eluding, we intersected. Penetrated to intimacy.

We crouched over the huge clawless track in the patch of snow by the trail we'd been following. The sense of it jumping inside me, I looked, rapt, across it at him. He spoke across it, his voice tinged with the hush of significance. "A lion," he said.

Still Point . . . .

TO THE MEMORY OF KATE FRANKS KLAUS

Horse chestnuts have great candles, tapering upward, bright white. So do sweet buckeyes, but theirs are yellow — sometimes even red. You come upon one in the green wood: Christmas in May.

Sumacs, when leafless, are like the tracings of stair-steps — particularly *Rhus copallina*, the winged sumac. Black outlines on the sky, their branches zig and zag up and sideways, then up and then sideways — vertical angling abruptly to horizontal, horizontal then vertical. A conglomeration of zigzags — in counterpoint, intersecting, topsy-turvy — they are like the doodles of an artist obsessed with the profiles of stairsteps, scrawled every which way across a sky-colored page.

Liquidamber is the genus of the sweet gum. The leaves are shaped like stars. On a single tree in fall there can be uncountable colors, no category of the chromatic spectrum left unrepresented, every leaf sporting some gradation between one category of color and another, the gradations limitless, defying language to delineate. Once I pressed a sampling of forty-some such-colored stars and gave them to a wild-life ecologist who'd always lived in places populated mostly by ever-greens. Among the colors included were candy-apple red and peak-of-spawning salmon. Three variations of burnt orange, and three of chartreuse. Sunflower gold, spruce green, and midnight purple. Guernsey-cream-laced-with-lemon and anthocyanin-black. A grown man, his eyes welled with tears when he saw them. He mounted them in a display box in his office, where they remain to this day. A common tree on the inner coastal plain of New Jersey, the sweet gum does well near water. "Liquidamber," the ecologist said. "Even the sound . . ."

Prunus maritima commonly goes by the name beach plum. I like to call it, playfully, "maritime prune." It grows in sand, loves the beach, where it thrives among the secondary dunes. A husky shrub, when left to its own devices it bristles and spikes out in every direction, like a dark starburst against the white. But that's just in winter. In spring hard green globules bead up all along the dark branches, and one day just as the brown thrasher is thrashing in the dead leaves way in under at the hub of the starburst, the globules start their own bursting, and the maritime prune breaks out into a splash of bridal spikes, white on white in the dunes. The purple-blue fruits of the fall are where it gets the first part of its Latin name from. Although, looking at the name from a punful perspective, you might say it's called *Prunus* for the fact that its easternmost flank very often slants up from the sand in a very straight line, at a very curt forty-five-degree angle, all its twig tips having been sheared by iotas of halite in the sea breeze—that is, salt-spray pruned.

The sycamore's appeal is commonly held to reside in its mottles — in the splotches of cream, green, and taupe that marbleize its peeling trunk like an antique book's endpapers, and in the smooth white-washed blotches that predominate in this motley as the tree gains in years. But, having reached a venerable age, the sycamore has another charm, not as commonly noted and visible only in winter. Its boughs sprout branches that jam up at their ends in big knobs, each knob sprouting a spray of fine sweeping twigs like willowy fingers, radiating not from a hand, but all from one big gnarled knuckle instead.

Such distinguishing qualities make up the charm of these woody life-forms. They are in a way reminiscent of the kinds of characteristics dwelt upon early on in human courtship, during the initial, most immediate and superficial, phase of coming to know. To say this is not to make light of such qualities. It is not to say that such charms — in plants or in people — are irrelevant; they are not. It is, rather, to say that the idiosyncratic charm that captures the attention at first may be relevant as more than just a fetching detail.

For although the charm is not itself the plant's essence, it is connected to that essence. It springs from that essence somehow. And sometimes, by enticing you into musings on its raison d'être, a charming detail can lead you into the heart of the plant. Musings that may issue in questions such as, Why candles? Why splotches and peeled blotches? Why every color of the rainbow and branches that step like stairs? Lifetimes of work go to probing such questions on the biology and physics of such characteristics — to pursuing insights into their evolutionary rationales.

In the cases where answers to such questions have finally been tracked down, we find each charming trait indeed has a deep-seated reason for being. The flower, of course, is there to attract the pollinator. But that fact just scratches the surface of the affair. The color, the odor, the shape, often the very texture of a given bloom is adapted, sometimes mind-bogglingly precisely, to exactly whom it would attract. A night-blooming flower just big enough for a night-foraging bat to stick its head into. A tubular corolla curved to fit the curving beak of a particular species of bird. Wispy streaks on petals pointing the way down into hidden nectaries, visible only to insects graced with a faculty for detecting ultraviolet light. Traits are nested within traits, functions within functions — each refinement of a characteristic correlated with a refinement in its reason for being.

All this can telescope and telescope to tinier and tinier traits and details of traits, and to mechanisms successively more subtle and refined. A flower with the yeasty odor of wine, which attracts beetles. A flower (dull red or brown) with the odor of rotten meat, which attracts flies. Microscopic threads dangling from pollen grains down inside a red trumpet-shaped blossom, which catch in the tiny stiff hairs on the beaks of hummingbirds. An orchid petal resembling a female bumblebee, which lures a bumblebee male, who during his attentions to this decoy ends up with a sac of pollen stuck to his head.

In the answers that have been tracked down there is this kind of pattern of meaning. But what a mere speck in the sea of ongoing questions are these painstakingly hard-won discoveries. The candle explained,[1] but what about the stepping branches? There's so much we don't understand.

For even as attention to the detail can lead to a grasp of essence, it can lead us to miss the pattern that unifies details, as well — and probably a good deal more easily than not. A detail is but a fragment, and, our attention divided by and isolated in fragments, we have to be very lucky not to lose the whole.

So much detail swirling in every direction that you could run yourself ragged, darting here and there, running in circles trying to find the reasons for it all. Peering, hypothesizing, experimenting, only to have to repeat the whole round over and over again. A detail seems to point to this explanation, here, for its being; then it's found to point to that explanation, there. Later, on another level, it seems to point to both explanations at once. Did those little blisters of oil inside the blossom precede the little toothed squeegees on the legs of the bee that pollinates it? Or did the squeegees precede the pockets of oil?[2] Such an infinitude of variations, of eddying detail. Seeking reasons — meaning — you could drown in the chaos of it.

. . . . .

My father taught me about trees when I was very little. He started with their leaves. He took me in the truck, on foot, atop the tractor; into woodlots, alongside swamps and hedgerows and streams. Stopping along the way, he showed me leaves shaped like tulips, leaves shaped like hearts, leaves shaped like mittens. He said their names — yellow poplar, catalpa, sassafras — teaching me to differentiate the green.

Traipsing along behind him those spring Saturdays when I was five and six and seven, I watched him plant trees, species after species. He planted whole lines and groves of some (white pine, dogwood, sugar maple), and of others (sourwood, cucumber tree, eastern redbud) he planted just one, as if just to be sure they would not be forgotten, but counted as they should be among their native kin. Gradually, he scattered trees all over the farm's two hundred acres, allowing many of them room to develop into specimens, individuals that exemplify the shape a species will take when unencumbered, when not crowded by the branches of others, not starved of light by overshadowing — in short, when given free rein. He planted them for the love of them, of each species in its distinctiveness, of their collective variety. Now, after fifty years, the farm is like an arboretum, a park full of specimens of dozens of species of trees, each teaching whoever sees it what at its best and freest its species can do and be. He always spoke their names with seriousness, as if each species were a weighty topic. Sometimes he even told me a tree's Latin name (*Taxodium distichum* for bald cypress, *Nyssa sylvatica* for tupelo gum); and sometimes he placed them in families — birches and alders in Betulaceae, pussy willows in Salicaceae. At the same time he told their details — a habit of sap perhaps, a quality of wood, a proclivity for growing "knees" — with affectionate admiration, and often with a chuckle of delight at the fantastical, idiosyncratic habits of these fine companions of ours who sport such solemn, esoteric names.

And so, my father introduced me to trees as serious beings, initiated in me an awareness of them as both individuals and families. He laid trees down in my consciousness, impressed them there as a locus of attention and regard. One effect of this was that when the lessons came at school on xylem and phloem and cambium, they stirred a zealous interest in me. In a boarding school where I was miserable, and where my efforts misfired repeatedly, I got my only A in botany. Another effect perhaps was that, eventually, I began sometimes in the presence of trees to envision certain less tangible arboreal qualities, ones that might be called meta-botanical, or even meta-biological maybe.

. . . . .

The first episode of this kind occurred one night in the forest decades after those lessons of my father, when I was on the cusp of middle age. In one of those hours when dejection and affirmation combine impossibly within you, and the pitch of emotion strains accustomed boundaries, opening new doors.

Bridget and I were camped there, in the taiga, by a stream. In a pensive mood, she'd gone off for a walk, up an old two-track in the dark. In a mood of my own, I'd stayed behind, perched on a log in a little clearing surrounded by Engelmann spruce trees, pondering amidst those still giants towering patiently above me, the painful treasure her friendship had given me.

There was a generation between us, but we were not (as knee-jerk prediction might have it) like teacher and student, mentor and protégée. Despite our difference in age, it seemed what each of us brought to the friendship put us in a kind of balance with each other, which helped us transcend any age-related discrepancies that might have precluded a full, ripe rapport. If she was considerably younger, she brought to the friendship a precocity of soul and a prodigiousness of intellect tantamount to the wisdom of maturity. If I fell a good distance short of her genius, I brought a ragged but rich life experience and a reflective habit of mind. And so we'd found ourselves on a peculiar kind of equal footing — firm basis for friendship — despite fundamental natural disparities.

And yet there *was* a generation between us. And there were times we were inexorably aware of it.

For me it was painful to think of: could she in all her shining manage to avoid the pitfalls? She had a life to live, like the most ordinary of us. The answer, pure and simple, was that.

For her too, it was painful, not so much to conjecture, but to see what was: the waste in my life, the squandered opportunities, the potentials unfulfilled.

I'd gone off track in my youth and now, hamstrung by a chain of self-inflicted losses, it seemed that just halfway through life's journey I was bereft of prospects. I was trying to come to terms with this state of affairs — the fear and humiliation, the hopelessness, of the beached whale — but everyone I knew declined to notice my beached-ness; and this had the effect of suggesting that my pain must be out of proportion to my situation, that a fumbled life didn't merit the desperation I felt. Though it may be that my friends averted their eyes in the name of friendship, in a gesture of supportive denial intended to shield me from suffering, they declined so completely and politely that my struggle to come to terms was all the more difficult. For as their insouciance seemed to suggest my predicament must be at best trivial, perhaps unfounded entirely, I'd come to feel deprecating of my pain. And so I'd been pushing down on it, balling it up in a stunted bundle, denying myself the validation that pain has the power to confer on experience, however misguided. Pushing down on it, that is, until earlier that day, when Bridget had affirmed it to me. That same afternoon she had told me, her face and voice contorted with the effort of unvarnished honesty: "I'm so sorry to say this to you, I'm so sorry. But I don't want to end up like you."

It was a gift no one else had had the courage to give to me.

Bridget afforded us both the dignity of not pretending. She spoke the hard truth because unsaid it would be a wall between us, and because to fail to acknowledge openly what we both knew would have been demeaning to us both. Beyond that, she afforded me a dignity I'd completely lost sight of: the simple dignity of *what is*. While others were too delicate to speak of my woundedness, she put a hand right on it. She ratified my pain. In doing so, she ratified my experience and its very misguidedness — the source of that pain. It was not only real enough to be noticeable, it warranted attention: a thing that could happen to others, so possible that she even feared it for herself.

I looked up from my log to the patch of night sky above. The Engelmanns, which in daylight were straight as tent poles, seemed to lean in ever so slightly overhead. Their spiked spires were like spears against the darkness. Darker by far than the sky they were profiled against, they eclipsed its dark infinity, and shuffling ever so slightly, they seemed to enclose me in a circle of arboreal amity. Always I'd felt a comfort in trees in the forest. Looking up from a campfire to see their spires listing above me, their great boughs swaying thick and furry against the night sky, I'd feel almost as if there were a serious intent in them, almost as if they extended goodwill toward me.

This time no campfire, just the little clearing. Coyotes howling somewhere on a ridgetop as they picked up a hint of glow from the oncoming moon. The round of sky overhead ringed by spruce spires seemed to constrict further, as if the trees were leaning in further still. Always I'd felt a comfort in trees in the forest. But never like this. The once balled-up pain was now liberated inside me. And flowing freely, it had assumed its dignity. I had a sense of the worth I was now free to earn of it, and I felt for the first time deserving of the comfort of the trees.

And if it was indeed true that they were extending goodwill toward me, I thought I glimpsed the source of their capacity for that.

All the trees around me had stood there through every night for decade upon decade upon decade. As the darkness came on and as it lifted, came on and lifted thousands of times, they stood. This was just an everyday fact — physical, material, tangible. But that night that fact had something beyond the tangible about it for me.

At the root of my waste and loss was a tossing and turning, a seeking every which way. A deep not knowing which way to turn or go. A leaving this which really is here, and pursuing that which isn't. A continual dashing toward, then dodging away. But the trees around me were getting it all continually. Midnight, torrents, sunshine, ice — and winds that both rip limb from limb and make the sap flow. What I sensed of the trees that night went beyond goodwill and the capacity for goodwill: *With no choice to dart or dodge, think what — if they could — they might know.*

They seemed to have sentience. Not just the sentience that belongs to the various botanical tropisms — the sensing of (and consequent moving toward or away from) light, temperature, gravity — but something along the lines of the sentience more customary to my own species. As if they took in things similar to what we take in, and in similar ways, they seemed to have a knowledge of something.

Of course, this was all in my mind — this tree philosophizing. A sort of reverse projection, perhaps, a roundabout sort of wishful thinking. And yet . . . And yet . . . What was it? What was it in *them* that made me feel that? That they had a kind of knowledge of something. That they were my friends, truly, despite fundamental natural disparities.

. . . . .

Along with us humans (and a number of representative species from other phyla across life's five kingdoms), *Arabidopsis thaliana*, a tiny wild mustard plant, has had its genome sequenced. In the process, this unassuming forb has revealed itself to be complicated in ways we'd never have dreamed possible for a plant. *A. thaliana* has only five chromosomes, but after the sequencing of just the first two of them, we'd already gained significant insight into the plant's biological sophistication via the density of its genes. Nearly 8,000 genes were found to populate these two chromosomes, as compared with an estimated 550 genes on human chromosome 22. And the sequencing revealed the long arm of one of the chromosomes to consist of sixteen million bases, making it the second longest continuous segment of DNA yet found at that point, after a piece of human chromosome 22. With a five-chromosome limit compared with our twenty-three, it's obvious that this simple plant could not surpass humans in general genetic complexity. But it surpasses worms and flies. Commenting on these findings, a molecular geneticist reminds us that unlike members of the other biological kingdoms, plants adjust their development to the conditions they're born into. "You get a very different plant in cold or warm, light or shade — but a fly is a fly every time," he says.[3]

A different plant every time, indeed.

The first plants conquered land about four hundred million years ago. About a hundred million years later, five hundred distinct kinds had evolved, and by the end of the Cretaceous (sixty-five million years ago) there were at least twenty-two thousand species. Since then, vascular plants (so called because of the internal fluid-conducting vessels that disseminate water and food throughout the plant body) have increased about twelvefold, with around 260-some thousand species now identified;[4] and grouped with the twenty-three thousand known nonvascular species (including mosses, liverworts, and hornworts — plants only partially adapted to land), this number rounds off to about three hundred thousand known species of living land plants.[5] And these great numbers represent a myriad of forms, sporting a staggering variety of adaptations that have allowed plants to penetrate every habitat on Earth, and every niche and micro-niche within every habitat.

For example, in desert plants there's the range of designs to minimize the water loss that occurs through transpiration (a process by which water pulled up from the roots evaporates through little holes in the leaves, called stomata, which also serve to take in the carbon dioxide necessary for photosynthesis). In some cases, leaves are reduced to little spines, decreasing evaporation by decreasing surface area. In others, the stomata open only at night, storing up CO_2 for the next day's photosynthesis, while avoiding the higher rate of evaporation that occurs during sunlight hours. In others still, a thick waxy covering (the cuticle) protects the plant from drying; or an extraordinarily protracted taproot siphons a deep pocket of water; or flattened stems grow facing every which way, so that while at any given daylight moment some necessarily face the sun, thus surrendering water vapor, others in the very same vicinity face away from the sun, thus remaining cool and reserving water. Some cactus, like the saguaro, store water in stems ridged with pleats, which not only expand and contract as the amount of stored water varies, but also provide lines of evaporation-minimizing shade all up and down the plant.

These represent just the tip of the tip of the tip of a vast iceberg of adaptations to desert conditions, and for every habitat there's another iceberg, with an equally spacious tip. Adaptations to alpine and tundra conditions include cup-shaped flowers that compensate for freezing conditions by concentrating sunlight, raising their internal temperature 4 to 18 degrees Fahrenheit higher than that of the surrounding air; and root systems that compensate for thin soil by proliferating to four times the volume of above-ground shoots; and leaves shielded from the abundant ultraviolet light of high altitudes by a covering of light-reflecting white hairs — or by a high concentration of the pigment anthocyanin, which absorbs the dangerous rays before they can destroy the chlorophyll necessary for photosynthesis. The problem of freezing in temperate zones is dealt with in countless other resourceful ways: by leaf abscission[6] in the deciduous plants; by an antifreeze of concentrated sugar that protects tree trunks and branches, as well as the leaves of herbaceous evergreens; by food storage (for example, in roots and rhizomes, bulbs and corms) for the plant to draw on during the cold season when photosynthetic leaves and stems have died back; and many others.

And as for adaptations to light or shade, different plants in different situations employ varying combinations of phototropisms. In plants exhibiting positive phototropism, for example, the shoot tips grow toward light. The shoot tips of other plants, however, grow away from light, as do many roots, exhibiting negative phototropism. Some vine seedlings at first grow toward a dark object, such as the base of a tree. Once the vine touches the trunk, however, the phototropism reverses from negative to positive, and the vine climbs lightward, sometimes delaying leaf formation until it has arrived in the sunny upper reaches of the tree.[7] In some plants, in a phenomenon called phototorsion, only the leaves twist to face a light source, often following the course of the sun throughout the day. Whereas phototropisms involve growth and are prompted by hormones (which often operate by inducing different rates of cell growth on opposite sides of the stem, causing it to curve), phototorsion does not involve growth at all, but is prompted by specialized motor cells at the base of the leaf blade.

Beyond adaptations to the broad habitats of widely differing climate and light zones, plants have adapted to microhabitats you'd never imagine. In order to live in acidic peat bog soils lacking in the nitrogen they need to build protein, some species of plants have become animal-eaters — for example, the pitcher plant. Although the hollow tubes of its leaves do photosynthesis, they also lure insects down into a deadly pool at their base, where bacteria digest the bugs' bodies and release their nitrogen for the plant's use. Another group of species has taken to growing not in soil but on other plants, often for the advantage of being closer to the sun. Some of these, called epiphytes, are adapted to growing on the branches of trees, high up in the air where they get lots of extra light.[8] Aquatic plants take advantage of water's high heat capacity to resist rapid temperature changes, to filter out dangerous ultraviolet waves, and, in some cases, to provide them with a steady store of nutrients that they absorb directly from their surrounding bath. Some aquatics, like water lilies, might be called "bi-ambiential" (to coin a term), for they've adapted to living in two environments at once, realizing the benefits of water-living via their nether parts, while their above-water parts provide them easier access to oxygen than water affords. In fact, since oxygen is not readily dissolved in water, many underwater plants (like the millefoil common in ponds) have evolved finely divided leaves to increase their absorption area — as well as to resist being torn by the motion of water, which is heavier and has greater impact than air. And in a turn of events I find particularly astonishing, at least one vascular plant has even adapted to the absorption of that plant anathema, salt. *Spartina alternifolia*, or smooth cordgrass, has membranes in its roots that filter most of the salt out of the estuarine water they drink; but for the salts that do cross the membrane, they have special cellular compartments to store them in until they can finally squeeze them out of glands in the leaves, returning the salts to air and water once again.

"A different plant in cold or warm, light or shade," said the molecular geneticist. I reiterate: Indeed. A different plant, as well, in acidity or alkalinity, on the ground or in the air, in wet or dry (or both), or even in saltwater or fresh. And as I said earlier, I haven't scratched the tip of the tip of the tip of the iceberg of plant adaptations, haven't even touched on vast groups — for example, the some twenty-three thousand species of nonvascular plants. So much swirling detail in the plant kingdom — so many species, so many unimaginably intricate adaptations — that you could run yourself ragged trying to find the reasons for it all.

And if the ability to make such environmental adjustments is proving to require such genetic luxuriance in a little mustard plant, think what must be true of some of these more bizarrely adapted species. Or simply, think what must be true of a tree.

. . . . .

Early spring has a special feel at the interface of coastal marsh and upland forest. There's a state park in New Jersey named Cheesequake that somewhere between mid- and late April is rich with this feel.

The coastal marsh there is a wide, flat, muddy bottom, cut by a tidal creek. Walled by steep, naked mud banks, this creek and its tributaries are flanked by sweeps of phragmites, fifteen-foot-tall reeds flying graceful seed heads like fluffy flags.[9] The phragmites march toward the ocean for scores of acres, until at a certain point they sense more salt in the water than suits their taste; and so down near where Cheesequake Creek flows into Raritan Bay they give way to the aforementioned, salt-adapted smooth cordgrass.

The upland forest there is an up-and-down place, all ravines and ridges, populated largely by various species of oaks, under which you'll find blooming, in their seasons, lady's slippers, trailing arbutus, and high- and lowbush blueberries, among other plants woody and herbaceous that like sandy soil. This soil having been scooped and mounded by the last ice age, the upland rises a good thirty feet above the marsh in most places, jutting in great steep-sided promontories into the bleached reeds of the early spring marsh, like headlands into a wheat-colored sea.

The ecotone of these promontories is a favored site for *Amelanchier arborea*. A small tree with exquisite bark — smooth and silvery and faintly streaked with stripes that narrow and broaden like those on a tiger's back — it is commonly known in New Jersey as the shadbush because it blooms just when the anadromous shad are running up the estuaries into freshwater to spawn. At that time, all the undulating edge where marsh meets upland is dotted with sprays of their frail lacy blooms, airy white poofs here and there against the grey and brown limbs of a forest that any day now will fuzz over with green.

One late April day I'd gone there for a respite from grief and confusion through the sight of their ethereal flowers. I trailed along through the forest. I smooshed through black swamp muck, where the skunk cabbage leaves blared shiny and green. I picked my way along root-veined ridges, among oaks and beeches, backed by the sea of phragmites as if by a yellow screen. My heart hissing with the facts of my life at that juncture — the tormented decline of aged parents, the downward spiral of former family good fortune, the struggle to keep family connections from bursting apart under the stresses of both — I peered down the slopes for a glimpse of the sparse white foam of shadbush bloom. I scanned the little humps of forested islands out in the ocean of reeds. In and out along the promontories I ambled, scanning. But I had come too late, they were gone.

Big things were on the way out in my life then. I'd been charging about, trying this, trying that, vying to stem the tide of change, but these things would be on the way out from now on until they finally just vanished, and this was a fact I was going to have to stick with. My parents were not just waning, but transfiguring, the colors of their very natures changing before my eyes. My mother, reputed all my life by all who knew her to be a paragon of sweetness, now seethed with hostility, her spirit gone mean. My father, too, always a bastion of perspicacity and good judgment, had begun to reveal worrisome sides. While she complained incessantly, scorning everything she had always seemed to love, he wore a vapid mask of denial, pronouncing obsessively on the family blessings, protesting far too much. Fundamental facts of our life were being called into question — the foundations of our accustomed good fortune, the cherished family bonds. What courses had really been running under our lives? It seemed that the very basis on which I'd built my sense of myself was deteriorating, as the family myth seemed to writhe into shocking new shapes I'd never have thought possible for us. Love turning hate turning love-hate. Certainty turning doubt turning fear. Even the farm was threatened, with its perfect specimens of a spectrum of native trees. Our very ground might be lost to us, to be itself transfigured, quite possibly beyond recognition, going from fields and trees to concrete and boards. In an effort to get things back to what they'd once been, I'd been reasoning, cajoling, begging, putting my foot down. Talking to doctors, talking to lawyers, accusing, sticking my head in the ground. I'd been snatching at one thing, then another, in an effort to shore things up, while more and more all I wanted to do was run. But the one thing that was really getting through to me was that running was useless: I barely knew where I was, much less where to go. I was losing my bearings, my grounding, my understanding. Aware once again, this time on a completely new level, that always, at every moment — in the most certain of certain moments — there's just so much we don't know.

And we have to bear it — what we don't know, can't understand, can't change. We have to try not to be whipped around by every unknown, by every affliction, by every bump in the road. We have to try not to be whipped around by the road.

And then there was something — out in the phragmites. A big smear of color — pink!? Beside a blotch of bare shrubbery, a dense cloud of color, white maybe, but with an edging, an elusive, shifting tracing of pink. Not pale pink but a pink deep and full-colored, that changed places, now here and now elsewhere, I saw as I looked harder, elusive yet at every second showing up somewhere along the contours of this startling wash of color out on the wheat-colored sea.

What is it? How did it get there? Go down in there through the muck and see.

At the edge of the forest, my view no longer obstructed by brush brake and tree trunks, I saw it down in there. It was a tree, of course. Old and big and all covered with blossom. Smack dab in the marsh flat. Astonishing.

I descended the promontory, exited trees into sunlight. Crunched and sloshed through the towering reeds. Right there on a hump of firm soil in the midst of the muck it was blowing, an immense cloud of pink in the spring wind — like a liquid of one color eddying into another-colored liquid, the two curling together; like a vapor reeling in air — swirling in place.

I'm weak on fruit trees. Unless they're old natives, unexotic, un-hybridized, I do not know my flowering trees. And this was not an old-fashioned apple. Too intensely pink along its contours where the flower buds hadn't yet opened. Too diaphanous, too limber and fluid, and no simultaneous green (as comes with old apples) of new leaves. Too fluid for peach, a cherry maybe — maybe some hybrid, some horticultural product perhaps, but this is sure: no human planted it there. And it did not belong there in any sense of human logic. A bird had planted it with its dropping, perhaps. Somehow its seed had settled in this most unlikely of places, burrowed in and clung and survived there, a stranger in a strange land all these years.

The outlandish expanse of color was one thing, but more entrancing was the sheerness of it. The tree, in parts a thick cumulus cloud, was in just as many parts a mere haze. Pink in the phragmites, wildly curious, seductive, the tree was like a colored gas in the wind, like a chemical reaction suddenly materialized on the air.

No, like a fire. That was more it. In the wind it was steadily roiling, like a fire blazing out of an oil drum, a fire that stays put in the oil drum but roils and roils in the air above it, and you can see through it where it roils in the air. Here for a moment you see through it and then not, but you see through it then somewhere else. That's what the tree was like — a transparent fire in the wind. Roiling, yet frozen. A bonfire of blooming, blowing in place; a frozen fire, growing in place — all alone in an alien territory.

Like the burning bush, the frozen pink bonfire of a tree seemed to have something to offer. It seemed very much to know some kind of thing. What it could possibly know, I hadn't the foggiest, but for a moment it seemed to be saying: *You are where you are. It's good enough as it is.*

It seems as I was rounding my middle years, I was becoming ever more impressionable where trees were concerned. Ever more open, responsive — not to say, vulnerable — to the meta-botanical qualities of trees.

. . . . .

If even a plant as humble and inconspicuous as *Arabidopsis thaliana* shows such genetic complexity, it seems we must chalk this advantage up to what may look to us animals like every plant's disadvantage: its state of plantedness. Of course, the various tropisms represent movement toward or away from a stimulus, but only by a plant's appendages (so to speak), while the plant itself remains affixed to one place. Although some plants manage to take a baby step over the threshold of circumambulation — like the aspen, which can amble a bit into its surroundings through cloning,[10] or the parasitic dodder, which can wander a tad over the local territory by wrapping up neighboring plants in tangles of its vinelike haustoria[11] — most every member of Kingdom Plantae is anchored to a substrate, be it soil, rock, or aquatic sediment, or even another plant's branch or leaf. Even if only by tiny filaments called protonema (as in the case of bryophytes), or by rhizoids or rhizomes proper in those plants that lack bona fide roots, most every plant is stuck in one place. To us mobile animals, this seems a gross limitation: how do you get food, how do you protect yourself, if you can't move away from and toward? How do you manage genetic diversity — how do you mate? If despite this condition of rootedness plants have radiated throughout every biome in such overwhelming numbers of species, it must be due to a vast genetic cleverness, a voluminous bag of tricks for dealing with fixedness carried in the genes.

The problem of food is, of course, solved in most cases by photosynthesis, that ingenious cellular operation that takes inorganic substances immediately at hand and, in the presence of sunlight, transforms them into the organic stuff of plant bodies. The tiny minority of plants that don't photosynthesize[12] come with other built-in schemes for getting nutrition: some directly parasitize other plants (for instance, mistletoe); others (Indian pipes) live on nutrients from other plants that are transferred to them by a fungus symbiotically bound up with their roots; still others (coralroot) are saprophytes, deriving nutrients from dead organic matter, often also in symbiosis with fungi.

The problem of protection against harsh elements is solved by physical adaptations along the lines of those mentioned earlier, but also by chemical ones.[13] In the desert, the seeds of some annuals, for example, contain chemicals that prevent them from germinating until enough rain falls to wash the chemicals out, thus assuring that the seeds will lie dormant until there's enough water to ensure growth. Similarly, plants employ chemical as well as physical tactics for self-defense. If some produce spines to keep from being eaten, others produce chemicals that taste bad, or that sicken grazers — killing them, even, sometimes. And while the creosote bush holds intruders at bay by sucking up all the water in its vicinity via wide-spreading roots, brittlebush uses a chemical to get the same result. Its leaves contain a substance toxic to seedlings of most other species, and as it sheds them in a wide skirt around its base, the brittlebush secures a wide margin of territory all to itself. Then again, the genetic programming of some plant species is so tricky as to enable the plant to enlist the aid of other species against intruders. One *Acacia* enlists ants by offering them an irresistible nectar. In exchange, the ants attack all organisms that threaten the *Acacia*, even killing encroaching plants by girdling them.

Perhaps the toughest nut to crack, however, is the problem of reproduction. Think of the lone cherry tree blooming in the Cheesequake marsh amidst the phragmites, with not another member of its species in sight. If you've elaborated yourself to the point where you can't reproduce by fission like the simpler microscopic organisms before you, and you haven't the means to mosey up to a potential partner and rub noses or some such thing, how do you get your sex cells combined with those of a like other — in animal terms, how do you mate? This is a fundamental problem of all plants, of course — not just those who find themselves isolated like the Cheesequake cherry tree, but even those who find themselves with a suitable mate just inches away.

One solution is to be monoecious — to carry both male and female gametes (that is, sperm cells and egg cells) in your body — and to fertilize yourself.[14] But self-fertilization can impede healthy genetic diversity, so most plants don't go this route. In some monoecious plants, the male and female reproductive structures mature at different times to prevent conjugation. In others, these structures are so positioned as to prevent contact of male pollen with female pistil (the structure that houses the ovules, equivalent to eggs). Still other plants are chemically "self-incompatible,"[15] with a means of physiologically blocking any self-pollen that alights on the pistil from growing the little tubes by which it would bore down to the ovules. In short, even when both male and female gametes occur on the same plant, they are often intended to conjugate not with each other, but with the gametes of other plants.[16]

But how, when one plant can't approach another?

For hundreds of millions of years the wind alone facilitated cross-fertilization. Plants released spores (later, pollen as well) in great masses to float on the breezes, perchance to light on the right sites on the reproductive organs of another plant of the same species. To this day, many plants rely on the wind for pollination,[17] but since there's a limit to how far the wind will carry a grain of pollen, wind-pollinated plants need to grow in dense stands for their pollen to be assured of meeting its mark. And so, since a solitary individual doesn't stand a good chance of reproducing by this means, it makes sense for a plant to do as the aforementioned *Acacia* has done: enlist help. Get the aid of an animal who can carry the pollen from plant to plant over fair distances.

But how to get the animal to cooperate? What's in it for him? When you're dependent on others to pass your genes along for you, you have to beguile those others into visiting you, and this is where the ingenious evolution of flowers that occurred in the Cretaceous comes in. Blossoms evolved to attract animal pollinators with their color, fragrance, or shape; eventually many of them even began offering nectar as a reward for a visit. Ultimately these characteristics — and others even more particular: for instance, the location of a blossom on its stalk, or the schedule of its nectar offerings — became adapted precisely to attract particular species of animals, which in turn became adapted to respond precisely to them.

Such a gamut of particulars, specializations. So much detail swirling in every direction — of structure, function, purpose. Such a swirling detail of relationships — intraspecies, interspecies, interkingdom, even. Over time flowers came to attract beetles, flies, ants, bees, wasps, moths, and butterflies. They came to attract true bugs and mosquitoes and thrips. They came to attract birds, bats, and even lemurs. And various marsupials, and in one case at least, a reptile, even.[18] At this point in evolutionary history a given angiosperm may offer a given animal anything from food to shelter to mating grounds to beneficial chemicals. An example of the latter: an orchid gets a bee to "mine" it for its scent, an arrangement that not only is sexually useful to the orchid (as in the process the bee transfers pollen from flower to flower), but also helps the bee get its own sexual job done. Male euglossine bees use flattened hairs on their front legs to scrape scenty chemicals from the petals of tropical orchids, then, using their hind legs, mix them with chemical secretions of their own. Why? As Gary Paul Nabhan puts it, these bees "have come to depend on the spicy perfumes of orchid flowers as precursors for their own sex pheromones. . . . stealing the orchid's sexual message and transforming it into their own aphrodisiac."[19]

Sometimes pollinator and pollinated are rigidly linked, as in the case of the *Yucca elata* and moths of the *Tegiticula* genus, which only have eyes for each other. (A good thing since, like all other organisms in a relationship of obligate mutualism, both would go extinct if this weren't so).[20] But pollination is seldom a one-moth-one-flower kind of affair, or even an affair between one bee family and one flower family, despite the flamboyant case of orchids and euglossines. More often, sets of flower species with certain general characteristics invite fits with sets of animal species with certain general characteristics. For instance, birds (such as hummingbirds) usually visit bright red blossoms (such as those of the ocotillo), often tube-shaped and full of nectar to meet the birds' high demands for energy. However, ocotillo blooms are pollinated not just by hummingbirds but by certain bees as well, and the hummingbirds that pollinate ocotillos may, in addition, pollinate plants from *eight* other completely different families. Often a whole *guild* of pollinators (frequently from several different phyla) "collectively focuses on . . . flowers that have similar floral forms and presentations but may either bloom sequentially or overlap in space and time."[21] Certain bats switch through a variety of nectar plants as they migrate; and carpets of myriad, simultaneously blooming, subalpine species often compete for the same potpourri of pollinators, as these sundry animals buzz, float, flap, or crawl through their colorful arrays. Again, all this is the tip of the tip of the tip of an iceberg. Innumerable cases illustrate that matches are seldom exclusive or inflexible.

The point, once again, is the dazzling complexity of how plants adapt and function. A seeming infinity of arrangements and causes for arrangements, patterns of meaning exquisitely difficult to tease out of a seemingly chaotic sea of detail. Why does the profile of the sumac's branches on the sky take the form of the outline of stairsteps? Why are the sweet gum's leaves shaped like stars? In almost any case you could name, we haven't yet fathomed the reason why in a particular plant a particular physical or mechanical feature has taken hold. There's so much we don't know. So much detail swirling in every direction that you could swirl, yourself, forever, trying to keep up with it, let alone trying to find the reasons behind it all.

At the same time, we know something big, however. Over the ages we've delved into enough cases, come up with enough answers to be damned close to certain that in each case there *is* a reason, whether we've fathomed it or not. If we can't explain to what purpose the sweet gum's starry foliage comes in so many colors, or to what end the bark of the sycamore is mottled and blotched, we've fathomed enough through the questions we *have* answered so far to know that the idiosyncrasies of the sweet gum and the sycamore are connected to the deepmost identity of each of these plants. To each plant's unique role in nature's immeasurable web of interdependence. To each plant's own particular way of interacting with factors biotic and abiotic to make its own particular living. To the very particular way it, and only it has evolved to survive, each as one particular part in a vast, swirling but unified whole.

And beyond this, of course, we know something else. We know that behind each specific, tiny feature's specific, immediate reason for being there's a broader reason — an overarching reason why each and every one of these innumerably diverse variations has taken hold. For every characteristic (from flowers to branching patterns, from spores to rhizoids to leaves to bark) of every plant species (woody to herbaceous — from sumac to *Arabidopsis thaliana*, from maritime prune to cordgrass) is tied not just to the deepmost identity of that specific plant (as one that must survive a bit of salt in its water, for example, or as one that must attract ants, or bees, or bats), but ultimately to the core identity of plants in general, of the plant kingdom as a whole: the fact of being a stationary life-form, rooted (most commonly) in earth. How could we be surprised that plants would turn out to be biologically sophisticated, genetically dense? They have to be clever — there's no better way to put it — for from the mightiest sequoia to the lowliest

Arabidopsis, they have to suffer the winds of chance like the rest of us; but unlike the rest of us, they have to do so quite literally *unmoved*.

The problems of being stationary abound. Despite this we have the radiations of plants throughout all the biomes, their voluminous bag of tricks for dealing with everything from flirtation (even if by proxy) to self-defense (also by proxy sometimes). Being immobile, it may behoove you to become beautiful, seductive. Being immobile, you have to fine-tune inner defenses — develop the power to poison, if need be. Despite all the problems of being stationary, we have the extensive success of plants, as they have taken the "disadvantage" of stillness and turned it into a wellspring of wonders, a source of ingenuities beyond imagining.

. . . . .

Breakfast in the parking lot at McDonald's, feeling desperate-depressed in a world of compartments and pieces, feeling myself the island that John Donne said no man is. A gull there with the telltale black-tipped bill of a juvenile, a second-year herring gull probably, the immature mottling of its back feathers just turning mature grey. The gull was injured, one leg pulled up with the foot dangling limply, a cut at the "ankle," the look of something severed, irreparable. Though gulls are not creatures of forest and this McDonald's was surrounded by pitch pine, smack-dab in the thick of the biggest single stretch of forest in the state — despite this there he was, alone, dangling, and I decided to feed him, though it's not my habit to feed gulls in parking lots. Threw him a crumb and in a flash others assembled shrieking on the asphalt, appearing out of who knows where. Something askew here, these gulls surely not where they should be, but rather displaced somehow from their natural habitat, natural tastes. Instead of wafting above broad expanses of open land and water reconnoitering for their sustenance, they'd been reduced to loitering in the shadow of plastic arches, awaiting the discard of bits of McMuffin in a pinched little black quad of human-concocted rock.

My gull hopped on one foot and slapped his wings at the others, defending his crumb. I threw more, precisely in his direction but closer to me this time, thinking that he, being desperate, might brave coming closer and that they might not. I'd throw and he'd first hop, flap, dart at the others defensively, then turn to grab the food. I was

brokenhearted for him, though it would have seemed presumptu-
ous to me, that morning, to say this. That morning, self-conscious,
self-suspicious—self-proscribing, self-circumscribing—I'd have felt
obliged to say something more along the lines of: the sadness belongs
to the situation, to him and not me. But that would have been the depression of dividedness speaking, the opposite of presumptuousness
in a way, and worse: a flaccid acquiescence to this world's prevailing
notion of the essential separateness of that gull and me.

It had been the theme of the year, it seemed, in all the journals and
magazines that showed up in my mailbox from the first to this very last
day of the year: the splintering of the green land into islands by con-
struction; asphalt and concrete spreading like lava, first in discrete
streams, which then widened, joining one with another into broader
streams, lakes, oceans, covering everything in their path. And it seemed
that this year, on this my annual, end-of-the-year, stock-taking day,
what I had to take stock of was this: mourning the land I grew up in,
lamenting the cleaving of the former vibrant domain of it into a mere
sprinkling of soft, green keys adrift in a hard man-made sea. Contemplating how, by isolating the once-green ground into mere islets of vegetation, we've separated nature from nature — contemplating the evidence throughout the land I grew up in of how this very isolation
works to decimate species after species of that very vegetation, and of
the creatures that depend on it.

Breeding out of this separation of nature from nature is, of course,
the division of people from nature, and amidst those stray gulls darting and diving about on the macadam I was feeling both splits that day.
I'd been feeling them both acutely for a good week at that point, until
on that morning of my end-of-the-year, stock-taking day I'd come to
the point of feeling like an island myself, cut off from any sense of the
pattern that unifies life's details, bereft of the whole.

It had begun in the aforementioned park named Cheesequake, that
park not far from the city named New York, where the shadbush
blooms in the ecotones and acres of phragmites march toward the sea.
There in that park that I'd always held as a place of comfort, the theme
of the year had taken a visceral hold on me. In a little pocket of the
Cheesequake woodland, there's a tiny Atlantic white cedar swamp. Me-
andering through it, there's a boardwalk (its wood treated with anti-rot
chemicals) with a couple of little wings coming off it where you can sit

and dangle your feet a while to take in this little ecosystem's mystique. That's the idea, I think, but when I'd tried it a week earlier, I'd just ended up feeling blue. For although the park bills it proudly as the state's northernmost grove of Atlantic white cedar (a.k.a. eastern white cedar, southern white cedar, and swamp and post cedar, too), that day I could not help but see it as a mere puny fragment, severed, as the woods and wetlands dwindle, from the prolific stretches of its past.

Rare, precious wood of an "odd, amphibious"[22] tree — they even made pipes from it in the old days, when bored Atlantic white cedar logs constituted the water systems in many early American cities and towns. Wood close-grained and impervious, in New Jersey bogs they've even mined it — great trees, some of them centuries old, and some among them six feet thick, a dimension no longer seen in our times. Mined it like bog iron (and from the same locales), like coal, except from water. This mining is possible because of the decay resistance inherent in the wood itself, of course, but also because of the conditions where these trees grow. Beneath the Earth's surface in Atlantic white cedar swamps, a layer of clay prevents water from draining. The trees grow in extraordinarily dense stands, obstructing sunlight, and in the perpetual gloom beneath them the accumulation of leaves in sodden soil makes that soil acidic in the extreme. The water standing upon it is the color of rust, any decay is creeping-slow (so slow that it was the water of choice to take on the months-long voyages of old sailing ships because, virtually free of microbes, it was the only water that wouldn't go bad), and in this water fallen trees remain intact. It's said the supply of buried cedar may run to a hundred feet or more. But it's said, as well, that at some not-too-distant point there may be more Atlantic white cedar trees beneath the soil than above it. For we've been cutting them and cutting them — by the early 1800s it's said that around the cedar swamps "sawdust piles rose higher than the trees" — and we've been steadily, steadily, ever more steadily draining their swamps.

A week earlier, for the first time, it had hit me: it was a puny fragment, the Cheesequake cedar swamp. A sparse smattering of trees, their branches sparse and only sparsely dressed with sparse, sickly specimens of their characteristic intricate scaly leaves. Lacy you might say, if you didn't know better. Minimalistic, you might say, appreciatively. A grove you might say, thinking wishfully. But what I saw that day was a gathering of twenty or so spare trees, deprived and struggling for what they need, clinging together at the edge of a megalopolis in a tiny pocket of a rag of land spared by humans from human development. I'd ended up feeling blue, and in the weeks since my visit had come to feel bluer still, as the Cheesequake Atlantic white cedar grove had burned itself into me as an emblem: a specimen, in its sickliness, of the isolation that kills. An emblem that brought home, like a stone to the earth it's been dropped on, the messages scattered about in the deeper levels of my consciousness — the messages all the magazines and journals had promulgated on their chosen theme of that year — bringing them all together, bringing me down.

Which is maybe why this New Year's Eve day I found myself heading south. Breakfast in a pine-bound parking lot on the outer coastal plain, then farther south still, down the parkway named for the Garden State — New Jersey — a state long-since dismissed as a mere "industrial corridor," though only by the unknowing, only by those on a callow zip through. Turning off then, eventually to wander the back roads through trees and trees and trees, a realm of trees, wherein the patches of human development are the islands rather than vice versa — here and there a little burg. In one of them, waiting for a light to turn, on the bumper of the truck before me, a sticker: *Proud to be a Piney/From my nose down to my hiney*. The guy in the truck cab was dressed in camouflage, not the hip kind, the real kind. This was not the "corridor" NJ.

No. With the theme of separation reverberating in me, I found myself, this morning of my annual stock-taking, in the heart of the Pine Barrens, the biggest stretch of vegetation still in one piece in the state where I was born.

In the forest, the lakes are black sinks, their nether shores bristling yellow-green with *Pinus rigida* from my vantage on a strip of causeway. I edge along between these black waters, among the skeletons of swamp plants. Or among their semiskeletons, rather, for these skeletons are not of the plants themselves but merely of their latest incarnations — skeletons merely of the leaves and flowers of this has-been year. The sweet pepperbushes, stripped of all but their desiccated racemes of seeds, to reveal all the birds' nests they hid so well when there was the need. The sweet pine, the miniature saw blades of their leaves cold-blackened but still stiff and clinging, sawing at the air.

Grasses like stumps of old worn-out broom stuck upside down along the sandy center of the causeway. And most exotically, along the lakes' fringes, clumps of pitcher plants, big bunches of leaves still jutting out of the squishiness, which while still looking leathery have become paradoxically brittle. In their lingering look of leatheriness, and in the vestiges of purple in their browned-down flowers, they are reminiscent of the February spathes of skunk cabbages that will, just two moons from now, be jutting up again, also out of squishing ground. The unique hollow leaves of the pitcher plants are like tough cellulose horns inverted in the muck, untapering upward to a perilous gape molded in the seductive shape of a heart, which lures little bugs (their molecules microscopic storehouses of plant-nourishing nitrogen) on an irrevocable journey down their throats. On this cold dark day, I find myself heartened by this plethora of skeletons in such variety, skeletons only of that part that passes — that darkens, hardens, then decomposes back into the surround — while the plant itself — its root, its bulb, its meristem — stays firm.

Heartened, too, by the persistence of this far-flung piney "barrens" in the most densely populated of the fifty states. A spark of hope against the hopelessness of saving any wholeness from being sundered to bits. For though New Jersey's land has been fragmented long ago, as have even the Pine Barrens some, they're still home to little victories. Although not impervious to our poisons, these "barrens" still seem to defy our grosser colonizations, remaining, by today's standards anyway, relatively un-encroached-upon and intact. And essentially, when you think about it, the Pine Barrens are a big victory.

A plane of sand turned biotic through the slow work of vegetation, ever complicating and embellishing the landscape through a process we've dubbed succession, in which one plant community creates conditions for the accommodation of a different plant community to follow it, one plant community after another elaborating the land into a patchwork of different stages of vegetative life. A big victory. The power of plants. To blacken and acidify water. To alter the composition of soil. To support birds, to eat bugs, to have reincarnations. To create the very air we mobile creatures breathe, and to feed the world.

At the water's edges, the air is grey but cracking clear, the images blunt around me, and I can feel the ice just fixing to form in and form up that squishy mud. But back in the forest it's all different, less distinct or firm, more fluid, equivocal. An abandoned two-track, all but erased by plant growth, leads in. The air is grey and misting. The ground is spread with a pale and finely spiked lichen, masses of creeping slender wires, and here and there an evergreen ground cover with shiny oval leaves. The two-track gets narrower, and spongier, and puddlier. The air has become close-grained with infinitesimal rain, and back in the scrub pine there is a denser fog still. The two-track becomes an animal trail for a brief stretch, and then disappears altogether, and so I begin listing landmarks in my mind to remember how to get back out of here. The base of a trunk with a thick coat of moss on this side; over there a hunter's blind made of old gates . . .

When I came upon them it was eerie, the light almost gone, and the lambent air was green. A green in the misting, in the fog, like a glow from within. A green light and green darkness, seeming unreal, magic — real New Year's Eve magic: last day of the year, down to the sparse, pale, dark end of things, but green. Atlantic white cedars — *Chamaecyparis thyoides*— old and girthy, tall and straight, stood before me in a grove.

In the eerie green light that they stood in — that seemed, in fact, oddly, to be emanating from them — the grove of Atlantic white cedars seemed somehow primeval. Thin strips of bark streaked their boles, running barely but surely on the diagonal, faintly peeling, intriguingly. There was a whitish lichen on the cedar trunks, little pale flecks of it, as if blown from whatever the machines are that fling fake stucco up onto motel ceilings — little flecks, as if spewed over the trunks like the last dregs of ersatz stucco blown from a machine. Down lower, thick bright moss, velvety, shiny in the dingy light, almost blinding — patches of it on the swollen bases of Atlantic white cedars, on fallen logs and roots, and on all the humps and bumps of things — glossy green.

I went in among them, until I had nothing but Atlantic white cedars on every side. Farther into the grove a flared-bottomed cedar trunk had a whole skirt of the neon green moss, the little bryophytes feathery when I bent over to touch it — the skirt of moss dense on the base of the trunk and on up it for several feet, cushiony when I pressed it, as if there were a layer of air between it and the trunk. Here and there a tree had a gall — an eruption of bark carbuncle balling out on it, mounding around some insect's interference with its tissues. One tree, dead, was stepped all up its trunk with little terraces of bracket lichen, all of them covered over with a transparent veneer of algal green. Grouped there together, the Atlantic white cedars felt like some ancient clan in an old watery world, an island of brawny archaic plants with the primal concoctions of life, still raw and blatant, oozing out all around them.

Magic, late, dark, greenish air, and the dark green, scaly boughs of the tall Atlantic white cedars hovering as the trees stood there in cohort, and it made you think of the nighttime there, of sitting there in the black night and what it would be like — the trees there in the dark, glowing green down along their roots where they entered the ground. It made you think of how these trees just stood there in cohort, growing in consort, and never moved except to grow or to blow, just stayed there all through the dark and the mist and the lifting fog and the dawns and dusks and midnights and never moved ever, and how year after year they were there growing and declining and coating over with mosses and lichens and thin films of algae, their roots anchored in the soggy black soil. Stalwart in the night, in the grey winter day with the snow spitting, in the humid summer among clouds of mosquitoes, liverworts sprouting down in the spongy mire at their feet. Always there, still (and quite possibly sentient), living in one place, and watching that place, and watching from it, all their lives. Dropping their seed, to be joined by their offspring; housing, serially, throngs of species of insects and birds; watching a neighbor slowly crumble before them . . . . *We are missing a point here*, they made me think, there in the gloaming. *There is a point here that the plants seem to be getting, while we are missing it.* They felt ancient and deeply forebearing against the fog in the background that was just turning now to a glass-powder sleet. They felt like the center of things. In the crystallizing grey fog sliding forth from the surround of scrub pine, they were making the meaning of New Year's. In the green light all around them, which seemed to emanate from them, was the light of meaning of all New Year's Eves. The light of the dying of the year, but green, and the Atlantic white cedars will be here tomorrow, to watch throughout another year.

On the way home that evening I thought of the proposed wilderness corridors I'd read about in the past year's magazines and journals. A dreamed plan to connect the remaining islands of wilderness, semi-wilderness: corridors to keep species fluid, to put them in touch with

a various enough pool of their own kind to ensure that all those species keep viable — corridors for things to brew in.²³ And I thought
back to the site of that robust group of cedars: the simmering stew of
the Pine Barrens, a place where life's variety thrives. A plane of sand
turned biotic, the Pine Barrens are not the "corridor" NJ in any way
that the passers-through mean it. But in another sense, possibly yes.

. . . . .

In Alabama, on the eastern shore of Mobile Bay, there's an ancient
tree, a distinguished individual of the species *Quercus virginiana*, that's
been dubbed Inspiration Oak. Some five hundred years old, it's 27 feet
around, with a branch span of 192 feet, and it stands in the center of
its own tiny park, on a piece of land that not too long ago was private
property.

In the late 1980s, in a dispute with the county over the price they'd
offered to buy her land — *and the tree* — as a vindictive gesture the
owner of the property paid a man to come cut this tree down. The man
cut into its trunk with a chainsaw — no mean task, he found, as he cut
first here and then there and then there. He never managed to cut too
terribly deeply — relative to the diameter of the tree, that is — but he
cut pretty widely before the word spread on what he was doing. And
what happened then is interesting.

People arrived in trucks, toting guns. They came from all over the
area and encircled the tree with their trucks, and they stood guard on
it, camping there for days with their guns. Although these people were
not what is commonly called "tree huggers," they formed a committee
to protect the tree, and soon they had set up a booth to disseminate information aimed at saving it. Eventually, of course, their effort drew
attention from environmental groups and foresters, who joined forces
with them in raising the money for the county to pay the asking price
for the land.

This victory ultimately proved hollow. The man with the chainsaw
had effectively girdled the tree. Although the cuts were relatively shallow, they had penetrated the cambium, the thin layer of tissue from
which a tree grows, so that despite the bridge grafts and the elaborate
sprinkler system that foresters devised to try to save it, the tree began
to die. Now it stands surrounded by a chain-link fence, slowly shed-
ding bark and limb tips. Foresters estimate that its massive limbs will
begin falling in five or so years. The tree has stood there since the time

of Christopher Columbus. Who knows, if left to itself, how much longer it might have lived.

This story is a compelling one for lots of reasons. But what I find most interesting about it is this: the original response to the violation of Inspiration Oak came not from environmentalists, but from people who likely would wince at being so labeled. It came, simply, from local country people, whose ancestors had lived for generations close to the Alabama soil.

Why did these people do this? Why does a tree mean so much?

Maybe we know in our blood, even when we don't know it in our brain, that plants made the world livable for us. That eons before we made our appearance, they were preparing the air. One plant recently determined to have played a pivotal role in the oxygenation of the atmosphere was a Devonian[24] tree called *Archaeopteris*. Although we once thought this tree dropped its branches after only one or two years, through newly discovered fossils we've ascertained it held many of its branches up to fifty years, a finding that changes our view of the role of *Archaeopteris* in the scheme of things. According to scientists, such a lifespan in a tree as abundant as the fossil record shows *Archaeopteris* to have been may qualify it for the title "the tree that changed the world." Its long-lived branches vastly increased shade, cooling streams and promoting the evolution of amphibians. As the tree proliferated it pulled greater and greater quantities of carbon dioxide from the atmosphere, thus cooling that too, while at the same time pumping unprecedented quantities of oxygen into the air. Thus, in addition to helping propel the evolution of vertebrates, *Archaeopteris* also helped prepare the environment for them to live full-time on land. Says scientist Steven E. Scheckler, commenting on the implications of these fossils that he and his team have found and studied, "In the beginning of the Devonian, we would not have been able to breathe without apparatus, but by the end of the Devonian, we would have been able to breathe."[25]

Even though it hadn't yet been revealed at that time, mightn't this *Archaeopteris* story be a clue to why those Alabama country people indulged in a brand of political activism so atypical for them? Even when we have no specific knowledge of such stories — or of the role of plants that they stand for — mightn't such actions as those of this group of Alabamans be linked to a subliminal human knowledge of the debt we owe to trees?

And maybe there's another reason, still more subtle, that prompts an action like the defense of Inspiration Oak: a significance of plants for the human psyche, perhaps, which deep in some old place in ourselves we intuit, even when we don't consciously acknowledge it.

Time is motion. Time is the sun coming up and the sun going down, it is the Earth going around the sun. This is the time we know, we engage in, the time we make for ourselves as *we* move — keeping always on the move. This is the time we measure by changings — our experience broken into compartments and pieces, that we move in and out of and among. The time of toward and away from, bringing disaster but escape also, bringing pain but also respite, relief. "Gotta keep on the move," said the desperate protagonist Morgan, in the 1967 movie of the same name. Over and over he said it, in the face of what he couldn't bear — over and over, as he kept up a frenzy of activity, moiling to put time/change between himself and what he couldn't bear.

We run to and fro — for brief stretches, at least, forgetting temporal pains abounding. But even as we accomplish this, we "forget" the overarching eternal glories, any sense we may have of them evanescing with our motion/time. For while we run, immersed in present moments — immersed in discrete fragments of the time of our discrete lives — we are cut off from the universal truths of time unchanging. In much the same way as, when we're fixed on details — immersed in discreet fragments of the space we live our lives in — we are frequently cut off from the truths of the universal pattern behind those details.

We may glimpse those eternal truths betweentimes — in strange, paradoxical moments-out-of-time. In a fleeting vision, we may find ourselves betweentimes at "the still point of the turning world,"[26] glimpsing the timeless pattern — of life, within life, behind and under and at the heart of life's motion and detail. As T. S. Eliot put it,

> . . . at the still point, there the dance is,
> But neither arrest nor movement. And do not call it fixity,
> Where past and future are gathered. Neither movement from nor
>   towards,
> Neither ascent nor decline. Except for the point, the still point,
> There would be no dance, and there is only the dance.

I sometimes think that the night in the forest with Bridget, when I fell to sensing so keenly what I identified as a meta-botanical quality in the trees, was one such paradoxical moment-out-of-time in my own life —

that I found myself at the "still point" that night. As I did also, I believe, during that interlude in Cheesequake when the startling cherry seemed to tell me something, and that hour of the green light in the Pine Barrens, when the Atlantic white cedar grove made the meaning of New Year's for me.

This truth glimpsed betweentimes might release us from suffering for all time, if we could tolerate the burden of All In Every Moment — if, instead of just glimpsing it betweentimes, we could bear to contemplate it steadily. Yet how can we do that, being each of us but an infinitesimal piece of the All, always swirling here and there with all the swirling other tidbits in all the millions of moments we live in — how can we do it when our experience is so divorced from stillness, oneness, by necessity? Amazing that we can grasp this truth at all, even in fleeting snatches; but we cannot take it in doses too frequent or too large. For, although to perceive the eternal pattern might confer an end to our struggles; although to feel our synchrony with that hub — which is neither moving nor not moving, which is connected to, and connecting, all — might free us from our suffering; still, our frail, moment-bound flesh can't endure the extremes of it, the Allness of that Oneness — in essence, "human kind/Cannot bear very much reality" — and so we can't sustain communion with the truth behind the scenes.

"Gotta keep on the move," said Morgan. Over and over he said it, as he became more and more disconnected from reality. Morgan is a kind of moving emblem of humankind in the inexorable animal habit of motion, which protects us while at the same time foiling clear understanding. But a plant instead just, always, stands there with reality streaming down.

Earlier this year sand miners in Michigan uncovered a spruce forest that lived during the last ice age. The entire forest was still standing down inside the sand — the spruce needles, spruce cones, and even the mosses of the forest floor, fossilized but intact. It seems it was flooded by water from retreating glaciers, buried quickly, thus preserved. Some of the trees were 145 years old when buried, but at this point they've been standing — in the same spot where their seeds first germinated — for 10,000 years.

Drowned, buried. Through whatever turmoil, that 10,000-year-old forest has stood, frozen in time. Still standing down deep in the sand even as its Engelmann relatives stand this very day at the Earth's surface in soil long ago elaborated by plants from a similar, original sand. An emblem of constancy and change together, united — like the axle with the wheel. Like its Atlantic white cedar brothers and its cherry cousins, frozen even in motion, and joining them as a manifestation of the pattern — each like a kind of still point in the turning world.

And maybe this is what I was sensing that night in the taiga under the Engelmanns; maybe this is what I meant by the meta-botanical quality of trees. Perhaps I was sensing a kinship of plants with the still point of the turning world, and perhaps we all sense it. Which is to postulate another explanation for the Alabamans' behavior: a symbolic significance of plants for the human psyche that, even if perceived only through a glass darkly, might readily inspire such actions as the defense of Inspiration Oak.

. . . . .

I am meditating under the broad skirt of an Engelmann spruce in the presence of three little shoelike flowers. *Calypso bulbosa*, commonly called fairy slipper: a little magenta orchid, more diminutive than the lady's slipper, the toe of the shoe sleeker, more streamlined, and topped by a hood and five little pointed flags. These grow in a line, easing up from under a rotting log beside me. Before us the stream is roiling, swollen with meltwater. Across the river bottom, the snow runs like veins of silver over the dark mountain among the trees.

Seated on my Gore-Tex jacket in the lotus position, I chant two notes of OM over and over, one higher, one lower. For a while I chant with my eyes closed. Then I open them, focusing on the veins of silver on the mountainside opposite until they all run together, blurring out the dark strokes of tree trunks with a sea of shine; and then, in a reversal, the black tree strokes take over and the silver recedes as if sinking right into the ground.

I close my eyes again, and in my mind's eye as I OM, higher then lower, I begin to visualize each OM emerge from my mouth like a petal, the petal of a fairy slipper. One high, curving up and out and looping down like the hood of the fairy slipper; one low, curving down and out and looping ever so slightly upward like the toe. One looping up, one looping down — over and over, one OM then the other, as if blooming and dropping and blooming and dropping, as the petals of fairy slippers do.

Sitting there, I feel planted in the midst of things. The stream rushing before me, the trees swishing in the wind over my head, I am there at the center, staying where I am while stream and tree stay where they are, but the water moves inside the stream, and the sap stirred by whipping branches moves inside the tree as my blood moves in me, and the birdsong circles around and the insects trail through the bark's crevices and the wind wafts side to side.

How centered a plant is. Everything around it moving — wind, clouds, water; insects, squirrels, and birds a maelstrom of life around it — and the plant itself is also moving, but moving in place. Water pulled from the roots via capillary action streams steadily up through the xylem tubes toward evaporation through the stomata in the photosynthetic leaves. Food manufactured in the leaves continually pours down through the phloem into the trunk and roots of the tree. And the hormones are moving in their cycles. Some gush in summer, holding the young leaves on tight. Then as the leaves begin aging, these hormones ebb, to be replaced by other hormones, which in response to environmental changes in autumn direct the closing of the threads of leaf-lifeline. At the base of every leaf, then, pectin is dissolving, cell walls becoming unglued one from another, until with the breaking of the last microscopic threads of xylem, the leaf falls away. All this time, the plant stands in place. Visited by animals and weather — being the visited one — and knowing in its own way, I'll bet you, exactly what other things stay in their places, and watching, in its own way, all the rest go by.

What am I doing here, doing this? What am I hoping for? An ingenue at meditation, most of the time I OM out my time, impatient. I wonder whether I'm doing it right. I feel like a pretender, an impostor, most of the time. As if I'll never really be doing it, as if I'll always be a waster of my own time. But today, in the presence of Engelmanns and *C. bulbosas*, I think I know what I'm doing here, what I'm hoping for: a snatch of just what I feel at this moment — a little glimpse of the essence of plantness, of what it must be like to be a plant. To take the world in and accept it. (For there are no other choices, really.) To take what comes in time — like the pain that, in the time when it comes, seems to be the only thing in all the huge world, but isn't. To take what comes in time — however painful and however joyful — and, for all its seeming onliness, to know it isn't everything, even as, in the thick of it, you feel as if it will always be there. And to know at the same time that it *is*— everything. And that it *will be*— ever there. In this fleeting moment I sense something of what it must be like to be a plant. I feel at the center of things. Not in the sense of the hub of which all other things are extensions; but of the hub that is still even as it's turning, and connected to what touches and turns around it.

What the plants have is what I want to strive for. To be in our fragmentary time of discrete units, as we must be, but to be (now and then) in that time in a different way, without being driven toward or away from. To accept those discrete moments through a broader knowing (to know, as in "to be in union with," as in "Adam knew Eve, his wife"). To stand amidst those discrete moments merely blowing, merely being whipped or caressed by the weather, merely glistening golden after rain or dangling branches broken by the weight of ice — adapting to the frenzy of those discrete moments by remaining myself unfrenzied.

To be able to do such a thing as all this betweentimes. To go in and out of (now and then) what I feel the essence of plantness to be.

. . . . .

And yet plants are, of course, like humans, subject to the slings and arrows of time.

It wasn't until quite some time after that day I meditated alongside the *Calypso bulbosas*— not until long after that night camped with Bridget among the Engelmanns, and that New Year's Eve twilight spent in the company of Atlantic white cedar trees — that I found out about all the studies done in the past century on plant sentience. And based on experiments done by a score of scientists, it appears that not only are plants subject to time's slings and arrows, but they most definitely *feel* them, very much the same as we do.

Darwin felt sure that plants must be sentient, but he failed to prove it. A few decades later, however, Sir Jagadis Chandra Bose succeeded in illustrating the sentience of plants in a myriad of ways. He reasoned that since plants managed respiration without lungs or gills, digestion without a stomach, and movement without muscles, they might very well undergo the kind of excitation that animals do, even without a complicated nervous system. The problem was to measure this excitation visually, a challenge Bose met by designing over several decades a series of increasingly refined machines. The earliest version, designed shortly after the turn of the twentieth century, picked up plant movements via a delicate lever attached to a set of mirrors. When a plant made its infinitesimal movements, the lever moved, thus moving the mirrors, which reflected onto paper a beam of light. This shifting spot of light was traced by a sliding inkwell with an ink sponge projecting from it, thus visibly charting plant movements never before detected by the human eye. After elaborating on this basic concept many times, each elaboration producing a machine increasingly sensitive to plant reactions and/or increasingly precise in its recording of them, Bose eventually produced an instrument with ten-thousand-fold magnification that could record plant growth and other changes occurring in a period as short as one minute.

With his machines Bose demonstrated how the digestive components of insectivorous plants work like animal stomachs; how the light response in leaves parallels that in the retinae of animals; and how the skins of tomatoes, grapes, and other fruits and vegetables behave similarly to the skins of lizards, turtles, and frogs. Applying a range of stimuli, from heat and cold to anesthetic and weak current, he demonstrated that in plants electrical excitation produces a mechanical response, which is exactly what happens in animals (albeit instead of occurring at the cellular level as in plants, it occurs in animals in the nerve-muscle unit, with the nerve carrying the electrical impulse and the muscle contracting in response). One of his experiments showed that too much carbon dioxide could suffocate a plant, which could then be revived with oxygen. Another showed that plants could be made drunk with alcohol — made to sway, pass out, and revive, even to suffer hangover. A variety of experiments demonstrated the paroxysms of plants in response to injuries to their tissues, suggesting their capacity to feel what we call pain. In one of these, when Bose hooked two electrical wires to a carrot strapped to a table and then pinched the carrot with forceps, the carrot's wince was magnified on a wall for viewers to see: as a pinch was delivered near the right wire, the light beam on the wall traveled eight feet to the right, then as a pinch was delivered near the left wire, the beam jumped an equal amount to the left. One of Bose's last machines detected growth rate as infinitesimal as 1/1,500 millionths of an inch per second. With this instrument he demonstrated that plant growth proceeds in rhythmic pulses, then went on to show how that growth can be retarded by touch in some plants and stimulated by touch in others.

Praised by the likes of Lord Kelvin and George Bernard Shaw (who dedicated his own collected works to Bose with the words, "From the least to the greatest living biologist"); hosted by all the prestigious scientific societies of his day, from the Linnaean to the British Royal Society, of which he became a fellow; nominated along with Albert Einstein to a prestigious League of Nations committee; and knighted in 1917; in his work on plants, Bose united the fields of physics, physiology, and psychology and found correlations never before identified between the animal and vegetable worlds (and the mineral world, too, for that matter, but that's another story). Even the conservative *London Times* said he had "swept the universe into a synthesis and had seen the *one* in all its changing manifestations."

And he prepared the way for all sorts of research on plant sentience to follow. The extensive experiments of Dr. T. C. Singh established a detailed picture of how music favorably affects the life cycle of plants, including growth, flowering, fruiting, and seed yields. Following his lead, many researchers demonstrated a positive effect of music on crop yields, reporting results such as heavier seed, earlier sprouting, thicker and tougher stems, and increases in production of up to 66 percent. Still other researchers experimented with nonmusical sounds, subjecting plants to different frequencies, cycles, and decibels, all of which were shown to affect plants, sometimes positively, sometimes negatively.

Other researchers experimented with plant reactions closer to those traditionally believed exclusive to the animal world. The work of a group of Kazakh scientists with beans, potatoes, wheat, and crowfoot suggested that these plants had the capacity to "remember" the frequency of flashes from a xenon-hydrogen lamp, as the plants were "conditioned" to repeat these pulsations with a high degree of accuracy. The same scientists conditioned a philodendron to "recognize" a mineralized rock. First the plant underwent a "training" period during which it was given a shock each time this mineralized rock was placed beside it. Thereafter, even though the shocks had been discontinued, whenever the ore was placed next to the plant, instruments attached to the plant recorded excitation corresponding to the excitation of a human being subjected to an emotional stimulus. And further experiments, in which a *barren* rock similarly placed elicited no such excitation, indicated that the plant could distinguish between the two different rocks. Yet another experiment on memory, by a member of the former Soviet Academy of Sciences, also elicited a reaction similar to human emotion, this time from a geranium. The plant was repeatedly exposed to two men — one of whom pricked its leaves, dripped acid on it, cut its roots, and burned it; and another who watered it, treated its wounds, and otherwise cared for sit. After this conditioning, the instruments electroded to the plant went wild whenever the abusive man approached it, but traced out smooth lines in the caretaker's presence. Some researchers even devised experiments that purported to show plants responding to human thought and to the wounding and killing of other organisms, claiming thereby to have revealed a form of empathy in plants.

These are but a few examples representing a body of experimental work that validates Darwin's intuition that plants must have sentience.[27] Although a small portion of this body of research is loose and fringe-y, thus understandably controversial, hundreds of experiments have confirmed in plants electrical impulses analogous to the nerve impulses in humans. And the best of these experiments have produced an accumulation of evidence to establish not only that plants perceive and react to their surroundings in ways far more complex than our unaided senses can grasp, but also that they exhibit sentience not at all unlike that found in animals, and in response to stimuli from both ends of the pleasure-pain continuum.

Not always as still as they might look to us, our vegetal companions. And some may allege that the revelation of such plant-animal parallels as the capacity for some variant of both elation and suffering might undermine any notion of the plant's affinity with the still point of the turning world. But I'd say on the contrary: evidence that a plant can experience its own form of joy and sorrow only serves to elaborate the metaphor. A still point that simultaneously reaches down into the earth and up toward the sky, assimilating bits of each in its body, the plant is a figure of the union of opposites. A still point, the plant stands quiescent, even as, receptive to both pain and pleasure, it churns internally with a distinct flurry of physiological response to each. At the mercy of both light and dark simultaneously — at the mercy of *whatever* force might happen to touch it, no recourse to flight — the plant betokens transcendence as an animal perhaps never could, simply by standing in place.

. . . . .

In the wake of my father's death, I retreated to an island. Twice in the early weeks after his departure, in fact, I took off to the longest barrier island in the Atlantic, the southern tip of which has been preserved long enough that the vegetation there is much the same as it was centuries ago. After the funeral I went there for five days in the dead of winter. Two months later, when — finally and officially — we lost half the land we grew up on, after signing my name to the papers, I went there again, in spring.

Both times I stayed in a motel north of the coastal preserve. Both times I took my usual gear. My bike on the bike rack, binoculars, backpack. But I didn't use any of them.

One morning I sat for hours at the edge of a heather bald — an open swell in the midst of dune thicket, a breast of sand spread over with the velvety grey growth of beach heather, a small, ground-hugging plant whose shallow, wide-spreading roots hold the sand around them the way magnets hold iron filings and commandeer to their own use every drop of water that falls on that sand. Keeping company with beach heather, I contemplated that little plant's ability to hold down its world, to anchor it steady, to preserve amidst a jumble of the twistings and twinings of much larger plants a calm clearing. I contemplated its ability to make its own territory, and then to preserve that territory from any onslaught whatsoever by the rapacious tangle of the other dune plants. In the company of beach heather I thought about beach heather, and then in the company of beach heather I moved on, my thoughts seeping elsewhere, out of both bald and thicket and off beyond thoughtfulness.

One afternoon, as the jumble of ice plates floating along the bay shore clinked and clattered in the rocking water, I sat in a forest of bayberries, once-shrubs that, given enough time undisturbed, had become trees. The clouds of their twig tips rose ten feet higher than those of any bayberry I'd ever seen elsewhere, and their boles were as big around as the boles of mature aspen trees. Even in the cold, which was enhanced by the ice's clattering, I sat among them for hours, and sitting with nothing but them in my consciousness, I passed beyond them.

One day I wandered in the maritime forest where the boles of whatever species that lived there had all come to snake like vines. A sassafras like a shepherd's crook. A shadbush intertwined with a holly in a smooth-skinned double helix. A coarse-barked black cherry bole a foot in diameter that, in brunt of wind, had forsaken the upward effort, to weave sinuously, horizontally over the sand. And as the surf pounded steadily beyond the dunes at the edge of the forest I wandered, I saw that even the limbs of stolid red cedars, and of red maples too, grew crooking and corkscrewed as they worked their way onward and upward into habitual wind. My mind meandered along them, tracing their arcs and loops, and then it went itself arcing and looping off into the wind.

One evening I sat three feet off the ground on the bough of a wide-spreading southern red oak tree. All around a spring drizzle fell. Beneath me patches of moss blazed like green satin, and black earthstars, their leathery points long since sprung, speckled the sand. A palm warbler darted, nut brown and goldenrod yellow. The gabble of brant drifted in from the bay. Catkins in bunches dangled like earrings from all the nude branches all around.

Through these sojourns I sat with the plants and saw my father. I sat with the plants and was with our family's lost land. I saw my father's noble attainments twining into the future, green and growing, and I saw his trespasses, shriveling and brown. I saw the land I'd grown up on as it had been. I saw it as it might have been in the future, advancing further toward wildness, and I saw it further divested of wildness, as, instead, it would be. I sat with the twisting boles, the slow-creeping roots, the giant specimens — the true specimens of an earlier time. At morning, afternoon, evening, I sat with them, sometimes in fog, sometimes with the sound of ice clattering, surf crashing, sometimes in pale sunlight, sometimes in wind, the wind raising sand and salt and blasting the plants and me with them, my scarf streaking behind me, straight as an arrow. I sat with the plants blowing in place. I was getting it all continuously. I was getting my father, all the irreconcilable pieces of him in juxtaposition. Without dodging, without darting, I cursed my father and ignited with love for him. I sat with his young face, his old face, his gifts, his failings, whirling around me in a maelstrom — winds that rip limb from limb and make the sap flow. Roiling in my mind as if in the air around me, clashing and melding, I felt all these images of him turning around me, inside me. I saw the whole intolerable show. In a triumph bequeathed me by plants, I stayed put for it. In the company of plants I sat tight with it and, gradually admitting every part of my father to the round of him in my heart, I gained access to new reaches of love.

. . . . .

Among its own unique set of swirling details, the mature silver maple has a scalier bark than other maples. The thin grey scales strip off rather easily. The leaves are notched with more graceful crenulations, their sinuses deeper, more sinuous, and their green is paler than that of most maples, greyer, and they are whitish on their undersides. When the wind blows, these leaves flip more readily than the leaves of other maples, flashing this silvery white. When we were kids, to see the silver maples turn white was dramatic, excited us with the portent of a coming storm. And although some told us the tree got its name from the way the scales of its bark catch the light, shining, I always thought these maples were designated "silver" for their habit of flipping their leaves to the silvery-white side before a storm.

The flipping is due to the fact that their leaf stalks, called petioles, are somewhat flattened. The physics of flattened petioles is that the impact of even small breaths of air sets them twisting, so that the leaves at their ends are flung over or seem to spin. We know this is the physics, but as far as I can discover we don't know why the physics of flattened petioles has been applied in the case of this tree while not in other maple species. It is one of those charms that must be linked to the silver maple's deepest identity, but its deep-seated reason for being, as far as I know, has not yet been revealed.

But I wish it had been, for then they might not have senselessly sawed down the mile-long string of silver maples along Longbridge Road.

The short, portly form of their trunks was typical. But the girth of those trunks was not. Although some deride silver maples for being short-lived, these specimens must have stood along that road for close to two centuries. I've never seen even a single specimen anywhere else that could boast the circumference of any one of those hundred or so silver maple trees.

I drove down Longbridge Road one spring day to find them, quite simply, gone. Just naked sky over the big rolling farm they'd bounded, the exposed fields looking bleak and forlorn.

Until not long ago, the electric company managed to live in peaceful coexistence with the plants at the roadside, snipping out little sections when necessary, once in a while felling a tree. But now, out of what?—a laziness called preventive maintenance? a relish for working their newfangled hacking machinery? (a relish never exhibited for working the manual saw)—they are mangling all the plants by the roadside indiscriminately. Trees and shrubs that have grown along the roads since my childhood are suddenly reduced to raw stumps, or at best to lopsided deformities, one side still sporting a full set of limbs and the side facing roadward shaved down to a naked trunk dotted with eyes of raw wood where it's been stripped of its branches, or to a cluster of split and frayed twigs. With the newfangled machines making it so much easier now than before, we can, therefore we do. And the huge old silver maples of Longbridge Road lie in fat cylindrical sections, rotting by the side of the road.

Bringing home once again the fact that plants live in the same aspect of time as we do, and are struck down by its motions as all of us are. Nevertheless, they have a lot to teach us about being still. If I've finally learned to sit and wait (and wait and wait) for the animals to come to me when I want to study them, it's due in part to the example of plants. And if I'm now able—sometimes—to sit tight with the bad-feeling truths instead of running off toward a feel-good, it's due not in small part to the example of plants. If once in a blue moon I now manage to keep truly living through the worst times, to live the good simultaneously without trying to deny the ultimately inexorable bad, I could be a lot further off target in my thanksgiving than to thank the plants.

As vulnerable as plants may sometimes be to whatever destructive vagaries of nature, and to all our poisons and hacking machineries, they still suggest something of the stillness beyond our motion, the oneness beyond our allness, the timelessness behind our time. In their morphology and their adaptations to it, in their modus vivendi, they are closer to timelessness than we are, and along with their autotrophic ability, that's another way they might be considered more scientifically elegant beings. Even the swirling detail of characteristics comprising even the simplest of the swirling variety of species of plants stems from their condition of plantedness. In plants you can see it: stillness as the source of swirling detail.

And short of being sawed off at the root tops the way the Longbridge Road silver maples were, they adapt elegantly to the mutilations time inflicts upon them, as witnessed by multitudes of even the humblest of trees and shrubs these days, to anyone who travels the roads. With half as many limbs and leaves as they once had, they continue to feed themselves out of water and air and sunshine. Lopsided as they may appear to those who lament their maiming, they continue to swarm with birds and insects and to sway in the breeze. Deformed as they are, they heal their wounds over and, standing in place, steadfastly grow on.

Notes

1. I don't know whether the advantage of horse chestnut "candles" per se has been determined, but the advantage of some candle-shaped flowers has. Using principles of aerodynamics and plant biomechanics, scientists have devised experiments showing that the upright, conical structure of some female flowers greatly increases their efficiency in capturing pollen grains.

2. Stephen L. Buchmann and Gary Paul Nabhan, *The Forgotten Pollinators* (Washington, D.C.: Island Press, 1996), 92. Hairs on the forelegs of certain anthophorid bees have evolved into "squeegees," which rupture blisters inside certain tropical flowers. The blisters contain nutritious oils that the bees mix with pollen and feed to their developing young.

3. An article on the sequencing done on *A. thaliana* up to that point appeared in the December 16, 1999, issue of the journal *Nature*. The research is summarized by O. Baker, "Chromosomes show plants' secret complexity," in *Science News* 156, no. 25 (1999): 389. As of December 1999, two of the plant's five chromosomes had been sequenced by nearly three hundred researchers working in Europe and the United States.

4. As E. O. Wilson and others note, however, there are untold numbers of species, especially in the rain forests, that we have yet to identify.

5. The nonvascular plants — mosses, liverworts, and hornworts — may be found on land, but they need surrounding water, even if it's just dew or rain, to live. Not only must their sperm swim through water to reach their eggs, but lacking xylem and phloem, these plants depend on surrounding water to provide them with the fluids and minerals that sustain them, which they absorb directly through their surfaces.

6. The process by which leaves are shed, summarized below in this essay.

7. Many other plants exhibit similar reversals in phototropism, depending on circumstance. Bermuda grass stems grow upright in shade but parallel to the ground in bright sunlight. The flowers of a particular rose species that lives on rock walls grow toward the sunlight until they are fertilized, at which point they grow away from light, so their developing fruits end up buried in dark crevices where they can germinate.

8. A subgroup of epiphytes, the bromeliads, drinks water collected in little tanks

at their bases, formed by their own incurving leathery leaves. Still other plants that grow *on* plants choose leaves and stems to settle on and so are called epiphylls (meaning "upon leaves").

9. Despite its aesthetic appeals (among them the pleasure of walking through expanses of it in winter, between walls of soughing dry straws that wave their torn flags high above your head), the common reed, *Phragmites australis*, is an invasive exotic, undesirable because it chokes out important native species of marsh plants.

10. By sending out suckers called ramets, an aspen can produce a whole grove of itself, sometimes measuring in acres, with every member the genetic twin of the originating tree.

11. Dodder lacks chlorophyll, thus the power to photosynthesize (see the subsequent paragraph). To make a living it penetrates the food-conducting tissues of other plants with rootlike projections, called haustoria, and steals its nutrition from them.

12. Since some plants don't photosynthesize (for example, Indian pipes, coralroot, pine drops, beech drops), and since several nonplant protoctists (for instance, euglenas) do, photosynthesis is not what sets plants apart from all other organisms. The distinguishing features of plants include the orderly alternation of haploid and diploid generations in their life cycle, and two unique characteristics of their cells: cellulosic cell walls and the inclusion of plastids among their organelles. Lynne Margulis and Karlene V. Schwartz, *Five Kingdoms: An Illustrated Guide to the Phyla of Life on Earth* (New York: W. H. Freeman, 1988), 260.

13. "If it seems that there are far fewer plant than animal groups, it is partly because plant and animal taxa are defined by morphological rather than chemical criteria. . . . The differences between many plants are invisible — plants produce different chemical compounds called secondary metabolites . . . [which] play a role in the plant's defenses against fungi, animals, and other plants. . . . They include feeding deterrents, toxins, psychoactive compounds . . . respiratory poisons . . . even gaseous compounds" (Margulis and Schwartz, 260).

14. The alternative to the monoecious species is the dioecious species, in which the male and female plant each takes an anatomically different form (with differences usually restricted to the flower).

15. E. J. H. Corner, *The Life of Plants* (Chicago: University of Chicago Press, 1981), 191.

16. The fertilization of some plant species falls under the heading of "having your cake and eating it too." In these cases, the *preferred* pollen of another individual develops more quickly on the female pistil than does self-pollen, thus reaching the ovules first. But if such cross-pollination fails to occur, the ovules eventually receive the slow-developing self-pollen, which is better than none at all. For more detail, see Corner, 191, and/or Neil A. Campbell, *Biology* (Redwood City, Calif: Benjamin/ Cummings, 1993), 739.

17. Wind pollination, although archaic, is not as much a matter of chance as it might appear. Recently, scientists have discovered that the architecture of certain

plants facilitates their capture of pollen. For example, leaves shaped like rabbit ears extending above the female flower of the jojoba intercept air in such a way as to make it swirl around them, thus breaking its speed, with the result that a pollen shower falls out of the air onto the female flower's pistil, ensuring fertilization quite effectively.

18. A species of gecko in New Zealand sticks its tongue in flax flowers to suck nectar and in doing so brushes the flower's male reproductive parts with the scales of its throat. These scales have increased surface area effective for pickup and delivery of pollen, which the gecko then often carries to other plants distant from the first (Buchmann and Nabhan, 100).

19. Buchmann and Nabhan, 50.

20. *Tegiticula* moths collect the *Yucca elata*'s pollen and place it into the pistils of its flowers, where they lay their eggs. Thus they ensure the plant will produce seeds to feed their larvae, which develop within yucca fruits. Evolution has arranged that the larvae eat only a modest portion of the seeds, leaving enough for yucca to reproduce. Moreover, it has arranged that these yuccas *shed* flowers that contain high numbers of eggs, and so natural selection favors only those moths who lay just enough eggs to get by. Together, these two "arrangements" keep the symbiosis between the moths and yuccas stable over evolutionary time.

21. Buchmann and Nabhan, 60.

22. Donald Peattie, *A Natural History of Trees of Eastern and Central North America* (Boston: Houghton Mifflin, 1991), 71. The other quotation on Atlantic white cedar, later in this paragraph, is also from this source.

23. Robert MacArthur and E. O. Wilson established that fragmentation of habitat decimates species, and subsequent studies have bolstered their findings. If, when confined to an "island" (either bound by water, or in some other manner geographically isolated) species can expire by the clade-ful, and if we've so fragmented habitat that extinctions are now proceeding pretty much at full tilt, then at this point we actually *need* corridors for the fullest possible array of species to thrive. The Yellowstone to Yukon Conservation Initiative is one example of several projects now afoot working to connect core areas of wild land, thus to permit wild species the fluidity of movement they need to ensure the health of their gene pools and the space they need to find their requisite foods and practice their requisite habits.

24. From the Devonian Period, 408 to 360 million years ago.

25. "The tree that changed the world," *Science News*, 155, no. 20 (1999): 319.

26. All lines of poetry quoted are from T. S. Eliot, "Four Quartets," in *The Collected Poems and Plays of T. S. Eliot* (New York: Harcourt, Brace & World, 1952). In this long poem Eliot draws on the ideas of a range of philosophers from Heraclitus and the Stoics to St. Augustine and on tenets of both Eastern and Western religious thought.

27. The bibliography in *The Secret Life of Plants*, by Peter Tompkins and Christopher Bird (New York: Harper and Row, 1973), includes, among other works, the primary sources for all the research on plant sentience referred to here.

Wolf Show, Truman, Ersatz Moon

TO CYNTHIA BOYHAN

We entered Lamar Valley from the west at evening. The wide river bottom was green-gold in the lowering light. The forested slopes were black up to the reddened outcroppings on the ridges, and ahead, against wider blue, a smear of rainbow burned on a leaden patch of sky. Dark bison clumped down near the river. Through binoculars I saw scattered bears digging at the edge of distant trees. Cindy drove and I did the glassing. It was early June and we were out looking for wolves.

Reports had it you were likely to see them around Soda Butte, a thirty-foot mound of travertine precipitated over centuries by hot springs on the valley floor. The springs warm the waters of Soda Butte Creek, imbuing the air around it with olfactory whispers of sulfur stench, and so even before you catch sight of the butte humped in the distance, you know you're close; but this time man-made markers signaled its proximity as well. About a mile short of the butte, the road wound through a third-of-a-mile-wide swath of land that was roped off either side and lined with signs that forbade stopping or walking. It was the corridor the wolves traveled from their den in the cliff above down into the meadow, to the elk and bison and pronghorn and deer and their vulnerable young.

On the far side of the corridor, flush against it, was a turnout jammed with vehicles. A jarring sight, though I should have been ready for it: since the inception of the Northern Rocky Mountain Wolf Recovery Program in Yellowstone,[1] jammed turnouts in this once sparsely utilized part of the park have become routine. A line of giant spotting scopes stood focused on the meadow. Crowds of people were milling around. My companion, an extrovert, soon had the dope on everyone. This couple had been there three nights in a row, that group every morning and night for five days. Everyone had been studying the situation. Everyone was continually passing the scoop.

— *Saw one this morning, big black one.*

— *Seen them out there about this time the past two nights.*

— *Members of the Druid Peak pack, word was yesterday. Soda Butte pack is down in the southern part of the park.*

A feeling was welling up in me, hard to decipher. Suddenly I remembered the previous year, when we'd also come up looking for wolves. We'd looked only in broad daylight then, and so the folks we'd mingled with had been mainly day-trippers, not savvy inveterate megascope-toters like these, but even so, all the turnouts had been filled with huddles peering through scopes. I'd had this feeling then too — how had I forgotten? Just like now, it had been something murky, unsettling, like the nasty cheap feeling you're in on something you'll be ashamed of.

Next morning at 4:15 there was the same-sized horde as had been there in the evening: in the pitch dark, people with coffee mugs, shouldering wildly expensive devices for extending their vision, telling stories of their experiences wolf-viewing in the turnouts.

The sky lightened, human activity heightened. Finally in the ragged grey dawn someone with a scope the diameter of a beer keg pinpointed something on the valley floor and the word went around. I looked through the binocs and couldn't see anything. The information line offered help.

— *That dead tree with just one branch on it — down from that branch and to seven o'clock, a grey one.*

Nothing.

— *It's moving east.*

Nothing.

— *Parallel to the stream.*

Nothing, nothing. Then, a little movement, a little moving patch of maybe a slightly tanner grey than the scruff of grey sage. Without all the steering from the big-scope folks I wouldn't even have seen it. And had I seen it, I wouldn't have known what it was. And had I been forced to guess (with a gun to my head, just to say something) I would have said it was a coyote. Even through a massive scope, enthusiastically proffered, I detected not much more than a greyish blur in the foggy bottom. How could anyone claim, based on this, that they'd seen a wolf?

How?—because it had been verified at the far end of the huddle by a wildlife biologist wielding an antenna. Word was coming down the line. She'd picked up the signal from the wolf's radio collar. It was wolf F107. Wolf F107.

After that, Cindy and I left the turnout. We went off through the mist on our own, on a trail toward the river and the black forest sloping up to the ridge. After a while some first rays of sunlight slid in slivers over the landscape before us. We saw free-ranging bison and elk and pronghorn; we saw a free-ranging badger and a Lewis's woodpecker with a sooty green back. We saw bear after bear in the distance, digging, until finally, nearing the river, we whiffed a thick, fetid bear smell that raised the hairs on our necks, and we changed our course.

For a while the murky cheap feeling I'd had in the turnout faded. For a while things seemed as they should in a wild valley. Us out there, moving around in it and through it, and the ungulates and bears and birds and badgers out there, moving around in it and through. Each maybe seeing and eluding the other, but all of us subject to each other and to everything else out there, linked in uncertainty. All of us out in it together — not them out there and us at the edge of it, the scene just about predetermined, watching them as if on a screen.

Then back around Slough Creek we saw two big white birds foraging in the distance. We'd heard that two migrating whooping cranes had come down in Yellowstone and were hanging out back in there. Slinking from willow clump to willow clump, we approached the birds. Sure enough, it seemed these were the whooping cranes. The only problem was their legs were bright yellow, and as far as I could remember whooping cranes' legs were black.

We crept closer, confirmed the telltale red on their faces. Their legs were black, all right, but each had one leg wrapped with a yellow tag. A leg band, actually, with a radio transmitter attached to it (which sends signals to a satellite, which relays to a computer the longitude and latitude of the bird) — the avian equivalent of the wolf's radio collar. Later I looked in Stokes's bird guide and even the whooping crane pictured there had its leg wrapped in yellow. *Of course*, I realized. Whoop-

ing cranes are one of the most endangered birds in North America. In
the early 1940s there were just fifteen left, and as of this writing there
are only about 180 in the wild flock, so of course they're monitored
heavily. At this point, I realized, probably every whooping crane left on
the continent is tagged.

"Well, we finally saw a wolf," Cindy said on the ride down out of
Yellowstone.

"I guess," I said.

She knew, as I did, that the failure to find them would have been a
far truer experience of wolves than the way we'd seen one that morning. But Cindy had worked hard to help get wolves reintroduced to
Yellowstone. She was exuberant that in the three years since being
transplanted to the park, they'd reproduced so successfully and had already so beneficially influenced the ecology there,[2] and she was flat-
out keen on seeing them anytime, anywhere. She conceded that the
turnout scene left something to be desired and that except for the
telemetry verification she'd never have known that the blotch in
the spotting scope was a wolf. "But it *was* a wolf, and we *know* that,"
she said. "That's the important thing."

"I don't know," I said. The bad feeling that had started to well up in
me the night before in the turnout was back again. I still couldn't quite
decipher it, but it had pooled substantially. And although I too wanted
wolves in Yellowstone, I found myself demurring. "I don't know
whether that's the important thing or not."

. . . . .

As we were "wolf watching" that weekend in Yellowstone, in towns
and cities across the nation people were watching a provocative new
movie. The subject of Peter Weir's film *The Truman Show* is a TV show
of the same name — "The Truman Show" — with an interesting twist:
a TV director named Christof has been filming the life of an unsuspecting fellow named Truman — from his days in the womb as a fetus
to this his thirtieth year — and broadcasting it live, 24/7, all over the
world.

Early on, the movie begins introducing us to various groups of
viewers of Christof's "Truman Show." Together with them we watch
a few scenes. Merry Truman walking to work through the sunny,

spanking white, island community of Seahaven. Truman saluting neighbors and business clients jovially. Truman in his cubicle at the office furtively riffling pages, ripping snippets of models' faces out of a fashion magazine. Truman coming home in the evening to his picture-book yard and dimpled wife. Truman hiding from his lovely wife/chipper life in the cellar with a trunk of old keepsakes, the trunk's lid pointedly lined with a map of Fiji — the country he attempted to telephone in secret, we recall suddenly, that morning from work. Here and there some such odd, intriguing detail — what's this composite picture of a woman's face he's constructing covertly? this clandestine fixation on Fiji? — but overall, a rather insipid stream of events.

Periodically, we cut back to the viewers. All over the world people from all walks of life are enthralled by "The Truman Show." Barmaids and their lineups of customers. Japanese husbands and wives and mothers-in-law. People drifting off to sleep on couches and soaking in bathtubs. Crowds watching drive-in–sized screens at the beach. Even as they go about their daily jobs, we see people laughing and crying with and at and for Truman. Why? we may at first find ourselves wondering. He's sweet, but he seems such a bland fellow. What's so interesting?

But very odd things keep happening to Truman, and if our interest isn't at first very much aroused by him, it's lured by these curious events. Out of a clear blue sky, a strange lighting fixture falls on the street in front of him. At the start of a sudden shower, for a split second a narrow column of rain falls on him only, before spreading into a ubiquitous downpour. His car radio suddenly goes phlooey, and after a bout of static, for a twilight zone moment he suddenly hears a strange voice detailing his every movement: "He's heading west on Stewart . . . He's turning on Lancaster Square."

Some of these mysterious events appear random. But many of them seem to be triggered by his efforts to leave his perfectly manicured, beaming community. First, he can't manage to leave by boat because he's terrified of water: caught at sea in a storm during childhood, he watched his father drown, and now whenever he goes near water, a sunken boat or some such detail seems strategically placed to remind him of his fear and thus to deter any notions he might have about ever venturing to cross that water again. When he tries to leave the island by bus, the bus's engine grinds, clanks, then steams hopelessly. When he forces his wife to drive him over a bridge to the mainland, walls of flame shoot across the road in front of them, and then men in insulated suits descend upon him and coerce him back home. What kind of eerie comedy is this? we wonder. If the spotless, jolly streets were a bit uncanny, this is downright surreal.

As the film progresses, we're gradually made privy to what's going on behind the scenes. And what's going on is that Truman's life is not exactly a real life. It is, quite literally, manipulated from above, from a sphere in the sky that looks like the moon but that is in fact a control center of great technological wonder, from which Christof directs Truman's world. Commanding the operators of giant switchboards, he orchestrates everything in Truman's environment, from the inhabitants of Seahaven (actors all of them, taking their cues through little receivers in their ears) to the five thousand miniature cameras (concealed in everything from pencil sharpeners to necklaces to rearview mirrors) to the weather itself (giant spotlights for heavenly bodies, massive sprinkler systems for rain). In fact, all of Truman's environment (ersatz moon included) is enclosed in one giant dome in Hollywood, the inside surface of which is a kind of great concave screen depicting the firmament.

It may be that — as trailers interjected periodically into the continuous TV show seek to persuade us — "nothing here is fake, it's merely controlled"; but after a string of such assertions, all variations on the same theme, one starts to feel that these trailers protest too much. For somewhere along the line the exercise of control passes a boundary beyond which the thing controlled is so controlled as to become inauthentic. And it seems that in his control of Truman, Christof has crossed that line.

We learn that Truman's wife had her fingers crossed during the wedding ceremony: she is not truly his wife. And his drowned father was not really his father, nor did he really drown, and the story on that is this: Truman was born an explorer at heart — as a child he wanted to be like "the great Magellan." In Christof's words, "As Truman grew up we were forced to manufacture ways to keep him on the island"; and ultimately Christof used the plot device of the aforementioned storm that "killed off" the "father" in order to frighten young Truman severely enough to squelch his craving to explore beyond Seahaven's bounds. The protestations of loyalty and heartfelt advice spoken by

Marlon, Truman's best friend since childhood, are lines fed into Marlon's earpiece by Christof to assuage Truman's suspicions that something's wrong somewhere — that someone's *watching* him — and to get Truman back in line so he won't (in both senses of the word) blow the show. But Truman's right. He's being watched, big-time. And this fact has made inroads not just on his privacy and freedom, but on the very authenticity of his life.

. . . . .

A few weeks after my trip to the Lamar Valley, I went to see the much-touted movie *The Truman Show*. Watching it, I was flooded with an eerie sense of what certain French poets called *correspondences*. Sunk in my plush seat in the dark theater, I was jolted time and again by the whiff of a bizarre, startling notion about that crazy awful stuff happening on the screen. Something to do with watching. Something to do with being watched. Something to do with authenticity, and the lack of it. Something to do with that turnout near Soda Butte.

That stuff on the screen was not just about Truman or his audience or Christof's manipulations. Somehow it had a bizarre, startling connection with the Yellowstone wolves. The unsettled feeling welling in me was eerily akin to the feeling I'd had in the Soda Butte turnout a few weeks earlier. *The Truman Show* was speaking to me of the wolf show.

Because when you think about the scene that takes place day after day in and around that turnout, that's what it feels like — a show. The wolves come down a roped corridor lined with people — like celebrities filing down cordoned passageways between gawking crowds. A hubbub, a flurry of commentary breaks out from behind binoculars and scopes:

— *Is that the alpha male? The alpha female?*

— *Is she the one they say has given birth to the most pups?*

— *They're heading down toward where we saw that cow elk earlier.*

— *You think they'll take her calf?*

"We watched three wolves on a kill yesterday morning," a pair of strangers had piped at me in unison that evening in Yellowstone, all charged up with their wolf-viewing experience. But there was something about the way they said it: wolves on a kill. It seemed it was just a kick to them, a mere shallow excitement at the materialization of a preconceived idea. A cliché, you might say, one-dimensional, untouched by any thought of the agony, strain, desperation of what was happening — its profound reality. The way they said it, it seemed clear that what they'd seen was essentially unreal to them, the way blood-and-guts on the screen isn't real.

In the turnouts the Yellowstone wolves have become a kind of spectacle. There's a wolf show at the Soda Butte turnout most evenings. A matinee at dawn.

In the traditional sense, a show is made up of two basic ingredients, the watcher and the watched, in particular relation one to the other: with the intention of entertaining the watcher, the watched is directed, manipulated in some way. "The Truman Show" is a classic example of this definition: the life of Truman is manipulated to entertain. Of course the wolves aren't intended as entertainment by anyone, neither by the biologists managing the recovery program nor by the rapt spectators themselves. But as an indirect effect of our manipulation of them, they've become a show anyway.

Since their relocation from Canada to Yellowstone in 1995, the wolves have continually been monitored, telemetrically and otherwise, by the U.S. Fish and Wildlife Service (the government agency that, along with the National Park Service, is in charge of the reintroduction of the wolves). The goal of this monitoring is scientific, to study their effect on the Yellowstone ecosystem, in order to "manage" the wolves for a greater goal still: to incorporate them into that ecosystem permanently, thereby rendering it fully intact for the first time in almost seven decades, thus securing for that ecosystem optimal health for the first time in as many years. This "management" involves a fair degree of manipulation of the wolves — baiting, trapping, and tranquilizing them in order to collar them, for example; or intervening when their behavior doesn't conform to the official wolf reintroduction policy (which, depending on the nature of the "nonconforming" behavior, can entail "eliminating" the wolves, as U.S. Fish and Wildlife puts it, or in blunter parlance, killing them). Although such activity in no way makes a show of the wolves, it paves the way for something that in effect does. For the information yielded by all this monitoring and "managing" — information that is covered by the media and posted on the Internet — ends up acting as an advertisement as if for a wolf show, as a kind of review or preview of it.

Before any of us in the Soda Butte turnout that June morning ever arrived there, we all knew all sorts of things about the wolves. Including the fact that we were likely to see wolves from that particular turnout. Including a pretty good idea of when. We knew the details of the wolves' Canadian capture. We knew of their subsequent confinement in chain-link holding pens in the Yellowstone backcountry for acclimatization, and we knew the details of their eventual release. If we'd been inclined to pursue the wolf information to a deeper level of detail, it was likely we knew what packs they'd established. If we'd perused still further, we might know the sites of the dens, and the genealogy of the pups, and perhaps even the ID numbers assigned individual wolves. Ultimately, in a case of one kind of watching preparing the way for another, thanks to the abundance and accessibility of this information, the Yellowstone wolves have ended up with bevies of tourists craning for a peek at their lives.

And when (as on that June weekend) we tourists are gathered in "audiential" circumstances — a group of strangers on the sidelines of a site where an event is designated as likely to take place — that background information tends to function for us like a stage set, rousing certain expectations for what we're about to see.

With their history recapped and their den site and corridor pointed out for us, with so much about the wolves labeled and interpreted a priori, the Yellowstone wolves are for us a story we humans have written. They are wolves whose fate has been shaped by us. And having written their story ourselves, as we enter the turnout in Yellowstone, we expect we have a pretty good sense of the gist of it. We know the particular episode we're there for. And — perchance conditioned by our habituation to the screens that dot our daily vistas — we're pretty sure we know how it goes: *The wolf leaves its den in the morning and goes out to hunt . . .*

We're accustomed to watching TV and movie and computer screens. We're accustomed to screenfare run rampant, screenfare produced to be quickly and easily consumed before and after every meal by everyone, screenfare produced not for art's sake so much as to feed the vast Screen Machine. We're used to story lines with a stripped-down focus, story lines disregarding any fuzz and buzz in the surroundings that don't seem to bear directly on the story at hand — in short, we're used to screenfare making an easily digested story of everything, used to screens presenting us with everything from current events to educational material to consumer products as if they were a show. Even live sporting events are "storied" for us as screenfare, as from a bank of screens behind the scenes certain aspects of a game are singled out for broadcast, while others aren't even shown. We're used to the organized, edited, exclusory focus of screens. To experience wolves truly you have to be out in it with them, the wolves and you two threads among countless others, all interwoven in the intricate, messy, erratic, unpredictable world. But standing in a group in a turnout focused on what you're expecting (focused, as it may often be, on expectations shaped by your habituation to screens), you have no access to the layered experience of wolves that you have a chance at if you're out there moving around in it with them — no sense of their elusiveness, for one thing, of the astonishing difficulty of finding and observing them in the wild. As we conceive it, watching the wolf go out to hunt is tantamount to being in nature: we're experiencing nature firsthand, privy to nature's ways. But actually, watching wolves from the turnout is less like being in nature than pretending to be in nature. In fact, it is a way of being out of nature, separate from it — like watching nature on a screen.

So it happens — detail upon detail of the situation coalescing until the whole is of a different order than the simple sum of its parts. Until the wolves become unsuspecting performers. Until the slightest flurry of wolf activity takes on the air of a show. We're in Yellowstone to experience the wild, but what we take in is something more like a "storied" screen event — nature in a sense organized, edited, and focused for us. Partly as a result of the fact of the wolves' manipulation. Partly as a result of a brand of expectation in us, a way of looking at and for things — a brand of expectation quite possibly subliminally influenced by our habit of viewing screens. And so it can happen that viewed from the vantage of an audience of lens-toting tourists, the wolves end up reduced to mere figures of entertainment — robbed of their serious complexity, like images on a screen.

· · · · ·

First and foremost *The Truman Show* is about screens and our involvement with them. It is quite blatantly a "venomous satire" (as Anthony Lane has called it) about manipulation of, by, and for screens.

Superficially at least, we're hip to the double thing of screens: paradoxically experiencing something without truly experiencing it, feeling it as if it's real when it isn't real. Sometimes even as we feel the reality of what's on a screen, we're simultaneously conscious that it's a contrivance. But sometimes that consciousness gets blurred, erased even, and we're so overpowered by the sense that what we're watching is real that we lose touch with the knowledge that it's not.

Traditionally, this getting lost in screens is what makes them so attractive, so perfect at accomplishing a primary goal of entertainment: escape. Some films, of course, have a more serious function. A film may help us to work out our lives, for example, as something in us not being lived out gets to be lived vicariously — as a film subjects us to the thrill of revenge or the catharsis of grief, for example, enabling us to process an experience internally without acting it out. Some films imitate life to help us know life more truly; some films reconfigure the world for us, broadening and deepening our experience of it by making the familiar strange — some films are art. More often than not, though, screen entertainment simply serves as a breather, and we go into it intentionally, consciously embracing the illusions of screens to forget for a while the problems of real life. But in Christof's "Truman Show" this dynamic has been somewhat altered it seems.

Whereas screens commonly immerse us in some realm of the exotic, transporting us to a distant jungle, a different culture, another century — to circumstances we wouldn't be privy to except via the film — the world of "The Truman Show" offers no such novelty. Truman is just an everyday married-guy, office-goer, and mower-of-the-lawn, the circumstances of his life as average as they come. And so in this case it's not the distraction of the exotic that captivates the viewers, but supposedly (and seemingly paradoxically) the promise of being made privy to real life. For Christof's shtick is that he's presenting his viewers with a bona fide real life, and they seem to be going for it 100 percent.

They seem to be going for it so absorbedly, in fact, you sometimes get the suspicion that many of these viewers are watching the screen in place of living, that watching the screen is tantamount to living for them. And if this is the case, then the appeal of Christof's "real-life" premise is not paradoxical — nay, it's clear why it should have a strong hook . . . The prospect of a surrogate real life that one can live through. That keeps the more intractable realities of one's own life at bay. That compensates, perhaps, even, for something gone missing in one's own life. Or for the elusive but haunting suspicion of some such loss.

"Many leave 'The Truman Show' on all night for comfort," Christof tells us at one point. And what could be more comforting than — at the click of the remote control, day or night — to be vouchsafed a kind of *participation mystique* with another real life that is simple and cheery and safe? Not an entertainment that in the end you must admit was counterfeit, but an actual human existence that — along with the consolation that it's aired continuously, in effect never ending — offers the double comfort of always working out better than real life while actually being real. In presenting entertainment as if it's real life, in presenting real life as entertainment, Christof creates for his audience an escape that's qualitatively different. An escape, as always, but with the added kicker that in this case the audience doesn't need to know that they're escaping, as throughout the show they're encouraged — nay, downright *licensed*— to indulge in believing that they're encountering, engaging with, contemplating the real thing.

But if real life is what they crave, you might ask, why would they choose to watch Truman, a man whose life might be said to epitomize bland emptiness and inauthenticity — a man whose every impulse is subsumed by a manipulator's plan? The answer perhaps lies in the shrewdness of Christof's manipulation. For while it's true that Truman's every impulse is kneaded or squeezed or clipped or channeled or blocked by Christof, to work not for the genuine life of Truman but within the confines of and for the perpetuation of *Christof's* "Truman Show," and while it's also true that this manipulation results in a character who often comes off a bit bland and silly, even sometimes as a bit of a dunce — while all this is true, it's continually offset by an unerring ingenious touch, for Christof always allows Truman's real heart just enough rein to keep the viewers in tow.

Among the stranger things that happen early in the movie is the sudden appearance of Truman's supposed father, whom Truman had supposed to be dead. The actor who once played this "father" appears one morning at curbside as Truman is walking to work. Unshaven and bedraggled, evidently fallen on hard times, he has presumably broken into the set to reveal the truth to Truman, perhaps as an act of revenge toward Christof for writing him out of the show — but he's whisked out from under Truman's popeyed gape by two "citizens" before he can spill the beans. And contriving to make this lemon into some lemonade, Christof decides that the return of his long lost "father" might serve to help quell Truman's recent eruption of wanderlust, so he writes the actor back into the show.

During a "heartfelt talk" between Truman and his "best friend" ("You're the closest thing I ever had to a brother," Marlon says and Truman's tortured eyes glitter with incipient tears), the "father" approaches for their reunion, advancing toward the young men through the fog. ("I found him for you. . . . Go to him," says Marlon; "Fade up music," says Christof, flourishing his arms like an orchestral conductor, on high in his ersatz moon.) "I never stopped believing," Truman breathes, his awestruck face zoomed in on by a "button-cam" on the jacket of his "father." As they embrace we see Truman's face over his "father's" shoulder, radiant with anguish and rapture, tense with tears. "Dad!" he exclaims, the word compressed out of him by a force of feeling as credulous and genuine as you could ever hope to see, and the audience goes berserk. Hugging, clapping, laughing, biting their hands through tears, they are beside themselves with emotion, as if Truman's life were their life, and as if it were real to the bone.

I have the eeriest feeling that something similar is going on in the turnouts of Yellowstone. Reviewing *The Truman Show*, as I watch "The Truman Show" audience respond to that "father-and-son reunion," the expressions of the many wolf-watchers I've observed — that June weekend and since — keep surfacing in my memory. People riveted by the idea of witnessing the real, live return of the wolf to its rightful place in an ecosystem. People with tears in their eyes at the sight of a real wolf's unspooling gait. People keyed up in suspense: will the wolves get that bison calf? People transfixed at the notion of "wolves on a kill." I think of these reactions in the Yellowstone turnouts and it strikes me that just as the viewers of "The Truman Show" seem to look to the screen to fill a void — seem to look to the show on the screen as a stand-in for something that feels, as it may be, disappeared, gone — so do the crowds in the turnouts seem to look to the wolf show. Driven by an awareness, conscious or not, that the true wild is going, going, about to be gone — a fact that has turned the archetypal natural state of the world into something exotic for us — we crowd the turnout, scrambling to get a look at it, to experience "the real thing" before it disappears from the world for good.

"There's nothing fake about Truman," trailers recurring throughout the broadcast of "The Truman Show" assiduously seek to assure us. They're free, wild wolves, we repeat to ourselves as we watch from the turnout in Yellowstone, feeling all jazzed at the notion that we're in the presence of the bona fide wild. We want to believe we're watching random wild wolves — in fact, I think we *need* to believe it. And kept in tow by the wild heart of the wolves, we're granted the illusion of it. The wolves beget and parent pups, hunt and kill before our eyes, and so we have this illusion. But this is not precisely a wild scene. For via planes, knockout darts, and radio collars, not to mention bullets and holding pens, the wolves' lives are clipped around the edges, in many ways channeled and blocked just like Truman's, and without these clippings and blockings we would never be privy to these views of them. Driven by a hunger to fill a hole in the world that we know to be ever-widening, we're there to witness wildness, but what we get is more like a film.

But so what? you might say. So what if we wolf-watchers come away from the turnout with less than a 100 percent experience? So what if we come away with a downright simplistic impression of the wolves — they're real and complex despite us, you may say. Despite whatever trumped-up, Hollywood-wild-and-free image whatever number of viewers might take away from the turnout, the wolves *really are* wild and free, so what harm does a false image do?

A question well worth pondering. But there are more *correspondences* between the wolves' situation and Truman's to go into first. For although *The Truman Show* was indeed speaking to me of the wolf show, that wasn't the whole of it. *The Truman Show* was speaking to me of more than just shows, just screens.

. . . . .

In his song "Billy from the Hills" Greg Brown laments that "people are fascinated with screens, no idea what's on the other side." What's on the other side in *The Truman Show* is Christof, and what strikes me as most chilling about the film is this: from behind the scenes Christof choreographs, directs, and determines not just what happens on the screen, but a good deal of what lies beyond it as well. For, as we eventually glean from watching the TV viewers in the movie, Christof manipulates not just the life of Truman, but in a subtle, insidious way he manipulates the audience as well. "We accept the reality of the world with which we're presented," says Christof. "It's as simple as that." Although he's referring explicitly to Truman here, this applies as well to his viewers. In fact, it applies to them most of all.

In mid-film Christof is the subject of a TV interview. In a pre-interview summary of highlights from his "Truman Show" (Truman in utero, Truman's first step, etc.) we're told that "as he grew so did the technology," providing more and more ways for manipulating Truman's life. As Truman eventually comes to remind Christof, however, it never grew to the point where they could get a camera into his head. And so there's a place in Truman that Christof hasn't intruded on, and it's here that his suspicion has been growing. This suspicion is what's behind Truman's desire to escape to Fiji, but so is something equally impervious to Christof's manipulations: the memory of a girl Truman once loved — the one whose face he keeps trying to piece together out of snippets of women's features torn from magazines. Christof had decided early on that Truman should "marry" the dimpled actress who now portrays his wife, but as it happened Truman's wild heart took a fancy to this other actress, and she went out of role and fell in love with him too. Just as she was trying to tell him the truth of his situation ("Everybody's pretending. . . . Everybody knows everything you do"), Christof had her whisked away by her "father," purportedly to Fiji, beyond Truman's reach; and now the more Truman mistrusts the world of his life in Seahaven, the more he remembers this girl and her efforts to tell him something, and the more he wants to go where he thinks she is.

All the actors try to steer Truman away from his suspicions. They throw countless hurdles in his path. But Truman's sense of truth and truthlessness is growing, and with it his yearning and resolve. Finally his resolve grows to the point where he is even willing to face his great fear of the sea, and he sets off in a sailboat to make the long journey to Fiji.

Up to this point, on the surface at least, the film is often slapstickishly comedic, but here it turns overtly ugly and terrifying. Up until now one might have made a lame argument that there was no harm in what Christof was doing—Truman was leading a comfortable life, a safe life, one might have said. Fixing on the surface of things, one might have dismissed as innocuous enough the emptiness of this too-bright, too-white life, and one might even have argued (albeit with a dearth of sensitivity and imagination) that what Christof was doing was beneficial—entertaining the world—or at worst neutral, harmless. But at this point any such argument would be invalidated completely. For when Truman sets forth in his little boat, Christof gives the nod to a technician to "access the weather program" and unleashes the wrath of "nature" on him. And although this "nature" is artificial, its wrath convincingly matches the real thing. All the filmed viewers of "The Truman Show" watch horrified as the "sea" Truman has feared from childhood turns on him a second time. And we, the live viewers of *The Truman Show*, watch doubly horror-stricken at the double spectacle of Truman battling the relentless storm bravely and of Christof willfully exposing him to death.

"We can't let him die in front of a live audience," says a technician.

"Capsize him," Christof says resolutely. "Do it!"

Underwater shots of Truman struggling. He's just about to drown. But then Christof surprisingly orders the storm terminated. Motivated by some odd love of his creation, maybe. Maybe, too, by curiosity. What will this creature he holds such power over try to do now? Christof is pretty sure he knows.

The sun comes out full and benevolent. The sea has turned, as they say, smooth as glass. And now, when Truman thinks he's finally broken loose from the prison it took him so long to learn he was living in—after having faced down even his great fear of the sea—what happens? The bowsprit of his sailboat quite literally pierces a cloud, and he finds that the boundless sky around him is only a shell.

And then, emanating as if from a cluster of white clouds on high, the voice of Christof, his "creator," begins to speak to him. Christof, who believes that "ultimately Truman prefers his cell." "In my world you have nothing to fear," Christof tells him. "I've been watching you your whole life. . . . I know you better than you know yourself."

Since this story is too terrifying and apocalyptic to tell in a straightforward manner and is therefore cast in the form of a comedy, what happens next is that Truman metaphorically thumbs his nose at his "creator" and, choosing freedom over the cell Christof was sure he was conditioned to, exits the artificial dome of his controlled life through a door in the screen of sky. Christof has lost his grip, it seems. In the end, he hasn't really got Truman, and this would presumably be seen as a happy ending if the film were to stop here. But it does not.

Next, after scanning the many TV viewers we've come to know over the course of the film, all of them exulting wildly over Truman's triumph, the film settles on two of these viewers, parking garage attendants in their glass booth. Having finished their exultation, they're about to get on with eating their lunch when one says, "What else is on?"

"Yeah, let's see what else is on," says the other without missing a beat. "Where's the TV guide?"

Only here does the film end, as at the instant these last words are spoken, the screen goes silent and black.

If Truman didn't buy Christof's manipulations, the audience did. In the end, Christof may not have gotten Truman, but he's gotten us.

The problem of screens is obviously the explicit concern of the movie. The film begins with this problem and ends with it. But the problem of screens is bigger than just screens themselves. Being arguably the most visible and widespread form of technological manipulation, screens function beautifully as the literal focus of *The Truman Show*. But screens also function perfectly as a giant metaphor for another, implicit concern of the film: technological manipulation writ large — that is, "what's on the other side" of screens. Christof is the director of a TV show, but his directorial manipulations depend on far more than just the capacity to command actors and cinematographers and to broadcast to the world's screens. Ultimately, the manipulated life that is "The Truman Show" hinges on Christof's power to execute just about any orchestrational whim he chooses, and thus it depends on the astonishing range of technological tricks from beyond the world of filmmaking, whose buttons Christof also has his fingers on.

And so perhaps the most troubling part of *The Truman Show* is that ersatz moon that Christof reigns from. That control center of such great technological wonder that — drawing on innovations from just about any field of research you can think of — allows Christof to produce everything from tricks of weather to flames leaping from pavement, from "implanted traumas about water and travel" (as Roger

Ebert put it) to "one big show binding the world in bogus bliss" (as Richard Corliss described Christof's show). What "gets" Christof's TV audience is not just the screen but the whole elaborate fabrication manufactured for the screen. And "on the other side" of that fabrication, at the very source of the manipulation of the audience, is the capacity for that fabrication — the whole moon-ensconced agglomeration of technologies, humming away behind the scenes.

. . . . .

As Cindy and I stood in the Soda Butte turnout that June morning, a little southeast of the park an aspect of the wolf show was unfolding that, for all our information, we were not aware of. You might say it was taking place on the other side of the screen. For even as we stood in that crowd "wolf watching," one of the Yellowstone wolves was being hunted to death via helicopter just outside our hometown.

The wolf was an alpha female. More than a year before, she and her mate had traversed the invisible boundaries of Yellowstone, and in a densely forested area at the southernmost tip of the Absaroka mountains they'd established the Washakie pack, the first Yellowstone-derived pack outside the park. They had chosen an eminently suitable place for their den, an area wild enough to be inhabited by such rare and endangered species as the grizzly and the lynx; but the problem was that a wealthy Easterner had also established his den back against that timber, and although one would think he'd have no need of raising cows for a living, he was going whole hog at playing the ranching game back in there. And so the previous fall, when this female's mate had preyed on livestock from this ranch, he had been shot by the U.S. Fish and Wildlife Service, in accordance with the wolf reintroduction policy. And then when some calves had been killed earlier this spring, U.S. Fish and Wildlife officials had set out again, this time to hunt down the alpha female. Just a week before our trip to Lamar Valley, siting down from their helicopter, they'd mistaken one of her offspring for her and shot him — a "legitimate mistake," as a biologist called it, since the yearling was running with the female and they looked so much alike. Then, the Sunday Cindy and I were up in the park, they rectified the mistake and shot the female.

Wolves are extremely elusive creatures. After his first twenty years of studying wolves in the wild, the wildlife biologist often cited as the world's foremost authority on wolves, L. David Mech, reported that — except by the aid of technology—he'd come upon no more than a dozen wolves on the ground. So how did Fish and Wildlife officials manage to find and kill those wolves so quickly in that vast, dense timber? As it turns out, fairly easily. Because all the original wolves in the Yellowstone wolf recovery program wore radio collars, they could be tracked by telemetry.

For when we decided to reintroduce wolves to Yellowstone, we couldn't just let them loose there and be done with it. There was too much opposition from folks outside the park who feared wolves would be wolves on their property, and the plan had to address their fears. We had to be able to study the wolves and document their impact in the park to justify their presence there. And we had to be able to kill them when they "screwed up."

In the car next to ours that evening in Lamar Valley was a lady from Texas, a little muffin of a lady with a sweet face. With a smile and a billowing of apple cheeks, she said she "just loved" the wolves. She said she'd driven the twenty-five-hundred-mile round-trip two years in a row now just to stand in a turnout every dawn and dusk for a week, it was such a kick for her to be able to look at them. But though she called herself a "major wolf fan" — thought it was "super" that they were here —"if they screw up and leave the park," she said, "they should be shot."

It was as if she thought they were like the cartoon animals we project our human traits onto. As if she thought they should know how to be good wolves by our standards and if they didn't do what was expected of them, they should pay. As if she thought they could somehow divine the U.S. Fish and Wildlife Service's agenda — could know that if they crossed over park boundaries and messed with livestock they would be tracked down by telemetry and "eliminated."

But of course they don't know our agenda. They don't know that even in the deepest forest we have our eye on them and can put even our trigger finger on them if we deem it necessary. Both the alpha male and female of the Washakie pack were radio-collared, and two of their five yearlings had been collared that spring, but that didn't mean a thing to them. They just thought they were seven wolves under god, and free.

Some might feel I'm making a mountain out of a molehill here. Although this population of wolves gets a lion's share of media attention,

it's small and unique, not typical of wolf populations — or of populations of any other species, they might say. Well, it may be small — and
in many ways it is, in fact, unique — but in a broad sense the Northern
Rockies wolf recovery population is representative of a number of
species we're manipulating these days.

For example, the pair of whooping cranes we'd seen that day in
Slough Creek hadn't simply "come down" as I thought at the time. Like
the wolves, they too had been released there by a wildlife biologist.

They were part of a project, an effort to establish for the rare species a second migration route in the Rockies, in addition to their accustomed flyway between their nesting grounds in northern Canada
and their wintering grounds along the coast of Texas. The idea behind
this project was that in case some environmental catastrophe such as
an oil spill in the Gulf of Mexico should wipe out the whooping cranes
using the original migration route, there would still be another population surviving them.

Like wolf reintroduction, this project is a well-intentioned and
noble effort. But it entails a good deal of technological manipulation
of whooping cranes. Eggs are hatched in incubators in captive propagation centers. In this particular project, these cranes were imprinted
as hatchlings on a wildlife biologist, Kent Clegg, who as their surrogate
parent taught them to fly, and ultimately to migrate south, using an ultralight. (In other projects, hatchlings are imprinted on hand puppets
made to look like the head of a whooping crane, and on people draped
in white sheets wielding them.) But migrating back north on their own
after wintering in New Mexico, in a show of bad judgment, these two
cranes put down in poor habitat. Alerted by the radio transmitters attached to their leg bands, Clegg had swooped them up from this ill-
chosen site and relocated them to Yellowstone, where Cindy and I
came upon them.[3]

One can't help but wonder whether cranes brought up in this way
can possibly be like the wild cranes that use the original flyway. These
birds may ultimately go free, but in raising them with planes and puppets, how can we manage to fully and accurately transmit their culture
to them?[4] Kent Clegg himself is asking these very questions. One of
the first goals of the research, he says, is "to determine if the birds can
be raised wild enough to survive" and to "act like normal cranes."

The lowland gorilla is another species we're manipulating a good
deal these days. At The Gorilla Foundation in California, a venerable

institution dedicated to research on primate intelligence and linguistic ability, the resident gorillas (the most famous of which is Koko) are treated with nothing short of love, but their life there is light-years from the life of free-living gorillas. They use human sign language to communicate with humans. They use toilets and toothbrushes. They play with a range of human artifacts, from fire hoses to steel ladders to an endless variety of dolls; and they even have birthday parties, drinking sparkling cider out of goblets, eating vegetable pizza and hamburgers and sushi balls, and opening wrapped gifts.

Like the ultralight-trained whooping cranes, this is a small experimental group of animals. But the group will be growing soon. Because the viability of free-living gorilla populations is severely threatened (by human population explosion, political instability, accelerated deforestation, and other forms of habitat destruction), The Gorilla Foundation is setting up an alternative habitat. Reminiscent of the whooping crane advocates who envision creating a population of cranes that would follow an alternative migration route, they plan to establish an alternative population of gorillas to preserve the species in the event that the natural (that is, untampered with) populations should become extinct.

This population will be located in a man-made compound on the island of Maui, an area similar in climate to their natural habitat but different in many other respects, not to mention that it's half the globe away. According to the foundation's journal *Gorilla*, the goal is to have the gorillas "experience a sense of freedom in a more naturalistic setting" than the one in California and "to foster the development of natural, healthy, and prolific family groups." Despite these good intentions, however, these gorillas will not be living as natural gorillas. Forage will be planted for them by humans. There will be man-made indoor as well as outdoor quarters, with human researchers eternally near. Discrete zones will be separated by hydraulic gates, and "gorilla-proof" steel mesh panels will surround the compound.

Cranes and gorillas are just two of many species that have been subject to manipulation via captive breeding programs, and it's a pretty sure thing that more and more species will continue to be. In these programs, the animals' lives are monitored day and night, just like Truman's. And just as Truman's desire for adventure is reduced to fantasies about mountain climbing acted out in mock conversations with his bathroom mirror, the natural impulses of these animals are also clipped, thwarted, and warped. But whereas Truman is manipulated for the gain of his manipulators (power, money, etc.), the manipulation of these animals is intended for their own benefit—to ward off extinction, to preserve the wild—and this motive makes manipulation a sight less offensive in their case. And it might be less offensive still if, in spite of itself, manipulation were regularly productive of its intended results. But it's not.

One hundred and forty-five reintroductions are documented for the twentieth century, involving 115 species. We hear a lot about such famous success stories as the Plains bison, the Galapagos tortoise, the bald eagle, the peregrine falcon,[5] leading us to believe that such programs are a panacea; but the fact is, these stories are among a small minority. Only a scant sixteen of these reintroduced species have been able to sustain themselves in the wild without human assistance. As for the other ninety-nine species for which unqualified reintroduction has failed, we just don't hear about them much.

There are many reasons for these failures, and often they're case-specific, but two broad reasons stand out. Most glaring and easiest to demonstrate is a lack of sufficient habitat for a species to thrive in after it's been reintroduced. A less obvious problem—one more difficult to prove, but no less likely for that—is captivity-induced alterations in the animals, which diminish their abilities to cope in the wild and thereby impede their thriving even when habitat is sufficient. Since healthy wolf populations still exist on the continent, we were able to use wild stock in the wolf reintroduction program. But many such programs involve species we snatched up just at the verge of extinction—for example, the California condor and the black-footed ferret—and in these cases reintroduced individuals necessarily come from a population raised in captivity over several generations. During this time the animals are cut off from their natural, wild environment—and from exposure to cultural traditions that would have been passed on to them by a wild population of their species. At the same time, they're subject to the manipulations of humans who, however well-meaning, know little about their patterns of development and socialization, or the way they perceive the world. A condor chick hatched in captivity, for example, might come into the world to the accompaniment of the clicking of surgical tweezers, as a biologist chips away at its shell to facilitate its birth. For sustenance this same chick is likely to receive chopped mice and chicken eggs in place of the regurgitated carrion that's a wild-born chick's fare — and this from a pigskin-and-fiberglass facsimile of a condor head, rather than from a real live parent. What psychological (and consequently behavioral) alterations such an un-natural upbringing might induce is anyone's guess.

And what constitutes a well-meaning attempt to simulate a natural upbringing can be even further divorced from nature than this ex-ample suggests. Preparing for a black-footed ferret reintroduction, bi-ologists worked first with captive-bred polecats, a close relative of the ferret — testing ideas on the more common species to avoid inflicting unnecessary trauma on the endangered one. In an attempt to teach young captive-bred polecats to avoid predators (a job accomplished in the wild by their mothers, who seemed, however, to have lost the in-stinct to perform it during this group of polecats' sojourn in captivity), the biologists subjected them to a stuffed badger mounted on the chas-sis of a remote-controlled toy truck, which zipped at the little polecats on tires instead of legs. When the animals failed to react to this whir-ring contrivance with appropriate caution, they were then simultane-ously assailed by rubber bands shot from toy guns each time the remote-controlled badger darted toward them . . .

However ingenious and well-intentioned such strategies may be, it's not surprising that some animals raised in captivity develop behav-ioral distortions that handicap them in their natural habitat, while oth-ers simply don't learn the requisite knowledge to survive. A female whooping crane who sat on the bare ground for hours "incubating" — while her egg sat exposed to the elements a few feet away — is an example of the former problem. As is the story of the captive-bred salmon, which, when released to the wild, were shunned by wild sal-mon, who refused to breed with them — evidence, researchers deter-mined, that the behavior of the captive-breds was somehow "off" (al-though the researchers failed to discern in what way). An example of the latter problem is the case of the Mexican wolves reintroduced in Arizona in 1998 from a captive-breeding program started in 1977. Al-though they quickly learned to hunt in the wild, these wolves didn't know enough to avoid people, and several were shot. In fact, these wolves had enough difficulty surviving out of captivity that, of the eleven released in March of that year, just seven months later only four were still alive in the wild.

An important aside here: I hope no one will construe my remarks as an attack on the wildlife biologists working to save the wild. On the contrary, I count them as heroes. Despite all I've said, I contribute to The Gorilla Foundation regularly. When I first read *The Whooping Crane*, Faith McNulty's 1966 book recounting the attempts to save that species up to that point, I was rooting for the project all the way, enthralled both by the stories of the humans dedicated to it and by the sagas of the individual birds used to bring off its goals; and earlier this year I rose with the rest of the audience to give the aforementioned aviator-biologist Kent Clegg a standing ovation after a film presentation of his work with the cranes. (It was only afterwards that it dawned on me that the cranes' migration instruction had consisted not just of Clegg and his ultralight, but also of a second aircraft flying along with them to make the film I applauded so enthusiastically. An example of the fact that these ubiquitous films, these technologies, are now so much a part of our world that often they don't even register with us — we accept them unthinkingly.) Like Kent Clegg, most often these scientists have the best intentions. Many of them work and care their hearts out. The earnest and astounding feats of people like Clegg (and Penny Patterson of The Gorilla Foundation, and Doug Smith and all his colleagues working on wolf reintroduction in the Northern Rockies) inspire the bejesus out of me. And as for wildlife studies, I don't want to appear to attack them either. In fact, I'm fascinated by them — and I concede the benefit of technology in executing them. I know the arguments for such tools as radio collars — both the scientific and political grounds for them, in terms of both research and reintroduction plans. And to fairly acknowledge the difficulty biologists face in conducting these studies, I want to affirm, as well, that the technologies I seem to vilify are often intractable — rarely as smoothly and efficiently powerful as I've made them sound here, but instead often frustrating to the point of heartbreak for those who work with them. But as much as I admire the biologists and credit the importance — the necessity — of the work they do, I'm concerned about the insidious spread of some of the technologies they use. I'm concerned that as these technologies make research and reintroduction easier and more possible, they have become the norm. I'm concerned, in the end, that as we come to depend more and more on manipulating species via such technologies, the very steps we take to save the wild may, ironically, further its demise.

Dr. Benjamin Beck of the National Zoological Park in Washington, D.C., has declared that it's better to move wild animals — as opposed to captive-bred animals — into new habitats, as was done with the wolves in Yellowstone, because the wild stock is better equipped to survive. But given the darts, radio collars, planes, and chain-link pens of Yellowstone — not to mention the unnatural degree of contact with humans (including habituation to going about their lives under the scrutiny of clusters of tourists) — one can't help but wonder whether Yellowstone might not ultimately amount to just another (albeit more subtle) kind of captivity, wherein our manipulations may very well alter the culture, nay the very instincts, of those wolves.

For although in Yellowstone a wolf's mate is still really her mate, her parent still really her parent and her prey still really her prey, if she crosses a park boundary and behaves outside that boundary as she does inside it, the boom comes down. It's her natural tendency to wander oblivious to cartographical boundaries (a wolf's typical range in the Rockies is two hundred miles, and some go up to five hundred miles) and to prey on bovid as well as cervid offspring; but for the Yellowstone wolves these behaviors are restricted, and if the wolves overstep these restrictions they're as subject to our bullets as Truman was to the "weather program." Obviously a Yellowstone wolf's life isn't as ubiquitously contrived as Truman's — the shell that confines her isn't as rigid or concrete. But although her shell is invisible, it's everywhere — wherever she goes — in the form of electronic signals emitted from the collar around her very neck. Screw up and the boundary of those emissions can be as concrete as the painted sky Truman's bowsprit pierces: she's come to a dead end.

And given that evolution favors those best equipped for survival, in the face of such irrevocable controls as these mightn't some of the natural tendencies of the Yellowstone wolves ultimately be tamped down? Not only are those wolves who prey on livestock "eliminated," but even wolves who are merely in the company of a wolf who does can be picked up and retained in holding pens for reconditioning, thereafter to be monitored — thus controlled — more closely than ever before. In Yellowstone, the pressures of artificial selection favor wolves who are circumspect in their ranging — in short, who learn to acknowledge boundaries never before acknowledged by wolves — and artificial selection can alter creatures a lot faster than natural selection does.[6]

Truman looked like a natural human being, and he had just enough wild contents left in him when he discovered the truth of his situation to ensure he remained one. But had he not escaped when he did, a few years later perhaps there wouldn't have been enough wild contents left in him to help him break from his prison. And if he hadn't broken free from a life of constant but unascertained manipulation, would he have been, after awhile, quite fully a natural human being?

Once-wild species descended from a lineage bred and raised in captivity for generations are considered neither domestic nor wild. And as groups of animals like the signing gorillas, the ultralight-trained cranes, and the Yellowstone wolves continue under human manipulation, is it not likely that, in addition to the behavioral changes we've induced in them, these populations will ultimately undergo genetic alterations that make them more adaptable to confinement or other forms of manipulation? Unlike Christof, who appropriated Truman's life to earn fame and fortune, we colonize wild species to save them. But are we really just saving an array of living taxidermy? Making sure that a certain number of *shells* of each species continues — shells that may look like wild creatures but that have had their wild contents hollowed out?[7] In short, is it not likely that as these animals continue under human domination, in time they will no longer be wild?

. . . . .

What is *wild*? What makes for wildness? Writers who've pondered this question (Henry David Thoreau, Gary Snyder, Jack Turner, to mention three whose ruminations command respect) have proposed a number of qualities. Self-willed, self-determined, self-maintaining. Self-regulating or self-organizing, directed by an order that has grown from within. Resisting domination or exploitation. Unmediated. Self-*authenticating*.

Authenticity is fundamental to wildness. In wild creatures, wildness is fundamental to authenticity: they're inextricably intertwined. If a wild creature's life is no longer unmediated, free of domination, directed by an order that has grown from within, it is no longer authentic — it is de-wilded. In regard to the Yellowstone wolves and the other species that still persist in the remaining wilderness, for me at least, it is this definition of *wild* that applies.

I'm aware that, semantically at least, wildness is not strictly an either/or matter. The range of animals as regards their association with humans covers a broad spectrum, from those captive in "ag-factories" and zoos (whose lives are thoroughly dominated by humans); to those cohabiting with us on our ranches and at our hearthsides (who, although their lives are systematically manipulated by humans, still have some degree of freedom to wander and conduct their own lives); to the likes of the robins in our tree branches and the deer bedding down in suburban backyards (whose wild ways are altering as they adapt to increasing contact with us); to the unequivocally separate and sovereign animals — whales in the sea, crocodiles in the Congo, wolves in Alaska (who, although they may not be exempt from contact with humans, deleterious or otherwise, are in no sense dominated or even much mediated by us). Viewed in light of this spectrum, wildness is, I realize, commonly considered as a matter of degree. But when I use the word *wild* here, I mean it in the pure sense of Turner and Snyder and Thoreau. When I speak of wild creatures here, I'm not thinking of the aforementioned deer and robins, even though such animals, being undomesticated, are commonly referred to as wild. I'm speaking of the extreme end of the spectrum, of those creatures that are unadulteratedly wild, and when speaking of them I *do* use the word *wild* in the sense of either/or. For the animals still on this part of the spectrum are the *last* wild animals, the *only* wild animals that — as long as humans dominate the planet — we will ever have anymore.

I'm not saying we should free our dogs and chickens, turn off the TV, and go back to dwelling in caves. And I don't think mere contact with humans need constitute the de-wilding of animals; on the contrary, I'm sure the survivors among the myriads of Alaskan wolves hunted from airplanes only become more superbly wild. But I do think the technological manipulation of the animals on the part of the spectrum in question does constitute de-wilding, by the sheer fact that it waters down the wild nature of the last and only purely wild animals we have. Which is to underscore that regarding the definition of *wild*, I take here a purist position. What other, if you long to preserve the last of unadulterated wildness, can you possibly take?

If a wild creature's life is no longer unmediated, free of domination, directed by an order that has grown from within, it is no longer authentic — it is de-wilded. And, getting back to the wolf show, if a wild wolf's life is no longer wild, is s/he?

At the start of *The Truman Show*, Truman comes across a bit dumb. Before his authentic heart really kicks in and he starts turning his fake life upside down, his behavior is dumbish because in this watered-down life shaped by Christof his most profound natural impulses (to explore the world, for example; to pursue the girl he loves) have always been squelched. Barred from the fullness of his nature, he's been *mediated* into a kind of puppet, a kind of cartoon for the screen. In essence, he's been dumbed down — de-wilded — by what Anthony Lane has called "the pressures of techno-pleasantry."

And in real life, under human control exponentially extended by our burgeoning technical capacities, the Yellowstone wolves — and the whooping cranes, lowland gorillas, and other remaining wild species — may ultimately be headed down the same path. All these creatures would, I'm sure, wildly resist domination just as Truman finally does, if like Truman they were able to detect its presence in their lives. But thanks to the ubiquitousness of technology, the de-wilding is often exercised from afar, and invisibly.

And since the technological means of de-wilding are rarely as direct or obvious as radio collars and planes, even we ourselves often fail to recognize their handiwork. Which takes us back one last time to that vast common stomping ground and symbol of greater technology, screens.

Being a film aficionada, I'd be the first to acknowledge that good films like *The Truman Show* bring aesthetic and philosophical order to experience, affording penetrating insight into the world. But as it shapes experience to its particular vision, even the "truest" film necessarily omits worlds. Which is, of course, as it should be — which is fine in the case of good films. Which is fine, probably, even in the case of the great bulk of mediocre screenfare that exists merely to feed the Screen Machine — except perhaps when screenfare becomes pervasive enough to begin to dominate our view of the world. Except when how we think about ourselves and the world is based less and less on what we experience actively firsthand, for our own selves, and more and more on what we get passively, virtually unconsciously — almost as if through osmosis — via screenfare. For as a film shapes experience to its particular vision, even if what it cuts out is a jumble of apparently meaningless stuff in terms of that vision, somewhere in that jumble (if we would sift through it) there's usually the potential for further insight into the very same truth the film would depict. Not to mention that jumble's potential (if we have the possibility to sift through it) for insight into untold other truths beyond the vision of the film. No matter how complex or true the image of the world that a movie screen or a CRT or an LCD manages to reflect, screenfare always manipulates and enormously oversimplifies the fertile maelstrom of reality. Even the truest image a screen can give us is a false image in that sense.

As I said, case by case this needn't be a problem — a film, a televised event, an Internet transmission can of course enhance our perception of the world. But we're exposed to screens day after day, year after year — screens that habituate us to accept fake life as real life, that distance us from real life by turning it into a show — and could it be that via this perpetual exposure to screens our experience of the world is subject to becoming, in some sense, oversimplified? Could it be that via the constant cutting and clipping and shuffling of so much of experience into shows/stories, screenfare could have the effect of cutting and clipping and shuffling the perceptions of those who view it — that in reductively shaping the world around us, screenfare could reductively shape our experience, too? We need stories, to hear them and to make them — we need stories the way wolves need to roam. But when it reaches the point where so much of what we take in is "storied" to screenfare, is there not a risk that screens have the power to water down our very concept of what life is, does, should be? Greeted by screens as we are at every turn now, could we become so inured to the screen's-eye view that, instead of just now and then slipping into the delicious escape of embracing screenfare as reality, we might fall into the habit of perceiving reality as a film?

In a word, could it be that, by habituating us to a screen-mediated view of reality, screens have the power to in a certain sense de-wild our minds?

I'm just posing questions. Could such a scenario come to be? In posing the possibility, I point once again, not without a due sense of irony, to a film.

At the high point of *The Truman Show*, when Truman exits the dome, the viewers don't even pause to absorb or contemplate this one un-mediated and purely wild act of his life. As if they no longer know the difference between the authentic and the inauthentic, they cheer and turn to another channel instantly. Has the truth really passed them by? we might wonder. Is it that they actually don't *know* what's real and what isn't, or that they're so addicted to screens that they simply don't *care*? Either way, this audience has been dumbed down.

This is screenfare talking. What should we make of it? Is *The Truman Show*'s layered reality layered enough to provide insight into the world we now live in — at the heart of our own firsthand experience, does it resonate? Or is its view oversimplified to the point of counterfeit?

For me, obviously, it resonates. Prompting further questions still. Such as: If this is an effect that screenfare run rampant might have on the watcher, what effect might it have on the watched? Reduce it to the level of an image on a screen, is my guess — undermining (for the viewer, at least) its seriousness and complexity. Which brings me back to that other question, left dangling earlier: what does it matter if the viewers in the turnouts of Yellowstone (perchance subliminally condi-tioned by a pervasive screen's-eye view) see the wolf as if it were an im-age on a screen?

If we in the turnout view the wolf as if it were an image on a screen, you might say that the wolf is thereby for us de-wilded. He's *mediated* for us, however indirectly, by technology. Not only by the technology that allows us to know where to find him — and to come watch him as if he were a show — but also by the technology that has disposed us to view him as if he were an image on the screen, that is, simplistically.

And a false image of a wolf is a false idea of the wild. Isn't it?

But what harm, practically speaking, does a false image do?

To give but one example: when the wolf becomes like an image on a screen to us, we're more inclined to take the manipulation of him for granted. Once the wolf has been de-wilded in our minds, it becomes more acceptable to us that he be de-wilded in other, more direct ways. The effect of having a watered-down idea of any part of the wild we were avid to connect with is that we are instead further removed from it. And the further removed we get, the easier it is — even for those of us who consider ourselves champions of wild species and wild habitat — to permit, and even participate in, the destruction of what wild remains.

In this sense, the de-wilding of a wolf is the de-wilding of the wild. Isn't it?

These are extreme speculations, I know it. But what could be more extreme than the way we've altered the wild in the past two hundred years? We've felled the bulk of old-growth temperate forests, leveled mountains, effected the expansion of deserts and produced new ones, and prodigiously polluted the water and air. We're fostering extinctions at a rate greater than any seen in the fossil record for two hundred million years, and much of the remaining wild is now judged in extremis by scientists all over the world. In 1992 the Union of Concerned Scientists, an international organization of distinguished academics and directors of scientific agencies, issued "The World Scientists' Warning to Humanity," stating that in no more than a few decades it will be too late to avert the environmental threats confronting us and "the prospects for humanity will be immeasurably diminished." Its signatories included ninety-nine Nobel laureates in science. Against this scenario, which once the most sound opinion would have held wildly implausible, can the scenarios I postulate be dismissed merely for being extreme?

When you broaden your focus to a biocentric view of things — the view that counts in the end — the truths of *The Truman Show* point eerily to the truths of the wolf show. Even to the most anthropocentric of us this should matter, for the wild is the matrix of all we are.

"In wildness is the preservation of the world," Thoreau said in his essay "Walking, or the Wild." Picking up where Thoreau left off, Gary Snyder, in his essay "Tawny Grammar," deliberates in depth upon how, specifically, the preservation of the world depends on wildness. Because "our breeding has never been controlled for the purpose of any specific yield" (a state of affairs that the advent of cloning has made vulnerable to change since he wrote those words), Snyder posits that humans are still a wild species. "Wild nature is inextricably in the weave of self and culture," he says. "Some historians would say that 'thinkers' are behind the ideas and mythologies people live by." But what's behind thinkers? "I think it goes back to maize, reindeer, squash, sweet potatoes, and rice," Snyder says.

It's obvious that primal peoples get their materials, myths, and methods from nature. With us, the sources and grounds of things have become less clear. Take the food in the supermarket. The body in the funeral parlor. At this point there are so many steps between the harvesting of food and our consumption of it, between the dying of the body and the image of our loved one arranged in her coffin, that we are buffered from the fundamental workings of nature even regarding such basics as food and death. With so much so highly processed now, we tend to think civilization is separate from the wild — that, if anything, it's civilization that creates order in nature and not the other way around. But if we were to trace back to the source of every manifestation of civilization's order, I imagine we'd find ultimately it *is* the other way around. Fuel fed into the system and burned for energy, resulting in the capacity to do work and the discharge of the by-products of fuel-burning: even that pivotal tool and erstwhile metaphor of our culture, the internal combustion engine, is modeled on a biological paradigm.

Engines, art, religions, and the vast web of linkages that is the Internet — at their source, all our orders echo patterns of wild nature. The wild is the root and the template of civilization and culture, and a wild grammar underlies our greatest accomplishments. "The grammar not only of language, but of culture and civilization itself, is of the same order as this mossy little forest creek, this desert cobble," says Snyder. To deny, to lose touch with wildness, is to deny, to lose touch with our very identity and the very meanings we create.

. . . . .

Sometimes it occurs to me that in some eerie science-fictionesque way we're becoming a global village in more ways than we might have expected. That perhaps what lies ahead is not just the homogenization of human culture, but of nonhuman culture as well, as everything, even nature at large, gradually falls under the direction of some version of the control center in Christof's manufactured moon. From feral beast to human soul, the whole world de-wilded. True wolf, true man subverted by technology.

But it isn't, finally, even technology itself, is it? For beyond the fabrications, and the ever-elaborating capacity for those fabrications, is human intention and the seemingly ubiquitous attitude: *Build it, and we will use it. We can; therefore we will.* It's not just that we've developed the power to water down the world. It's that we're using it without discrimination or foresight. It's that we're giving ourselves into its thrall.

And now that through overpopulation and the juggernaut of technology we've created so many problems, it seems that no one knows any way to combat them but to turn toward more technology, getting ever more tangled up in it. For how can we be like Truman and walk out the door in the sky? The wolves keep trying, and dying for it.[8] But we — as Christof puts it — we're safe in this world.

In the developed world, anyhow, most of us have a comfortable life, a safe life, and so what, realistically speaking, is there to do now? Take off the collars, stop watching, stop directing — let the wolves really run free? But then they'd do their wild thing in our unwild lives and we'd "eliminate" them. And as for the whooping cranes, gorillas, and all those other threatened and endangered species whose "wild thing" does not intrude so directly on our lives — how can they endure if we let them run collarless, tagless, unmonitored, untampered with, completely free? Humans are everywhere now, there's no room for wild creatures to be their wild selves, and so if we want to have wolves in Yellowstone, whooping cranes and gorillas in perpetuity . . .

We try to preserve the wild by manipulating species to fit de-wilded habitat. Perhaps the main reason for this is that via traditional economic reckoning it's considered more prohibitively expensive to preserve habitat than to work with small groups of animals. But since this approach isn't even workable for the great majority of species, and since even in cases where we can resuscitate species by captive breeding there's often not enough of their required habitat to return them to, it seems a misguided (and ultimately much more expensive) way. Shouldn't we look more comprehensively to nature to learn how to solve this problem? To the realities of nature that portray to us our own realities, and that have always shown us, in ever so many ways, the way? Biologists who do look to nature for solutions believe we must bolster the health of what wildness remains by providing corridors between existing islands of wild habitat.[9] They know from every detail they scrutinize in nature that the pattern of nature is interconnectedness. And if, despite this knowledge, many biologists continue to manipulate species piecemeal, it's because from every detail of the human world that they're confronted with, they also know this: barring the provision of adequate habitat, if we want wolves and whooping cranes and gorillas in perpetuity, then collared and tagged and monitored is the only way. Barring the provision of adequate habitat, we can't let wild species be truly wild.

But if we don't?

How far can we pursue the de-wilding of nature at large without de-wilding our own souls?

Do we want the hearts within us subdued, our wild thoughts and passions all watered down? I think the lens-toting tourists in the Yellowstone turnouts are prime evidence that we don't. Because I lament that watching wolves has become almost as easy as doing the laundry, and because I'd prefer that wolf-watchers be forced to confront the complexity of wolfness by doing the hard work of finding wolves the old way (even if that were to mean I'd never see a wild wolf myself), I may have represented the wolf-watchers less than sympathetically. But in the end I don't mean to disparage them. For one thing it would be hypocritical — I've stood often enough in those turnouts myself. But most of all, at bottom I respect what drives the wolf-watching folks. For I believe that knowingly or not, they are acting on a truth at the core of all of us: the need for wildness, for a connection with it. So in the end I have to honor the tourists in the turnouts as their own brand of hero, representing for the rest of us that profound human need.

In this they point up the gap in the overarching analogy of this essay: whereas "The Truman Show" is the work of a malign manipulator, the wolf show arises out of the actions of benignly motivated folks. Out of the wildlife biologists' efforts to preserve the remaining straws of wildness. Out of the lens-toters' efforts to grasp at those straws — at some contact with them. The wolf show is a product of the convergence of actions of people who love what they would manipulate, who manipulate because of love. But though we are not Christof, I fear our effect could well end up being similar to his.

"I am the creator of a television show that gives hope and joy and inspiration to millions," says Christof. The Yellowstone wolves also give inspiration, and hope for the restoration/preservation of the wild. But if we intend to grant them life only on condition of the suppression of their natural tendencies, then the hope is based on a lie, just as it is in "The Truman Show."

. . . . .

Yellowstone again, this time in winter — just a week ago, as I sit writing the last words of this final draft. This is precisely what I saw and heard there this last time, and once again it strikes me as an emblematic scene.

Two vans with U.S. Government plates in a turnout; biologists pointing antennas down at the gaping valley below. Looking for signals from the Rose Creek pack, "doing leadership studies." "Documenting who does what and so forth." No signal yet, they tell me. But "air support will be arriving soon."

On down the road vehicles clustered in a turnout. The usual huddle of laypeople narrating one to another a scene they're viewing through scopes. There is a group of canids — maybe six or seven —"on a kill" back in a gully framed by trees. At least two of them are "collared." Everyone is exulting over the wolf show.

Down the road a piece, two park rangers with radios. A yellow plane comes circling overhead. As I start off cross-country to view the canids alone, away from the roadside crowd, a ranger calls to me to come back: I'll "disturb the wolves."

Around and around, the yellow plane hovers over the valley, procuring the final scoop. The canids are coyotes, it reports to ground radios. No wolves down there.

"But two of them have on collars," contests a driver stopping by rangers. "They don't collar coyotes, do they?"

"Yes, ma'am," says the ranger. "They've got collars on everything."

Notes

1. The Northern Rocky Mountain Wolf Recovery Program's agenda to restore ten breeding pairs of wolves each to Yellowstone National Park, Glacier National

Park, and the wilderness of central Idaho, was put into action in 1995 with the release of Canadian wild wolves into central Idaho and Yellowstone.

2. Scientists agree that after only three years the wolves had already extensively influenced the ecosystem. Killing large numbers of elk, by 1998 they had reduced an overly dense elk population, culling weak members and so improving that species' gene pool. They had also reduced the coyote population by as much as half, leading to an increase in small mammals like ground squirrels, which in turn led to an increase in hawks, owls, and eagles. The increase in carrion on the ground throughout the year feeds large numbers of other species — from grizzlies, coyotes, ravens, magpies, eagles, and wolverines to 450 known beetle species that depend on carcasses to survive. These are just a few of the many cascades of benefits wrought by the presence of wolves.

3. As it turned out, this wasn't the last relocation. Since Slough Creek was too heavily used by people, he made another capture later, and yet another transplant.

4. Theirs is an intricate culture, including not just their migratory habits, but well-defined family territorial patterns and their elaborate dances. One remarkable example (from Faith McNulty's book *The Whooping Crane*) is the behavior of the mated pair Josephine and Crip, upon the hatching of the first chick in their nest: "Josephine called Crip, who had moved off to feed. He came to the nest. Both birds put their beaks together, pointing downward [at the chick], then slowly stretched their necks skyward and gave a long, bugling call."

5. Birds are among the greatest success stories because methods for fostering their recovery are often simpler than those required for other animals (except in cases where there are so few surviving individuals of a species that we must resort to captive breeding). To effect recovery of a bird species it's often enough to manipulate their eggs, without manipulating other aspects of their lives in the more invasive (and often counterproductive) ways used for mammals. Of course, if a bird's habitat has dwindled drastically, as in the case of the California condor, it may be that no amount of manipulation will help. We await the result of releases of captive-raised condors (in Big Sur and the Grand Canyon and a few other protected sites) to see.

6. As attested by the myriad breeds of cattle we've produced since we first tampered with the wild aurochs ten thousand years ago. And the myriad breeds of chickens, dogs, carrier pigeons, cats, horses, etc.

7. After generations in a captive-breeding program, a species can undergo physical as well as psychological changes. Two examples: red grouse in captivity for no longer than six generations were found to have intestines considerably shorter than those of wild grouse, a change that could affect their ability to survive on wild forage; and wild turkeys confined for several generations were found to have smaller adrenal glands than wild birds, a change that may account for certain behavioral alterations that prevent captive-breds from surviving in the wild.

8. In addition to the Washakie pack members mentioned above, as of November 1998 fourteen other Yellowstone wolves had been "eliminated" by or under the auspices of the U.S. Fish and Wildlife Service.

9. Examples of such efforts currently in progress: (1) the Yellowstone to Yukon Conservation Initiative (acronym Y2Y), working to identify and preserve/restore migration corridors from Yellowstone to the Yukon Territory; (2) The Wildlands Project (TWP), working to identify and preserve/restore corridors from Utah to the Mexican border; and (3) Restoring Wild Patterns (RWP), working to identify and preserve/restore corridors in the gap between Y2Y and TWP.

Men and the Blue Lights of Nature

TO LESLIE RYAN

I

lue-black hair combed back in a light-slicked wave, à la Elvis. Blue satin shirt a-gleam under blue-silver lights. The drumsticks smeared in his lightning hands, and the chrome of his drums flashed four-pointed stars as he played them. His car was a customized '56 Ford, two-tone, with a continental, a visor, and skirts. Friday nights when he wasn't playing drums he raced it down the strip along the boardwalk — the wax on its black-and-white paint job high sheen-y, its chrome flashing four-pointed stars.

Pretty soon he was vetoed by my parents. He was flashy and fast, they said. I gave him his ring back, coerced to, yet innocent of rejection — he was the obsession of my every hour. No matter, he got back at me in a flash. Up till then, when homeroom period ended, he was always outside the door waiting. At the end of each class, all day long, he was there to walk me to the next with his arm around my waist. But the day after I gave him the ring back, walking alone in the stream of students changing classes, I passed him going in the other direction with a drum majorette: and this time he had his arm around her. He held his chin tilted up, smug and solemn, his eyes above the crowd, and the brazen nugget of his ring flashed from a chain around her neck.

I fell sick with the flu that evening. For four days, I lay aching and burning with fever in the bed I'd slept in since childhood. Heavy with will-lessness, hopeless, I could not imagine ever getting up again. I had never felt such pain in my fourteen years.

The night he touched me where I'd never been touched before was a year after we'd first gone steady. Going to first base, they called it in those days. I was all new-found heat on the surface, a wonder of burning. But inside I went cold with desire. It could have been anybody, I think, once it got started — anybody, and I wouldn't have cared: I just didn't want it to stop. My parents would have been astonished at what happened next, though. He did stop, said this was no good. First that and then this, he said, sliding his hand down in a flash preview of second base. And then we're in trouble, he said.

I was already just about at the end of it with him by that point. Since the majorette incident, I'd been seeing him on the sly for six months, and I'd begun feeling trashy about it. Then too, some part of my parents' influence had begun seeping up insidiously now and then, and in spite of myself I'd begun to feel embarrassed by the hot rod and the blue satin shirt. Still, all the next day I walked around in a fever. In a one-track trance, I could think of nothing but the feel of his hands. Soon after, I broke with him, as my parents would have wanted. But at bottom, they'd lost that parently battle: I'd had a taste.

If you'd made me search my soul on it then, what I'd have come up with, I guess, was that it was sex. Which it was, but that was just the surface of it. As I'd explain it now, the sexual fever had unlocked an inkling of some ultimate that was waiting. The fever that froze me like a zombie, held me like a prisoner, promised at the same time some graced deliverance. I wanted that fast flashing heat again, and would have it. As if it were food, water — but to nourish, slake what?

J was fast and flashy. And from that point on, this was a strain running through my relations with men. The flash was rarely again so close to the surface. There were no more hot rods, no more satin shirts. Couched in the deeper, less scrutable parts of the men I chose from then forward, the wildfire was henceforth more likely to show up in their visions or convictions, their fixations or yearnings, their waywardnesses or tangled lunacies, than in their accoutrements. But though never again in the simple way J had been, still in one way or another, the men I picked from then on were flashy and fast.

. . . . .

In the night sky, there are all manner of blue lights flashing. Fall, summer, winter, spring, from sunset's end to the start of sunrise, they come into shining in the dark depths of heaven — most of them, most of the time, a deep silver blue. The moon and the stars, of course — the most obvious; but others, too, rarer — or if not rare themselves, then the sight of them rarer, requiring more time and more patience, more focus — and just the right vantage — to see. Some shine on with imperturbable blueness, but some flicker, wink, twinkle, and others hurtle, bolt, zip, while still others tantalizingly, incorporeally, evanescently shimmer and wave.

They arouse a blue longing down in our own darkness, their wild, cold, blue beauty, so out of reach. But if you could approach them closely enough to distinguish their sources, the blue gleam that can so trigger your longing would transform altogether — sometimes to a seething conflagration; sometimes to a cold airless body, a lump of rock bathed in void; and sometimes to nothing more than a scattering of minuscule ice chips suspended in air.

On close scrutiny you'd find some of the blue lights to be not lights at all, but mere reflectors. As for others, you'd find they were lights all right, though not blue and alluring, but rather blinding white rages of annihilating fire.

. . . . .

It's a beautiful thing, the moon's blue light. Sometimes soft, almost gauzy-absorbent, going to white; sometimes glittery, metallic, just short of silver; sometimes nippy and brittle — ice glaze over cornflower — verging on indigo.

J was like the moon. Everything he gathered around him reflected light, and the light was alluringly silver-blue. But there was something cold in him — that walk through the hall with the majorette, calculating. Or was the cold I connect with J in me, rather — that night I went blank and relentless inside, careless, with desire? Passion is not always hot.

Heat and cold are somehow part of each other, intermingled confusingly. When the hot water of the shower first hits my skin, I get goose bumps. The − 10-degree air of a winter night burns my face, as if slapping it with fire, and the touch of dry ice sears my hand, reducing the place of contact to a crisp of dead skin. Hot light on a cold surface can make a blue beauty. Cold beauty can make you hot.

Half a lifetime after J, I now live in a cabin in the mountains. High up, in the winter it is sunk in snow. On the two-track leading in, the winds whip new drifts up every half hour, barring the jeep for the season — no use to plow — and so I snowshoe in and out, walking over buck-and-rail fences, the only clue there's a fence underneath me the tips of the bucks now and then poking through.

Some nights I just snowshoe for the beauty of it: the snow with a radium shine on it, the blue lights spangled and spangling above. One night in the east, over the saddle between Warm Spring Mountain and the crest of her unnamed sister, I saw a fast flashing thing. A shaft of light shooting straight up between the two mountains. A thick if insubstantial column, blue-silver mostly, but with an elusive opalescence — faint green, yellow, pink, writhing almost imperceptibly over and through it, now here, now there.

I would compare what I felt at the sight of it to the birth of an ocean of photons just the shape and size of my body — as if the atoms of me were all suddenly heated to the point that their electrons were bouncing right out of their orbits,[1] making the quantum jumps that produce those little blips of light.[2] In short, I felt all aglow. It was not a usual thing I was seeing, this beam shot from solid horizon up into darkness in the midst of the mountains. Piercing, while at the same time vaguely unguent and flowing, it was an uncommon light. Then it was gone, as if suddenly fused with a growing glow there between Warm Spring and her sister, heralding the rise the next moment of a fuzzy cold blob of moon.

In their expositions on optical phenomena, the books on atmosphere I looked into made no mention of what I'd seen that night. Sun pillars were the closest thing to it — columns of light above the rising or setting sun caused by the reflection of sunlight off the flat, plate-shaped ice crystals found in cirriform clouds, or in ice fog near the surface of the Earth. No mention of moon pillars, but one book implied their existence. It said ice fog was most common in the northern latitudes of North America, then added that in the high, cold valleys of an intermountain region, ice fog crystals will sometimes form at night.

Like the moon its light came from, the moon pillar was a reflector of light, though in a much more rarified sense. For the light of the moon pillar was light twice-reflected, reflected light once removed. The ice-crystal plates of the ice fog were horizontally oriented. The rays of the moon, still below the horizon, hit the bottom side of one minuscule ice plate to reflect down to the top side of another ice plate below it, to reflect up then from the top of that one to the bottom of another, and so on, always reinforcing the oncoming rays vertically. Actually, the light of the moon pillar was moonlight not just twice-reflected, but reflected again and again and again, ad infinitum — from ice fleck to ice fleck to ice fleck and back again, moonlight reflected a zillionfold.

A rare sight, this iridescent blue shaft of reflection. Unlike the moon, a privilege few get to see. But even the moon, though — think of it: how many times in your life do you see the full moon? At the end of the movie based on his novel *The Sheltering Sky*, Paul Bowles makes a cameo appearance. His blue eyes milky with incipient cataracts, he asks this startling question. A few hundred times maybe, he conjectures, and the truth of it pulls you up, shocks you. The shortness of life. The cold blue passions so few.

II

The light flowed like liquid on his hair as he moved around the pool table bobbing and sighting, leaning across the green felt in the glow of the overhead lamp. His skin was the color of the Arapaho woman's standing at the bar beside me, but not quite. Long black braid with some kink in it, wrapped around with rawhide. Leather vest, cross-laced up the sides, silver tips of the laces whipping around his hips. Did I say the flash was rarely again close to the surface? In the case of H it went from down near his bottomlessness clear up to the top of his head.

I was nailed by the sight of him. Nailed, as in a spike pounded all the way through. The physical details of him told some ineffable part of me some ineffable something. It was like a story I'd written, that had come up from god knows where in me, and now here it was true.

He knew the Arapaho woman, came and passed a quick line of banter with her. Then out of nowhere he put out his hand at me and abruptly said his name. Hours after that handshake we walked down the center line of the only paved street in his town with our arms around each other. Back at my motel he got into bed fully dressed. He'd thought my old jeans and flannel shirt on the hook were my "old

man's duds," was how he eventually put it. He'd thought it was a scam
we had — lure him there, get him naked, take his cash.

Assuaged of that notion, he still slept with his knife in the bedstead
the whole time I knew him. In country where men customarily wear a
knife on their belt, he often carried his in his boot. He carried it always,
though if we were out and he was in the mood for serious drinking,
he'd signal me to a dark corner and hand it to me to keep. These behaviors had their own logics, and eventually he told me the reasons for
them — secrets, he said, he would vouchsafe only to me. But even as
he shared them with me, his wild secrets were, in the purest sense, safe.
I heard them from the outside only, as fast flashy stories all covered
with four-pointed stars, and although I thought I understood them, in
fact I couldn't begin to plumb their true meanings — so for all intents
and purposes, even as he told me them, they remained secrets even
from me.

Sex full of kink and fantasy. My life with him, too, full of kink, and
madness: the center of things never holding, things always flying apart.
He lacked the moorings of a known heritage. That he was multiracial
his adoptive parents had refused to validate; they raised him instead,
from an infant, to think he was white. Then he'd come home from
school one day crying because the kids said no way he was his white
sister's brother. "Just tell them you were in the oven a little longer than
she was," his adoptive mom said.

The only thing he could trust, he said, was his motorcycle — a low-
slung, vintage Harley. It was blue and shiny and it kept breaking down.
Sometimes when I was seated up behind him he'd ride it in a prone position: his head back on my lap and his fingers laced beneath his neck,
he'd steer with his boots on the handlebars at eighty miles an hour.
We'd meet up with his "club" outside barrooms, in park grounds, a
horde of V-twins rumbling. The final time he met with them it was on
his own, in a motel room: no ladies invited, the bed laid over with guns.
They banished him when he didn't go along with it. He had that back-
bone, along with his weaknesses.

When the demons flared in him, he'd put more demons in him. A
dose and he'd sit and read two days straight without sleeping — his
eyes and his heart speed-cold. Or with no word he'd click the door
after him, start the truck up, and speed off through the snow on

the black strip of highway, up the steep sloping snake of it and over the distant hill's crest. I'd lie wrapped in my sleeping bag on the couch through the night in vigil, watching for lights down the hill.

But so much that he put out felt like love to me — intimacy, passion, solicitousness. He knew how to shine with veneration, he struck from the first with single-minded attachment — nay, possessiveness — and I took his need for love. When his suspicion focused on me, though, he himself cheated. Betrayal was the central lesson of his life.

When it hit me, it flattened me in ways I'd never have imagined. Suddenly the implications of all the flashing detail of him came together, shattering my sense of things, splattering me across the landscape I'd contrived of my life. This was not love, this was no bright strike from heaven; this was the ravage of desolation. There was stone at the core of him. It had taken me a long time to catch on to the true state of his soul — distracted as I was by the constant bright rim of explosions whirling around the still dark hub of it.

. . . . .

At first, I thought I'd call this essay "Men and the Cold Lights of Nature." But then I got thinking about it. While some of the lights I'm talking about here are secondary lights — reflected, thus cold — most of them are primary lights, burning and hissing and buzzing, twirling and writhing and jabbing with heat. When I got thinking about it, I realized that what the lights I'm talking about here have in common is not temperature but color — they're all blue. At first, this is a little surprising: blue is a color we associate with cold. We think of blue fingers, blue ice. Yet, while perhaps in some sense all blue lights are cold in the long run — airless like the moon, icy like the rare iridescent blue pillars that owe their existence to it — even cold light comes from heat. Trace back to their ultimate origins, and even the reflected lights owe their existence to electrons jumping orbits somewhere, and orbit-jumping is both the effect and the cause of heat. And despite the association of red and yellow with burning, it turns out that where celestial fire is concerned, blue is an indicator of heat's greatest intensity: if reddish stars measure in at up to 3,000 degrees Celsius, blue stars measure in at more than 10,000 degrees. Not all the lights I'm talking about here are cold by a long shot, but virtually all of them are blue. From the cold airless moon to the constellation Orion's diamond-bright Rigel, representative of the hottest category of stars.

And although most of them are night lights, not all of them require the foil of darkness to impress our retinae with their flash.

. . . . .

As the boom of thunderclaps outstripped even the boom of the wind that was plastering every herbaceous shred of the vast subalpine meadow flat to earth, I dashed, bending before it my own self, into a stand of trees. Knees to chin, hands clasping ankles, I crouched imprudently among trees — though in the shelter of a beetling boulder, at least: impossible to think of lying flat in the open, as traditional wisdom would advocate, amidst that raving storm. I crouched among trees against all counseling — the park that was usually smooth and flower-spread transformed all around me to a fierce booming ocean of wind — and worried that here, just a few miles above my cabin, I might be stricken dead.

To the east the bald grey hump of Union Peak went pale against the sky's deep galena, and all the prostrate plant life of the park went an eerie green in the weird leaden glare. And then, hunched in the lee of my boulder with the limber pines snapping around me, on that mountain before me, I saw a monstrous blue light flash. Thick as my arm, even from that distance, and eerily straight — almost as a rod — a bolt of lightning rammed into the bare side of Union Peak — no trees there, just granite — flashing wide, liquid-pulsing and livid blue. It was hard to believe it. The hugeness of it, the starkness of the bolt and the mountain, the unswervingness of what should have been jagged, driving like a giant pikestaff into the bare side of rock — and the stolid unchangedness of the mountainside the moment after, no fire, no anything. What would you find there at the point of impact if you climbed up to look?

Weeks later, browsing through a book about weather, I stopped at a section on lightning and read about what goes on inside a thundercloud. Within that great ethereal anvil of pouf, everything is in tumult. Air currents rise and fall with amazing speed. As they do, an electrical charge builds up — three hundred thousand volts per foot, one source has it — and though we don't clearly understand how, it seems the charge is transferred through the cloud when particles such as rain-drops and ice pellets borne on these currents collide and scrape. The rising particles acquire a positive charge, accumulating a bank of positive charge in the cloud's upper reaches. The falling particles acquire a negative charge, creating a bank of negative charge down near its base. Lightning is the inevitable reaction that neutralizes these charges, in the process often generating as many megawatts of power as a medium-sized nuclear reactor does.

There's within-cloud lightning, cloud-to-cloud lightning, and cloud-to-ground lightning. What happens in a case of the latter, such as the Union Peak strike, is this: the charge of Earth is normally negative. Given that like repels like, the pool of negative charge in the base of a thundercloud pushes the negative charge of the Earth just below it outward, to the sides, repelling it away from the area the cloud covers, out to its periphery. The result is a kind of electric shadow of the cloud on the ground beneath it — a region of opposite charge. In the region of this electric shadow, positive charges now begin running up and down objects that protrude from the Earth — vertical objects, such as trees.

Meanwhile, the negative charge in the base of the cloud begins ionizing the air in its vicinity. It opens a channel of ionized air several hundred feet long, called a leader. Ionized air is a good conductor, and the negative charge at the base of the cloud runs down the leader. This process is repeated over and over — one leader after another is formed — until the chain of leaders reaches almost to the ground. Then, at about one hundred feet from the ground the negative charge is met by the positive charges running up and down those vertical objects — such as trees. The result is a jagged path of conduction between the region of negative charge in the cloud and the region of positive charge on the ground. In about the same instant that the negatively charged leader makes its hit, a positively charged ground-to-cloud streamer jumps back at it — that is, just as the leader provides electrical passage groundward, the streamer provides electrical passage up toward the base of the cloud. In these two strokes, so closely consecutive as to be inseparable to our eyes, the opposite pools of charge, negative and positive, are neutralized in what we see as a single lightning stroke. This process of cloud-to-ground lightning is essentially the same for cloud-to-cloud or within-cloud lightning, the only difference in these cases being that the positive shadow the negative leader connects with is in another cloud, or in another part of the very same cloud.

Beyond this account of how lightning operates in general, a few particulars I read that day helped me interpret the idiosyncrasies of that Union Peak stroke — the seeming singularity of the bolt, its massiveness and uncanny directness, which made it not only surpassingly terrifying, but also charismatic for being so rare. Most of the time lightning looks like a bird's-eye view of a river's system of tributaries, or a webbing of slender veins — or an illumined branch of slim crooked twigs against the sky. This is because the leader channels are usually multiple, with subchannels branching off from a main channel, causing the lightning bolt to be multiforked. As it turns out, though, strong wind can blow the ionized channels around, sometimes shoving multiple channels right up against one another, and evidently this is what happened that day on Union Peak. To me, that bolt appeared unprecedentedly thick — as thick as my arm, as I've put it, even from such a distance — but given that plastering wind slamming into the mountain, it's likely that what I saw was a passel of separate channels rammed and welded together, to appear to my eye as a single fat bolt.

And as for the straightness of the bolt, I thought I could deduce an explanation for that, too. Electricity takes the easiest passage. Which is why I had reason to be worried about seeking shelter in the trees. A leader forms more easily over short distances than long ones, thus a negative charge explodes at the closest contact it can find with a positive charge — that is, with the tallest vertical object in the vicinity — which was in my case that day (as I keep repeating) the trees. But there's another way in which the stroke takes the easiest path, I learned from my reading — and in this case the path is rarely related to the shortest distance. The moistest regions of air conduct with the least resistance. Such regions are often patchy, which is why a lightning stroke often zigzags — jumping around among the wettest patches of air. But the atmosphere above the patch of Union Peak that took the bolt must have been homogeneously saturated, I deduced upon reading this. For some reason, for a good hundred feet above that stricken patch of mountainside, the air must have been virtually uniformly wet. Thus the path of least resistance for that lightning bolt (or those many bolts that the raging wind plastered together) turned out to be an unusually straight one — a path, as it appeared to me, almost straight as a rod.

Even as I was gripped by fear, the marvel of this unusual bolt took me over. The thrill of seeing a flash so unprecedented in my eyes' experience — so flowing-bright and sure-targeted — held me transfixed. Though massive boughs ripped and bounced around me, no lightning struck me. All possible makings of lightning that hour must have gone into that massive streak. But though it did not strike me, still in some way it nailed me — how to express? It struck a tree of me and ignited my forest. It singed the bedrock of me. I emerged, who knows . . . wiser? Who knows? Different.

. . . . .

All I can say now, looking back over these adventures with lightning — all I can say from this cabin I've retreated to now — is this:

H was in many ways like a lightning bolt. I thought so from the start and I'd say so still. Perhaps we were lightning bolts to each other, another case of that hackneyed rule that opposites attract. Perhaps we were leader and streamer, each a conducting route for the other's energy — it seems so obvious, if endlessly mysterious, that even human explosions work like that. And to extend the analogy still further, perhaps the night we met we were in just the right patch of atmosphere both at the same time — the winds of both our lives pounding in confusion, resistance factors at a minimum — so that we went at each other unusually straight and thick. I often wonder, if I were to climb that side of Union Peak and range across it: would I be able to detect the point of impact?

But however much these analogies may ring with a certain truth for me, the matter seems less simple to me now than they used to imply. Less simple and much less exclusively about H. That Union Peak bolt — and, in fact, all my sightings of blue lights since I've retreated to this cabin — have tempered my original impression in this matter, rounded it off some, put a few more finishing touches on it. H was like a lightning bolt in ways, no question. But however many ways he was like a lightning bolt, he was not a lightning bolt, nevertheless.

Another point that book on weather made, which impressed me: Earth is continually losing its negative charge, which leaks off into the atmosphere. This negative charge is one of Earth's necessary characteristics, making Earth precisely what Earth is. Lightning storms help preserve this vital characteristic: they return to Earth much of its lost negative charge. A lightning bolt helps Earth retain its natural energy, thus reinforcing Earth's integrity, thus supporting the very identity of the Earth.

H did not do that for me. (Nor did I do it for him, I should acknowledge, though that's beside my point). In fact, as far as my identity goes, I'd say that when my encounter with H was over, I'd been stripped of it. And yet, in suggesting something to me about my blindness to something, you might say my encounter with H and its upshot pushed me to ultimately realize my identity, too. A contrived identity divested, a truer identity hinted at. H contributed nothing to my integrity — and he did nothing to support my identity, that's a fact. But I guess you could say that in a perverse and roundabout way he helped lay the groundwork for the work of the blue lights of nature that did.

III

In their effects, my encounters with other men were not as dire as my encounter with H was. He came along fairly late in the game, when my illusions were most rankly developed and thus most ripe for a hit. Nevertheless, the others took me, for however long they took me, by essentially the same manner, every one of them.

I repeat: in their visions or convictions, their fixations or yearnings, their waywardnesses or tangled lunacies, the men I picked were fast and flashy. More than likely this is why they came and went like lights in the sky. For like the constellations in their steady progression, if there was always one coming up, there was also always one going down.

There was a latter-day Beat poet — his work esoteric but oddly poignant — who taught in the evening, then from midnight till morning held court in the campus tavern as he romantically drowned in his cups.

There was a jack-Mormon cowboy who'd been banished from the fold when a wild bent flared out in him early — left to flash, streak, and amble across the high desert, aimless and cursed.

There was a man who played in a play, smeared colors on canvas, and blew an ancient wind instrument on city street corners, before finding an old view camera at a flea market — and his true calling: recording his vision in a precision of light.

Their clothes, for their time, were a bit the other side of conventional — sandals, shabby World War II army jacket, stained cowboy hat — but you wouldn't have called them flashy. Still, these men all had their lights, or their cannons, going off in them.

There was a white man who wore his dense curly hair in a wild, woolly Afro and had a string of credentials in the law. Leaving the right-wing hearth of his father as persona non grata, he worked in civil liberties on five continents, engaging in such activities as helping to write the constitution of a fledgling nation freed from colonial rule.

There was a working-class boy with a knack for the wit and learning of Dr. Samuel Johnson and a marked talent for the academy, who nevertheless up and enrolled in medical school for the sole reason that he thought money would fill up the holes in his life better than literature could.

There was a blue-blooded boy who read Leibnitz and William Burroughs and Tu Fu, and everything else in his path. He read them in Nepal and Bolivia and in the Szechuan Province of China — anywhere the path of the moment led. Turning his back on the family's firm and their expectations, he adjusted to traveling below-decks — couldn't stop exploring the world.

The lives of these men were nothing if not self-determined. Misguided or not, these men jumped borders, made their own rules — but in the traditional sense of the word, you would not call them fast. Still, they shot through the standards of their foundations. Sped right on past.

They couldn't be still or content with what the life they'd been born into would furnish — not one of them. They were too full of pain or yearning or striving, too lost or too driven, too empty of satisfaction. There was something always beating at each one of them, and what he made of the situation, he made. But the men I chose were too full of the urge to shine somehow — to shoot off trailing sparks, in a rocket launch or a nosedive, whichever — too engaged in bottomless questing to be yours even if they wanted to.

. . . . .

Throughout my youth, and beyond, there was always one rising, one setting — in that way, the men I chose were like constellations, as I said. And in another way too, as I saw it — for each of them struck me as a cluster of blue lights uniquely configured, outstanding against a drabber, more randomly arrayed foil. Though in some ways the constellation analogy doesn't hold.

For example, there's the cyclical aspect of constellations. As the Earth rotates, they appear to travel around it in a more or less circular path, and so the constellations are chronic, appearing repeatedly. True, rising as they do about four minutes earlier each evening, you will never see a given constellation in quite the same place at the same time from night to night, and as the seasons change the sequence of constellations on the night sky shifts. Although high in mid-sky in January (at least from the vantage of my cabin), Orion has disappeared from the night sky altogether by July, when the much less distinct, less flashy constellation Ophiuchus occupies about the same place. Still, within a twelve-month period, you can be sure that every one of the constellations will return to its former location — and in light of this fact, I'd have to say my beaus were less like true constellations than like a constellation conjured by my fancy one winter night.

On a February evening I walked along the flank of a hillside outside Jackson, Wyoming. I walked south, facing toward the old section of town that's nestled at the foot of the steep wall of Snow King Mountain. I saw the lights of the town, fuzzy in the fine snow that was falling, but I could not see the silhouette of Snow King — no accustomed black backdrop beyond the bright sand grains of townslights, no precipitous profile, no abrupt demarcation between opaque jagged ridge and lucidly glowing night sky. Instead, where the mountain should have been there was just the same black of the heavens, and hovering just above the townslights, as if it might almost skim them, there was a strange, low constellation. Blue lights in the rough outline of a great butterfly floating just over the town.

I stopped, rapt — overwhelmed for an instant at the strange sight of it. How had the stars come so low? Then I realized it was the ski runs on Snow King. Or not the ski runs exactly, but rather their border of pole lamps — the big flourescent bulbs shining in them. Like the contour of the mountain, the discrete white bands of the ski runs had been obliterated by the fog of fine snow sifting, so all that could be seen of them was a vague aura leaching through darkness in the form of a white sheen around the light bulbs — like the expanding shell of gas, called a planetary nebula, drifting out from a dying star. As mountain and sky had lost their distinct identities in one continuous blurred blanket of darkness, so those streaking white runs had lost theirs in a blurred milky glow, and all that remained distinctly visible were the bulbs of the pole lights, bluer than ever behind the scrim of fine snow, blue like the fiery star contracting at the center of a planetary nebula. In full assemblage they seemed to me to form the outline of a butterfly — a fanciful Constellation Papilio — just about to go down.

The men I chose were less like a true constellation than like this optical analogy I perceived in the lights outlining the ski runs of Snow King. Unlike a celestial constellation, they were not chronic, but flashed forth in a particular set of conditions, unlikely to appear again. They were more like my fancied constellation — a thing part really there, and part conjured. The facts one thing, the interpretation another — imagination's artifact.

But then, what is a true constellation but an artifact of the imagination, anyway? The stars are out there, of course, but contrary to what the ancients believed, those in a given constellation are not arranged like dots all on the same plane so as to inscribe a picture on the sky. In any constellation certain stars will be closer to the Earth, some perhaps a matter of just a few light-years away; while others will be more distant, perhaps by a factor of hundreds, or thousands, even. The only relationship among the stars in a constellation, really, is that they're all scattered in roughly the same direction as seen from Earth — that is, from our vantage. Their only relationship is their arrangement with respect to one another within the human eye.

And so, the constellation analogy turns back on itself. My beaus were less like true constellations than false ones, and yet even true constellations — being a human construct — are in a sense false. And so, by the very fact of being like false constellations, my beaus were like true ones. Like the pattern of stars we perceive in the heavens, the patterns I saw in the blue lights of their lives were more than likely just constructs existing primarily in this beholder's eye.

Even viewed in this light, though, the constellation analogy is limited. For anyone can see that even the brightest constellations have no particular dazzle, and as celestial motions go, theirs are pretty plodding and staid.

Stars move, of course, like everything else in the heavens. Some are approaching us, some are receding from us — and with telescopes we can deduce the speed of these so-called proper motions by measuring their Doppler shifts. And for stars very near to us we can detect the proper motions even with the naked eye. Barnard's star, just six light-years away, is the star with the greatest proper motion detectable in this manner. Even so, as perceived by the unaided eye, in 180 years it's moved a distance no greater than the moon's diameter — or a scant twelve miles a year. And so we can say that, just as they are not particularly flashy, constellations are decidedly not very fast.

. . . . .

Perhaps this is why I've never been one to pay much attention to constellations. I never paid them any attention at all until I moved to this cabin and began snowshoeing on winter nights. Then, of course, I couldn't help but be taken a bit by Orion — by the belt and sword of that hunter sailing so flagrantly above me, and by the diamond sparkle of the rare blue supergiant Rigel marking his heel. But even in summer, when I sit out for hours in the darkness, I pay little attention to constellations — they are just not vibrant enough for my taste. More compelling to me is the giant white rag of the Milky Way, unfurled across the top of the sky. Or the unexplained oddities I've seen from time to time closer to the horizon — strange lights that by their sheer unpredictability and flamboyance raise a ruckus in me.

Once when Ann was here we saw fireballs. I bring her into it as a witness, as evidence that I wasn't just out there hallucinating that night. We'd camped out, but the fierceness of the lightning storms that kept sweeping through scared us enough that we abandoned the tent and spent a good part of the night in her truck. With its tires for grounding, we huddled behind the windshield looking out toward the Absaroka mountains in the distance.

When lightning flashed on that distant horizon we could see their profiles. In particular, we could see one great promontory of peaks that jutted in our direction, the sharp-pointed, irregular triangles of its mountains tilting every which way in the flickering light like the silhouette of crooked black teeth in a huge black maw, or the silhouette of waves in a thrashing black sea. The storm there was terrible. Then it grew, impossibly, worse. The lightning flashed more and more often, continuously. And then in one wing-beat of an instant we saw the fire-balls — round, red, and rolling down the concave sides of the black waves of mountains, crest to trough, and again, crest to trough.

   — *Did you see that?*

   — *Yeah, did you?*

   — *Didn't they — weren't they rolling?*

   — *Weren't they — like fireballs?*

What we saw, as it turns out, would not properly be termed fireballs, because *fireball* is the technical term for a kind of meteor, which creates a very different kind of spectacle. From my reading, I'd gather that what we saw would properly be called ball lightning instead. What little the books say in common about ball lightning is that it's controversial. The descriptions they give don't much agree. One source describes it as a luminous ball that maneuvers like a flying saucer. I personally don't know what that means. Another source describes it instead as a rolling ball — which I can relate to, since that's what we saw. The ball may "commit a variety of pranks before it fizzles out," this source adds. A couple of other books note that, rather than fizzling, it some-times explodes itself away. Neither Ann nor I can remember how the balls terminated; it all happened so fast and it was so shocking, we didn't register such details clearly. All we know is that we saw what seemed to be balls of fire rolling, as if down the mountains — at least two, maybe three.

If sightings are to be believed and ball lightning exists, the books say, we don't understand how it can. We don't know how electricity can contain itself in ball long enough to perform such pranks as people have claimed to see. But Ann and I saw those balls of fire, one after an-other rolling. And we saw them there in the heart of the Absarokas — mountains wild enough to host grizzlies — no chance of man-made fireballs there. In that setting, and in the context of that continuous severe lightning, it seems they must have been a form of lightning themselves.

And as for the phenomenon technically termed a fireball, I may have seen some sign of one of those, too. I may have seen evidence of an official technical fireball twice in fact, about a year apart, and in al-most the same place.

Each time it was summer and I was inside the cabin, seated both times looking out the big southwest-facing window toward the silhouette of a long forested ridge. In the main room of the cabin I don't use electric lamps, I use oil lamps. In their brightness, electric lamps turn a room into a box of light inside opaque darkness. The windows reflect the room's bright light back at you — their glass, all full of reflections, becomes opaque like mirrors, and you can't see anything beyond them but blank black. But the light of oil lamps, being dim and localized, does not turn the windows entirely into sheets of reflection. Reflected merely as more or less discrete pools of light on the glass, the light of oil lamps does not entirely block the window's transparency, does not close out completely all the details veiled in that outer darkness. You can see through the dark, you can see into it, to perceive at least some of what it enfolds. And so both those nights facing out that big window, I could see what lay beyond it — that is, to the extent that human eyes can function in darkness, I could see certain goings-on of the night.

Each time, what happened happened so quickly that it was over before I could really attend to it. Each time, I saw through that southwest window what looked like a narrow trail of fat green rain falling ever so briefly over that forested ridge. The first time I went out to the porch and sat for a long time with my eyes trained on that southwest horizon. But it didn't happen again. And as time went by I began to question I'd seen it — perhaps it was a trick of my eyes.

When I saw it again a year later, though, I believed it was actually something. Something not in my eyes, but out there in the sky over the ridge. It was a quick series of light-dashes falling ridgeward, like the quick dashes of light that fall from dwindling fireworks, or sparklers — or the bright elongated dashes of illuminated rain. But these dashes were a lurid, neon green. Eerie, electric, liquid. Green sparkler rain over the southwest horizon. Not once, but twice.

I never had the slightest clue what these green showers could be, until I was trying to learn about those balls of fire Ann and I had seen. Since we'd thought of them as fireballs, that's the word I searched the indexes for, and a couple of them actually listed the word. A fireball, say the books that bother to mention it, is an extremely bright meteor. Sometimes such a meteor, they say, leaves a train — a path in the sky that remains for just a few seconds, like what I'd seen. Sometimes, when a fireball leaves such a train, the books say, it makes a hissing sound, in which case it's likely that, instead of burning up in the atmosphere, the meteor will hit Earth. I, of course, did not hear any hissing. But the way that green trail of dashes looked each time, I imagine it was making one. I think two years in a row I saw a bona fide fireball — a brilliant meteor falling to Earth somewhere up in the subalpine park above my cabin, beyond that ridgeline of trees.

These are the kinds of celestial lights that have taken me traditionally. Not the staid, steady, established constellations — but the weirdos, the renegades, the ones that move fastest and shine most bright.

And contemplating these strange light phenomena, I sometimes wonder: what of the Hubble stuff? What of the light focused by the lenses of that huge floating telescope — and to be focused still more acutely, revealingly, by the next generation of telescopes that are about to make the Hubble obsolete? What about all the celestial lights the naked eye can't see?

The naked eye, for example, only rarely picks up on the zinging fragments of metal and rock that are meteors. However many sightings are reported, they don't scratch the surface of the numbers of these cosmic shards zipping around in the solar system. Actually, these errant fragments come in three phases: meteoroid, meteor, and meteorite. A meteoroid ranges from the size of a sand grain up to several feet in diameter (anything bigger is an asteroid) and travels in space. If it enters Earth's upper atmosphere, its name changes to meteor. If it falls through that atmosphere without burning up and strikes Earth's surface, it becomes a meteorite. A hissing fireball trailing green rain is a meteorite in the making.

These fragments have a variety of sources. Some are chips off of asteroids; some are pieces of burned-out comet; and some have been found to be bits of Mars, and our moon, even — bits that evidently shot off into space, escaping the gravity of their parent bodies, when those parent bodies collided with other bodies, asteroids presumably, or very big meteorites. Many meteoroids have been floating unchanged in space for billions of years, and when they fall to Earth as meteorites they bring information about cosmic history. Supposedly the Earth gains twenty tons a day from the infall of these rock fragments as meteorites. If we don't see them more often, perhaps this is because few of them are fireballs big enough to leave a telltale train. Many more are mere bits of grit, which upon contact with air simply vaporize. But even these tiny bits show themselves sometimes — particularly when Earth's orbit crosses the orbit of the meteoroid swarms they're traveling in. The sparks of recurring meteor showers — like the Perseids of August, the Leonids of November — mark the vaporization of members of those swarms of innumerable sand grains circling the sun.

. . . . .

No, more than constellations — of any kind, imagined or real — most of my beaus were like meteors. Although some moved through my life at a leisurely pace, like a constellation slowly but steadily wheeling over the sky, most just came zipping through, burning up fast. The cowboy passed through for a summer. A boy aviator burned bright in my life for a week. A cop, a ranch foreman, a cab driver, a biologist — in explosions of varying duration they came, and went. And back when I was in graduate school in Chicago, a student at the Art Institute there stormed through my life periodically, in a rain of flashes much like the Leonids or the Perseids in one of their especially vibrant years.

He'd call me to his studio in the middle of the night and I'd drive up there. At that hour I could make it from the South Side to the Near North Side in a half hour only — weave the barrens of Lake Shore Drive giddily, lane to lane, if I wanted, as off to my right a red band rose between the top of Lake Michigan and the bottom of the black sky. Opening the door to his storefront, I'd hear him doing his gravelly pirate voice in the back room — "Me goood fraynd Jeem Awkings" — and barging in, in a torrent of Treasure Island dialogue, earring-ed and bandanna-ed and eye-patched, he'd pull up short in mock surprise at the sight of me: "Now, fancy yew be-en 'ere." Or he'd wheel himself furiously through the door in an old cane-backed wheelchair, raving melodramatically, in the guise of a man lamenting the loss of a limb, which he'd folded back in the trouser leg of an oversized pair of pants. Or he'd saunter in and with a flamboyant flourish tear open his shirt to reveal a glut of little fake flower tattoos he'd just plastered all over his shoulders and chest, exclaiming, "The beauty of 'em's worf the pain." He was a drinker, a charmer, a whimsical player — a rakish and burly little Irish ginger man. His paintings could dazzle your eyes from their sockets, and he was confused about love.

He drove my insides to a frenzy. Back down on the South Side, I couldn't do my work. The drafts of my thesis on *Endymion*—Keats's perplexing portrayal of a frenzied youth racked by desire for an ineffable something: Beauty? Love? Truth?—languished, unattended. For days after one of my trips to the Near North Side, Endymion lived in the book on my desk unlooked at, deprived of my former bemused contemplation as he sought his ineffable something in a protean woman whose essence is perhaps most succinctly characterized as the spirit of the unattainable moon. His elaborate trance now unheeded by me, he pursued his maiden in all her shifting guises, through realms above earth and below, all on his own at those times — without a trace of my former sympathy, empathy, or bewilderment for company, sometimes for weeks. He was in dire straits, Endymion, but how could I attend to him, when for days after my ginger man's meteor showers I couldn't shake my own trance — the trance he'd put me in with his lusty imagination — and I couldn't shake my own lust to bask in its light.

A crazy lot, these meteor fellows — these fireballs and lightning balls, raging to burn up the world, or to burn themselves up in a flash across the sky. Engrossed in their bottomless questing, they couldn't be yours even if — even when — they wanted to . . .

. . . Or was it in some way, just as much, that I didn't want to be theirs?

IV

I never worked when I was with them. I went to paid jobs of course, but I never did my own work. And I was never myself when I was with them — not my full self by a long shot — and I was with them, one or another, most all of the time. I could barely breathe for my obsession with them. I was enthralled, taken over completely by their bursting and glittering and streaking — but they were the cold airless death of me, those fast flashing men.

Filling me with heat, their light would then flicker, blot out, shoot off in orbit, leaving me cold. And worst of all, this was so in a metaphorical sense more than literally. It was not so much that they physically left, but that what I loved in them, yearned for, wanted to share of them, often went poof in a shower of green sparks.

The burn of cold, the shiver of hot. My body scorching, my soul on ice. Catch one of them flashing along in midair, and just as I'd grasp him, the possibilities he epitomized would flicker. He'd burn me up, speed me empty, put me out like a candle, just as I thought I might attain the grace of a steady blaze.

They couldn't be mine, even when they wanted to. I couldn't possess their lights. And how could I be theirs, if I was not mine?

Did I use them to skirt the search for my own fast flashing? Did I choose them to do the fast flashing for me?

. . . . .

Finally, I retreated to this cabin up in the thin air. I surrounded myself with the warm, steady light of oil lamps.

Strange to say, men visitors are the ones most taken with them. Women like them well enough, but they want to know how much work it is to keep them clean. Men, though, want to touch them, to look down through their chimneys at the flame. They go from one to another, often returning to hover above them again. Then, throughout the evening — through conversation and music and eating — you'll catch them time and again gazing off around the room at the oil lamps' soft glow.

But other people, male or female, are here at the cabin rarely. And the men who come are the men of my women friends — nothing more to do with my life than that. I retreated to the cabin in isolation. For all intents and purposes leaving men behind.

But here where I've chosen to stop, in this cabin up in the sky, the blue lights are with me always. Our silver satellite, the habitual constellations, the erratic planets, the Milky Way. The moon pillars and all the freak forms of lightning. The fireballs falling and the sparks in the meteor showers zipping to nothingness. How cold and killing for me were those so-called loves of mine. But that was my own self, really — the cold of my own so-called love. These blue lights now around the cabin make me see that. They remind me of those fast flashing men — bring them to mind for a little — but then they take me beyond.

One was like the moon, one like a blue light pillar, maybe. One was like ball lightning, one like a fireball, perhaps. But consider this, the blue lights tell me: a meteor burns itself out. And a meteor become meteorite ends up a cold metallic lump of rock. It was never a meteor or a meteorite that you wanted, the blue lights tell me. What you wanted was their light.

It was not the men themselves you wanted, the blue lights tell me. If it seemed that they spoke to your soul, it was only because of their fast flashing lights. It was the lights that were the message. It was the lights that held a promise of meaning for you.

I think back to J, to that first fever. One taste of that fast, flashing heat, and I wanted it over and over again. But what I see ever more clearly from this vantage is that the fever had indeed unlocked an inkling of some ultimate that was somewhere in waiting. The fever that froze me like a prisoner, *had in fact* at the same time promised some graced deliverance — of something waiting in me. I did not know this then. All I knew then was that I wanted that fast flashing heat, and would have it. I did not for one moment stop to question my desire. And so, I set off on a lifetime of pursuing — not the message, but a string of messengers, instead.

Yes, I used them to skirt the search for my own fast flashing. Yes, I chose them to do the fast flashing for me.

I know this now, for here alone with the pure lights, I find my electrons jumping orbit. I am aglow, I am burning, I am *nailed* — not by a man but by the blue lights of nature, by the refulgent range of them, born of the universe. Hot and hissing, or cold and mirroredly mute, they resonate with my own innate lights, long smothered in me.

I was seeking not the men but the flash and fast I saw in them. Seeking my own flash and fast, though I could not get at it through them. All I could get was the pain reflected off their frenzy. All I could get was my own questing pain flashed back at me, as they zipped off into the dark. All I could get was my own insubstantiality, my own tendency to spark and go poof, when, just as I grasped at them, those lights that I yearned for flickered and guttered before my eyes. Leaving me behind to find myself like nothing so much as an electron spinning in its orbit, its location a mere fuzz of probability. Is it here? Is it there? Where is it? Sometimes here, sometimes there, but actually, where?[3]

But here, now, at this cabin with its roof in the sky, where I've finally *stopped*, it's as if I'm the entire atom. With a nucleus, a center — a heart for the shells of my elusive electrons to center upon. Stopped here, surrounded by the blue lights of nature, I can feel myself. As they flash through the sky, flaring and snuffing and flaring ever again, these blue lights of nature illuminate my own buried lights, fan their flame, get me going — revealing in me the light and speed that I sought, as I finally stay still.

Working now — doing my own work. Working into being my own full self. Getting an inkling, a glimpse in my soul now and then, of some vague aura of what the Hubble's secrets might be like, even. Of the "stuff" that's out there, and in here, even if the naked eye can't make it out.

In the quiet here, I no longer smolder to quickly extinguish. In the stillness, I flare here, both the cold and hot lights in me blazing forth steadily together for the first time.

V

The most spectacular blue light of nature I've ever seen was Hale-Bopp. It was certainly the one I got to scrutinize the most. From January through May 1997, I saw it at some point almost every night, many nights looking out for it more than once, to register its location of the moment along its apparent course around the northern pole. In January I might spot it through the west window of the cabin around suppertime, skimming the breccia buttes on the northwest horizon. Then later, waking momentarily, at 2 A.M. maybe, I'd spot it out the little north window up under the eaves, now sailing high in the northeastern sky. It was a little wedge of light then, in early January — bigger than any star or planet, but yet not as big as the moon. A little silver-blue wedge with a snub nose and a vaguely blurred backside, which gave you the sense it was moving at breakneck pace, although that movement didn't translate to the human eye across all those millions of miles.

As time went by, it grew bigger. It appeared in similar locations but at different times. As I said earlier, I can't drive into my cabin in winter. As I said, the wind drifts my little two-track closed too regularly to make plowing feasible, so I leave my jeep where the snowplow stops plowing, back in the trees, and snowshoe in and out. Snowshoeing in one night at the end of March, I was stopped short by Hale-Bopp. Nailed fast in the frigid air.

It was midnight, much later than I'd ever stayed out during snow-shoe season before, and although we'd just passed the vernal equinox, it was −18 degrees. As I strapped on my snowshoes to make the trek home, I was cursing myself for not staying in town instead of plunging through snow in the dark in this cold. But when I emerged from the trees into the white clearing, all the cold went off me, like water evaporating under hot sun. There was Hale-Bopp — now sailing at midnight in just about the same spot where a couple of months earlier I was wont to see it at suppertime, buzzing the northwest horizon with its stupendous tail fanned out behind. And whereas a few weeks earlier it had been a hard little bright silver-blue wedge, it was now a colossal wing of light, the brilliant balled tip of it nosing, hard and blue, Earthward, the feathery tail of it spread long and wide like a silver peacock's tail trailing, its myriad vanes all gauzed together with barbules and barbicels of glowing gas.

Although I didn't know it at the time, this particular midnight marked the zero hour of March 22, the day Hale-Bopp made its closest approach to the Earth. A week or so later, when it made its closest approach to the sun, its tail viewed from Earth was between fifteen and twenty degrees long. A nice bit of serendipity for me, that the first night I'd ever stayed out until midnight in snowshoeing season turned out to be March 22, 1997.

Albrecht Durer and others used the comet as a symbol for melancholy. An ancient Chinese poet called comets "vile stars." But when, happening to glance behind me on March 22, 1997, I saw my snowshoe tracks side-lit by comet light, I thought the comet was the most ecstatic of all the blue lights of nature I'd ever seen.

In 1950, the Dutch astronomer Jan Oort hypothesized that comets come from a sun-centered spherical shell hundreds of times more distant than Pluto, where they all orbit endlessly, except when now and then the weak gravity of a passing star dislodges one and starts it moving toward the sun. That spherical shell has come to be called the Oort cloud. Another supposed ring of icy bodies in the outer solar system — the Kuiper Belt, between the orbits of Uranus and Neptune — is also cited as a source of comets.[4] Although the detection of argon in Hale-Bopp's tail in 1997 suggests this comet was born in the Kuiper

Belt, as things have turned out, Hale-Bopp is believed to now spend most of its time off in the deep reaches of the Oort cloud.

When dislodged from the Oort cloud (or the Kuiper Belt), a comet leaves off its habit of orbiting the sun more or less in a circle, at a more or less uniformly great distance throughout its orbit, and accompanied by its fellows in crowds. At this point it begins its own unique and far more eccentric elliptical orbit — one that affords the comet far more intimacy with the sun than it ever had circling with its fellows in the Oort cloud (or the Kuiper Belt), one that affords this outcast comet the opportunity to shine. That a comet sweeps past the sun in its own personal orbit was hypothesized in 1705 by Edmund Halley, when he published calculations to support his belief that a comet observed in 1682 was the same comet that had appeared in 1607, and in 1531, and in 1456 — and the same comet that would appear again, he predicted, in 1758. The comet did reappear in 1758 — to be known thenceforth as Halley's Comet. And calculating back, we've been able to track appearances of this comet on average every seventy-six years, to at least as early as the mention of it in Chinese records in 239 B.C. In fact, the famous comet that appeared just before William the Conqueror's invasion of England in 1066, and that is seen in the Bayeux Tapestry's depiction of this event, was Halley's Comet.

Ever since Halley's hypothesis was confirmed, we've been keeping track of comets. Eventually, it was the accumulated record of comets that enabled Jan Oort to deduce the existence of their nursery in that spherical cloud beyond Pluto, as he tracked the orbits of incoming comets backward to their point of origin. As our comet recording proceeded, we came to classify them according to the time it takes them to orbit the sun. Traditionally, a comet that completes its orbit every two hundred years or less has been called a short-period comet, and one that takes longer than that, a long-period one. Halley's is of course a short-period comet, which is why Halley was able to "discover" it by tracing its reappearances. So is Comet Encke, with a period of little more than three years. By this definition, Hale-Bopp is a long-period comet, completing its orbit only once in about four thousand–plus years.[5] Some are astonishingly longer. It's been calculated that Comet Kohoutek, spotted in 1973, takes more than two hundred thousand years to go once around the sun.

But what is a comet, exactly? As put by Fred Whipple in his "dirty snowball" theory, in the same year that Oort hypothesized his famous cloud, a comet is simply a lump a few miles in diameter made of frozen gases and dust. At aphelion (that is, at the point on its orbit farthest from the sun), this lump is cold, a mere dirty snowball, but as it approaches perihelion (the closest point on its orbit to the sun), part of its icy surface begins to heat up and evaporate. Upon striking the gas, sunlight energizes its atoms and they emit light, creating a halo of glowing gas and dust called a coma around the icy nucleus. Because the nucleus is bumpy, irregular, some regions of it attract more sunlight than others, and in those spots, as the icy crust gives way to sublimation, jets of gas and dust shoot away from the nucleus and out through the coma, sweeping back from the coma into one or more tails. Until Hale-Bopp came along, we had never observed more than two tails on a comet — a dust tail and an ion tail. But Hale-Bopp displayed a third type of tail made of sodium atoms, the generation of which has yet to be explained.

The closer the comet gets to the sun, the larger the coma grows, expanding sometimes to millions of miles across. And the dust and gas that leave the coma may sweep into a tail stretching *hundreds* of millions of miles. The tail faces always away from the sun, no matter whether the comet is traveling toward the sun or retreating from it — a phenomenon we attribute to solar wind, a mass of fast-moving, electrically charged particles ever streaming out from the sun. The solar wind moves faster even than comets, overtaking them even when they're moving away from the sun, thus sweeping their tails ahead of them, in contradiction to our traditional definition of a tail as something that follows behind.

But as the comet moves farther and farther from the sun and starts to cool, the tail starts to shrink. Eventually the coma collapses, and the comet is just a lump of ice again, a bit smaller on its trip out from the sun than when it was traveling in toward it. For each time a comet passes perihelion, it loses a little more gas and a little more dust to the burning, until one day it dies — in some cases, like that of Biela's Comet, first splitting into two comets before crumbling into a throng of small fragments eventually spread over the entire orbit once traveled by the comet itself — small fragments henceforth to be regarded as meteoroids.

And so the comet, like so many of the blue lights of nature, is fast and flashing, flaring for a time across sky, then flickering out. And yet, it is strikingly different, too. For me, anyway, the point about Hale-Bopp — along with its weird beauty, incredible size, and opulent light — was this difference. The point about Hale-Bopp — the point about any comet — is that as long as it lives it's returning, circling back.

Not in any daily, pedestrian sense of making its rounds via Earth's rotation, as do the constellations. Not even in any tightly predictable way, in fact. For given that its course is influenced not just by the pull of the sun, but also by the pull of the planets it passes — and even by the thrust, or propulsion, of those jets of gas and dust shooting out from the nucleus when its icy crust gives way — a comet's orbit is often erratic, and its period (as illustrated clearly by Halley's — sometimes seventy-five years, sometimes seventy-six, seventy-eight . . .) is irregular. A comet's voyage does not proceed like clockwork, but more dramatically, rather. We never know for sure what its precise path will be, or exactly when it will return. An idiosyncratic voyage, a voyage of extremes, it engenders suspense.

When a comet disappears from view (as Hale-Bopp did in November of 1997[6]), it is embarked on a cold, dark odyssey, to the ends not just of the Earth, but of the whole solar system. Along the way it loses its light, and its course is subject to fresh jitterings every time it goes. But having reached that dark destination, it will veer back, we know, eventually to burn once again as it nears the sun, emitting once again a bright coma, sprouting once again jets of gas and dust. (Sometimes, even — as in the case of the Great Comet of 1861 — that returning comet will come so near as to sweep us with those insubstantial plumes, bathing the Earth, though with no noticeable effect, in its long, flowing tail.) A comet is not a one-time light — which a one-time convergence of circumstances sets flashing — but a fast flashing light that does not burn itself out, does not vaporize to nothing in its burning. It is a light that can burn but still hold its substance, that can flicker out without losing its potential to burn again and again and again. A light that, though go as it must, is ever circling back, ever returning. A light that combines the combustibility of meteors with something close to the constancy of the moon — as flashy and astonishing as ball lightning, but with a kind of steadiness that for mortals like us just about amounts to permanence. True, with each round the comet is dissipating, its body ever wasting, quite literally blowing itself out. But un-til they waste away entirely — which will be long after I do — Halley, Encke, Hale-Bopp, and all the others will be coming back around. And even if I won't live long enough to see the return of most of them, I know always that they're coming, that I can count on that — that for all intents and purposes, in terms of my life anyway, these comets are always a light in the making, a potential for light that will last.

. . . . .

All night long I sat up writing him a letter. Next day I waited behind a door to the lab where he worked until he finally chanced to walk past on the other side of it, and, desire trumping trepidation, I swung that door open and thrust the letter into his hand. After that I waited in the parking lot by the woods until lab hours were over. The rain fell in sil-ver strings all during the time that I waited, pinging off my car's dark blue hood.

Then he was coming at me in the rain in his yellow slicker. Books tucked under his yellow sleeve, his dark hair sweeping out beyond the edges of his yellow hood. Coming and coming, his hair wetting up as he walked — I thought I could see the black of it peppering over with silver droplets, and the water slick on the asphalt was splashing up sil-ver around his boot soles. His hair going lank now, the rain soaking through it, long strands of it plastered black against the yellow slicker, as his feet kicked up silver, and his face was held always toward me where I sat inside my car, beyond the blue hood of it, behind the silver-dotted windshield, where he couldn't see me at all. He couldn't see me through the rain-dotted windshield, but his face was held al-ways toward me, at me, as he kept coming and coming, as if in a film loop that would never end. And then he was opening the car door, sit-ting down right beside me, the window behind him dotted with silver, the two of us in a blue shell wrapped around by a silver world. He pushed his yellow hood back, his face held always toward me. "I'm not ready for you," he said. "I've got a black heart."

Self-abnegation, I called it to myself, in my dream world — the heightened world of my own making that I believed was the real world — where I turned everything to nobility, myth. Self-abnegation, I thought, that streaming fall day that, whether we were ready or not, marked the hard-and-fast beginning for us. But as it turned out, it was true: he did have a black heart. Compounded not of evil, not of meanness, but of his own abstruse brand of torment.

His mind was like a tiger, burning. And so, even in its blackness, was his heart. Fierce, flashing, recondite — both of them. His vision was grand and labyrinthine, his conceptions — the projects he set for himself — always layered, metaphoric, demanding intricate research and articulation, while at the same time their aim was compassionate, their implications ecumenical: conceptions and projects rich in both mind and heart.

But then, often he abandoned these projects. In the heightened world of his own making that he believed was the real world, he turned everything — from the books, films, and sports that he studied, to his friends, lovers, family, and the students he taught — to impossible beauty and impossible doom.

For that, he was at some level furious at all of them. Furious that he loved them so passionately and that they somehow always seemed to betray him, that they could never live up to his vision of them, that they could not — as he could not, in his vision of his own self — work out. His expectations exceeded the world. But having such expectations, he exceeded it also — which was the fuel of his fast, furious burning, in every sense of the word.

I remember a March day in the garden. Planting peas as I'd always done, but in a new universe. In more ways than I knew yet that day, I had left my old life, and just months after the rainy day in the parking lot, I was there, planting in the garden, and he was there, too, working up inside the house.

Grey, raw, the sky on the verge of snow without snowing. My hands, in the cotton gloves, were blue. I remember kneeling beside the furrows. Placing the hard, white, wrinkled peas one by one with blue hands. I remember the heat inside me, flesh burned off to spirit — transubstantiation in an airless flame in the solid cold grey afternoon. This is not about religion, but the words are deliberately chosen. Those days I was graced, having found in him a figure of what you look for all your life. Looking up toward the house from my patch of turned earth, I felt the glow of him in there working. In the period to come I was to shortchange health and double-cross sanity, struggling to keep that light in my life.

When I came down in the morning, he was just going off to teach in his Yankee cap, having stayed up the whole night preparing for his class. When he was scheduled to tutor till noon, he was still there with a student at four o'clock. When he wrote criticism, it was on someone like Thomas Pynchon. When he read an author, he didn't stop till he'd read all that author's works.

My first birthday with him, the first gift came a minute after midnight. The next came at dawn, and so on, up to midnight the next night. A record album on the bathroom sink in the morning. A first edition signed by a favorite author at my breakfast place. A black scarf with a handpainted iris to use for a headband, hair combs of mother-of-pearl. A pottery bowl the color of sapphires, a red velvet peasant blouse. And, when I returned from work late that night, a field of candles burning on the table, circling a myriad of little potted plants that he'd raised from cuttings himself.

When it was time for friends, he bought Châteauneuf-du-Pape and lobster. He made the house theirs. He played the music to all hours, and everyone ended up staying through the weekend.

When it was love-making time, he took me off in the snow with a bottle of wine and a blanket, to a clearing in the woods where we lay with the whole of heaven sizzling over our heads.

He felt the pain of innocuous strangers, identified with the despair of his enemies. I always said that if I could ever write the best that was in me, I'd be lucky to manage a distant approach to Holden Caulfield, but if he wrote the best that was in him, he might do *War and Peace*.

Also, sometimes when he drank, he emptied everything he could get his hands on. When he got dark, he struck out at himself. When he wanted, he was unfillable. When it was at its worst, he looked at you with blank eyes.

When he decided to leave, he took one duffel and went two thousand miles to start over from scratch. And heresy of heresies, for all the grief and longing it was to cause me, by that point I was ready for him to go.

I was thirty-three when I found him. A few years later, he was gone. The years passed then to now are as many as it takes you to live through your youth. But the thing is, he's been like a comet. As far away as he's gone from where I've been, he's always been circling back. As it's turned out, there's no room in either of our houses for another.

For our two separate reasons, we've each stayed alone. But though we live far apart, every time I need a code for life's dealings, I make one based on his initials. On at least one occasion, he's designated me next of kin. We keep a hand on each other's lifeline. We range out in our lives, and we circle back.

Some may feel it's a sad state of affairs, this arrangement. As they may think of it, you should have someone near for a connection to be strong. I would say, look at the comets. Halley's, Hale-Bopp — even Kohoutek. Solitary they may be, and distant from the heart of their solar system, but the forces that connect them to it have not been broken yet.

VI

Lights reflected. Lights of white-hot friction, of gases burning, of the incredible burning of ice. Lights that strike, then vanish in a flash. Lights that strike and go on even after flashing, having set fires. Lights that blot out, lights that dwindle. Lights that cycle predictably, and lights whose cycles you cannot foretell.

Lights glowing warm on wicks, inside glass chimneys. Beckoning the snowshoe-er from the windows of a cabin collared by snow.

Lights long lost — squelched throughout a long journey, like the light of a comet — then igniting finally in the soul. Soul igniting as the blue lights reflect its image back to it, saying, The light of nature, born of the universe, is in you.

. . . . .

Like Endymion (subject of the thesis I eventually abandoned in favor of a less elusive topic), I've been a traveler in thin air. Up here in the cabin, in air literally thin, I see that in one way or another that's where I've always been. And I've stayed in thin air, even now. But not entirely. Up here, however thin the air, one is grounded in the natural world. And despite the transitory, ethereal quality of some of its manifestations, you can't know a greater reality than this. I'm still enthralled by light, that's a fact, and you can't grab it. But then again, light is as fundamentally real as it gets. After all, it's the by-product of electrons, albeit electrons dancing; and as insubstantial as they are, electrons are crucial building blocks of all the solid world.

Meanwhile, here at the cabin, I stay still now and do my own work. I range outside and inside, now learning new light, softer and subtler, more diffuse.

. . . . .

Evening, six o'clock, the end of February. At this latitude, here at the end of the time zone, it's still light out.

Usually, it would be pink now. It would be customary dusk. It is still dusk, of course, but with a less customary aspect. The sky is the color of snow.

It is not snowing, and snow does not threaten. But the way the cloud is, the light suffusing the sky is the exact same color as snow.

Most of the mountains around the cabin are covered with trees. Some, more distant, are ragged-topped with rock. One, though, is smooth, open, barren of protrusions. No rocks, no trees to break the even color of snow.

If you were unfamiliar with this horizon — if you didn't know that smooth mountain was there — the way the light in the sky is this evening, you might look at the place where that smooth mountain stands and not know it was mountain. You might believe you were looking at sky.

Even those who know this horizon intimately, as I do, are subject to wondering in such light as this. For all the beauty of the sky's whiteness at this moment, this is perhaps its greatest beauty of all: with the sky's light the color of snow now, where this smooth mountain goes up, though you may know it's there, you don't know where it ends.

An obfuscation on the part of light, to set you wondering.

Think where you can go now, this obfuscation by light whispers. Open the way now for other lights, and their mysteries. Like the color of this sky and this mountain and the light that makes it. So many more colors than blue.

Notes

1. I use the term *orbit* for simplicity's sake. More accurate terms are *shell*, often used by chemists; or, more precisely, *probability cloud* or *charge-cloud*, used by physicists.

These terms communicate more clearly the fact that electrons do not move in clearly delineated concentric tracts around the nucleus of an atom, but rather in indistinct energy levels, with areas of higher and lower density, which can overlap.

2. When the atom that it's part of absorbs heat, an electron jumps to a higher energy level; then, as it's pulled by the positive charge of the atom's nucleus back to its original lower energy level, it emits a blip of light called a photon.

3. This analogy is based on the work of two pioneer theorists of quantum mechanics. An equation of Erwin Schrödinger's enables us to calculate the probability of an electron's being found in a certain region of an atom. But according to Werner Heisenberg, the probability of an electron's location is all we can establish. His Uncertainty Principle states that there's a limit to the certainty with which the locations of electrons in atoms can be known.

4. Some astronomers would say that the Kuiper Belt is only the innermost fringe of the Oort cloud.

5. Some sources classify Hale-Bopp as a short-period comet. These sources have it that the orbital periods of almost all long-period comets are at least one hundred thousand years. Some sources also consider that a comet originating in the Kuiper Belt is a short-period comet, another attribute that qualifies Hale-Bopp for that classification, ever since the detection of argon in its tail, referred to above.

6. Hale-Bopp was visible to the naked eye for seventeen and a half months, the record for any comet. The final sightings of Hale-Bopp by naked eye occurred in November 1997 from the Southern Hemisphere, but the comet was still visible by amateur telescope for many more months.

sightline books . . . .
The Iowa Series in Literary Nonfiction